ROUTLEDGE LIBRARY EDITIONS:
WOMEN AND POLITICS

I0130548

Volume 3

FABIAN COUPLES,
FEMINIST ISSUES

FABIAN COUPLES, FEMINIST ISSUES

REVA POLLACK GREENBURG

Routledge
Taylor & Francis Group

LONDON AND NEW YORK

First published in 1987 by Garland Publishing Inc.

This edition first published in 2019
by Routledge
2 Park Square, Milton Park, Abingdon, Oxon OX14 4RN

and by Routledge
52 Vanderbilt Avenue, New York, NY 10017

Routledge is an imprint of the Taylor & Francis Group, an informa business

British Library Cataloguing in Publication Data
A catalogue record for this book is available from the British Library

ISBN: 978-1-138-36393-9 (Set)
ISBN: 978-0-429-39879-7 (Set) (ebk)
ISBN: 978-1-138-39054-6 (Volume 3) (hbk)
ISBN: 978-1-138-39060-7 (Volume 3) (pbk)
ISBN: 978-0-429-42333-8 (Volume 3) (ebk)

Publisher's Note
The publisher has gone to great lengths to ensure the quality of this reprint but
points out that some imperfections in the original copies may be apparent.

Disclaimer
The publisher has made every effort to trace copyright holders and would welcome
correspondence from those they have been unable to trace.

MODERN EUROPEAN HISTORY

Fabian Couples, Feminist Issues

Reva Pollack Greenburg

Garland Publishing, Inc.
New York and London 1987

Library of Congress Cataloging-in-Publication Data

Greenburg, Reva Pollack, 1940–
    Fabian couples, feminist issues / Reva Pollack
Greenburg.
    p.   cm.—(Modern European history)
    Originally presented as the author's thesis (Ph.D.)—
University of California, San Diego, 1983.
    Bibliography: p.
    ISBN 0-8240-7808-X (alk. paper)
    1. Women and socialism—Great Britain.   2. Fabian
Society (Great Britain)   3. Feminism—Great Britain.
I. Title.   II. Series.
HX546.G74   1983
335'.0088042—dc19   87-27719

All volumes in this series are printed on acid-
free, 250-year-life paper.

Printed in the United States of America

UNIVERSITY OF CALIFORNIA

SAN DIEGO

Fabian Couples, Feminist Issues

A dissertation submitted in partial satisfaction of the

requirements for the degree Doctor of Philosophy

in History

by

Reva Pollack Greenburg

Committee in charge:

      Professor Judith M. Hughes, Chair
      Professor H. Stuart Hughes
      Professor Kathryn Norberg
      Professor Andrew Wright
      Professor Donald Wesling

1983

DEDICATION

To my daughters, Beth, Joan, and Lara, who prompted me to investigate the "woman question," and for whom, I hope, such questions will no longer be vexing.

TABLE OF CONTENTS

Page

Acknowledgments v
Abstract vii

1. Fabian Socialism, Feminist Issues 1
    I.   The Birth of the Fabian Society 4
    II. The Fabians and the "Woman Question,"
         1884-1914 11
    III. Fabian Couples 46

2. The George Bernard Shaws 60
    I.   The Quintessence of Shavian Feminism 61
    II. G.B.S.: The Apprenticeship of a
         Critic at Large 86
    III. Charlotte Payne-Townshend: The
         Instruction of a Reluctant Bride 100
    IV. The Shaws: An Unconsummated Union 123

3. The Hubert Blands 163
    I.   Hubert Bland: The Fabian in the
         Frock Coat 164
    II. Bland as Anti-feminist 181
    III. From Daisy Nesbit to Edith Bland 194
    IV. E. Nesbit: Children's Author 205
    V.   The Blands: An Odd Compatibility 237

4. The Sidney Webbs 274
    I.   Sidney Webb: The Development of a
         Committeeman 275
    II. Beatrice Potter: The Apprenticeship
         of a Social Investigator 290
    III. The Partnership: One + One = Eleven 318
    IV. Metamorphosis: The Emergence of a Public
         Figure and a Reluctant Feminist 351

5. Conclusion 387

Selected Bibliography 397

ACKNOWLEDGMENTS

The writing of a dissertation is an enormous task, the enormity of which I had no notion before I began. This was, perhaps, fortunate. Never would I have attempted to scale such a mountain had I known how steep was the climb. En route many people have been helpful, many encouraging; to all of them I am grateful. With what little ink I have left in my pen (with the few bytes left in my Apple), with whatever brain matter has survived my effort, I would like to single out just two people without whom I would have long ago lost my way.

In the best of all possible worlds, all husbands are loving and warmly supportive of their wives' endeavors; all are amenable to difficult schedules, inconvenient arrangements, on behalf of their wives' distant goals. In this not so perfect world, my husband, Gerson, invariably has been just that, and I am lovingly grateful.

Whether all advisors are in the habit of exhibiting saint-like patience and offering painstakingly constructive criticism to their students, I do not know. My advisor, Professor Judith Hughes, managed to do so, even in the face of my occasional reluctance to cut purple prose or to make sense. Her encouragement has been crucial, her unfailing assistance keenly appreciated.

v

A final word on Beatrice and Sidney Webb, Charlotte and George Bernard Shaw, and E. Nesbit and Hubert Bland, whose skins I tried to inhabit, and whose company I very much enjoyed throughout this lengthy exercise. For all their inconsistencies, they are a fascinating lot; from them I have learned far more than I had hoped or expected.

ABSTRACT OF THE DISSERTATION

Fabian Couples, Feminist Issues

by

Reva Pollack Greenburg

Doctor of Philosophy in History

University of California, San Diego, 1983

Professor Judith M. Hughes, Chair

In the three decades before the First World War,
the relationship between socialism and feminism was both
curious and convoluted. Despite strong theoretical links
between these ideologies, class and sex seem to have
inspired conflicting loyalties and opposing demands. In
Britain, the uniquely middle-class, reform-minded Fabian
Society might have been expected to bridge the gap between
these movements. Yet, between 1884 and 1914, the Fabian
Society's record on the "woman question" was highly inconsistent and, at times, overtly regressive.

In part, the Society's behavior reflected the fits
and starts of the wider feminist movement and the disagreements among its own feminine members with regard to women's
issues. More important, it reflected the contradictory
notions and prejudices of the leading figures in the
Society, most of whom happened to be men. Three of the
most influential members--Sidney Webb, George Bernard Shaw,

and Hubert Bland--were married to women who were themselves active in the Society. To understand fully the Fabian response to the "woman question," one must understand the views of these prominent Fabians. These three couples, then, the Webbs, the Blands, and the Shaws, are the subject of this study.

On an issue as emotionally charged as is women's rights, however, stated opinions are not enough. To clarify both the ideological response of these six Fabians, and the experiences and attitudes which informed those responses, I have examined not only their works and words, but their marriages as well. My assumption has been that a partner's real feelings about the rights and responsibilities of each sex, and his or her own sexual identification, are nowhere more apparent than in the conjugal relationship. Thus, in discussing the biographies of these three Fabian couples, I hope to shed additional light on their views with regard to the "woman question" and on the correspondence or contradiction between their views and their life experiences.

Chapter 1

FABIAN SOCIALISM, FEMINIST ISSUES

In the three decades before the First World War, a curious often convoluted relationship existed between the feminist and the socialist movements. Developing almost simultaneously, both movements were philosophically grounded in egalitarian principles. Their adherents shared an optimistic view of human nature and of the possibilities of improving upon it. In working for what each called "the Cause," that is, collectivization for socialists, the vote for feminists, both groups formulated critiques of the same institutions, and each sought to enlarge the benefits derived from those institutions for their constituencies. Several socialist theoreticians pointed to the interrelation of the two movements, positing that only through socialism would women be truly emancipated.[1] Marx, in particular, stressed the connection between the oppression of women and that of workers. The abolition of private property, he claimed, would abolish "the status of women as mere instruments of production," just as it would end the alienation of labor from its own product.[2]

Recently, a number of feminist historians have examined the histories of socialism and feminism to determine if socialism had indeed provided a fertile soil for

notions of women's emancipation, or if socialists themselves
had been particularly receptive to feminism.[3] Despite the
theoretical links between these ideologies, the results of
these studies have been largely negative. While a formal
commitment to women's emancipation often existed within
European socialist parties, the programs to implement it
did not. Class and sex seem to have represented two conflicting loyalties which prevented a real merging of the
movements. Moreover, feminist concern with interpersonal
relations and non-work related issues did not fit well with
the socialist emphasis on the economic substructure as
manifested in the workplace.[4] In addition, most male
socialists tended to view feminist demands as irrelevant,
since all such needs would be taken care of "after the
revolution,"[5] while feminists themselves were usually
unable to combine across class lines to form a unified
front.[6]

In prewar Britain, the one organization which might
have bridged the gap between feminism and socialism was the
Fabian Society. Unlike its socialist contemporaries, the
Social-Democratic Federation, the Socialist League, and the
Independent Labour Party, the Fabian Society was almost
entirely a middle-class organization.[7] Its members may
have belonged to the newly emerging "intellectual pro-
letariat,"[8] but very few ever engaged in physical labor to
earn their living. The primarily middle-class feminist
movement, eyed with suspicion by most working-class

socialists, might have seemed less threatening to Fabians who shared many of the same professional and educational concerns as the feminists. Indeed, a large number of Fabian women were feminists themselves. Moreover, by its very nature as a reform-minded organization committed to constitutional change, the Fabian Society was not obliged to wait until "after the revolution" to consider the special problems of women or to offer remedies on their behalf. Yet, according to one historian, the attitude of the Society in the prewar period was "lukewarm" on the "woman question"; it was converted at "pistol point," and "rather late in the day, to overt support of women's suffrage."[9]

For the purposes of this investigation, the term "woman question" is not confined to the battle over the suffrage, however central that battle was to the women's movement after 1905. Rather, it is defined as, not one, but a series of related questions about the proper role, the needs, and the nature of women.[10] The diversity of the answers suggested to the "woman question" reflects conflicting views of women's needs, as well as conflicting definitions of equality. In order to ameliorate the conditions of women's lives, is it necessary that they achieve complete equality with men, or do women require instead special restrictions, special privileges? Given the complexity of the problem, it is not surprising that the members of the Fabian Society could not always agree on these issues or definitions, or that the women of the Society were themselves often split on a given issue. What _is_ at times surprising is the low priority assigned by the leadership of the Society to issues of such genuine importance. Why that was the case is the subject of this study.

I. The Birth of the Fabian Society

The Fabian Society had its roots in the ethical socialist enthusiasm of the 1880's. Inspired by the doctrines of Thomas Davidson, the peripatetic Scottish schoolmaster dedicated to fostering love and brotherhood through communal living, sixteen young men and women gathered in the rooms of Edward Pease, at 16 Osnaburgh Street in London, to discuss "Fellowship in the New Life." A second meeting followed on 7 November 1883, during which it was resolved to reconstruct society "in accordance with the highest moral principles," and to meet on alternate Fridays to do so.[11] In the course of the third meeting, a rift developed between those anxious to remedy their own spiritual deficiencies as a means of improving the world and those with a more materialist approach to the problems of society. The Fellowship of the New Life was formed in December to meet the requirements of the more spiritually inclined; its ranks included Havelock Ellis, Edward Carpenter, and Ramsey MacDonald. These members set up a communal home, while continuing to work at their respective jobs outside the establishment. Their general attitude toward this short-lived experiment was expressed rather succinctly by one of the participants: "fellowship is Hell."[12]

The more worldly of Davidson's disciples met at Pease's lodgings on 4 January 1884 and formed the Fabian Society. It was so named after Fabius Cunctator, the Roman general who was said to have defeated Hannibal with his policy of waiting patiently and striking when the moment was right. His nineteenth-century namesakes decided to hold meetings, discuss papers, collect articles from current literature, and thus to determine the proper course for their organization. The concept of socialism was not mentioned until the sixth meeting, when a Miss Haddon read a paper contrasting the "two socialisms," that is, that of the Social Democratic Federation and of the Fabian Society. According to George Bernard Shaw, however, the Society was, in its infancy, as insurrectionary as the S.D.F., if somewhat more intellectual and less Marxist.[13]

In 1887, the Fabians set forth a statement of their general principles, which by then were far from insurrectionary, and called it the "Fabian Basis," a document which all members signed upon joining. According to the Basis, the "Society consisted of Socialists," and was committed to the "reorganization of society, by the emancipation of land and industrial capital from individual and class ownership, and the vesting of them in the community for the general benefit." What differentiated the Society from other socialist bodies was that it sought to promote these ends through the "general dissemination of knowledge as to the relation between the individual and society."[14] In short, the Society's main concern was educational; it did require, however, a general commitment to the redistribution of wealth.

The Fabian Society was, from the start, a middle-class organization. Its members tended to be well-educated; most were employed as civil servants, clerks, journalists and ministers. Approximately one-fourth were women, many of whom considered themselves "new women," emancipated from Victorian notions of femininity. The only working-class individual in the early Fabian Society was W. L. Phillips, a house painter, but he did not remain a Fabian for long. As one old-time member noted, "proletarians were not at home in our company."[15] The restricted (and restrictive) nature of the Society was assured by its stringent membership requirements. Before becoming a candidate the prospective member had to attend at least two meetings, and to promise that he would do the kind of work the Society needed to have done. Two guarantors from the Society then had to attest to his socialist views. After a year's probation, if the candidate had convinced the Executive of his sincerity and ability, he was admitted to full membership. Thus, it is not surprising that the Society which began with approximately fourteen members remained small, save for two brief periods before the war.

The driving force of the Society was its Executive Committee, which, in its weekly meetings, did a lion's share of the Society's work. Members of the Executive had primary responsibility for determining the course of lectures to be given to the Society--often giving many of these themselves--and they determined the policy and direction of the Society, subject of course to a full vote of the membership. The Executive was elected by vote of the London members until 1894; thereafter a mailed ballot was instituted allowing members in outlying areas to vote. Members served a one year term, unpaid, beginning in April. The only paid member of the Committee was the General Secretary, a post occupied continuously from 1890 until 1915 by Edward Pease. His salary in the first year was £1 a week.

Although the procedure for election to the Executive was democratic, the result was oligarchic. In a ten year period only forty-five people served on the fifteen member Committee. The first fully-constituted Executive, which served from January 1885 to April 1886, consisted of five unknown young people in their late twenties: Edward Pease and Hubert Bland, two of the original founders, George Bernard Shaw, who had joined in September 1884, Sidney Webb, who had just become a member, and Mrs. Charlotte Wilson. Mrs. Wilson was the only one of the original five not to serve continuously on the Executive for the next twenty-five years, although she remained a member and reappeared on the Committee in 1911. In 1886 the Executive gained its most celebrated figure, the well-known author and lecturer, Mrs. Annie Besant. She, like the fiery anarchist Mrs. Wilson, remained on the Executive for only a few years, with consequences, one might argue, for the role and the importance of women in the Society for the next two decades. By 1888, with the addition of Sidney Olivier and Graham Wallas to the Executive, the "Old Gang" of Bland, Shaw, Webb, Olivier, and Wallas, which shaped the course of the Society, was complete.[16]

The mainstay of the organization was, from the beginning, its fortnightly lectures, which were delivered either by members or by an occasional well-informed outsider. The purpose of these meetings, many of which were open to the public, was to educate and activate the listeners. If a lecture was of particularly high quality, the lecturer would be asked to turn it into a tract for publication. Examined and corrected by the Fabian Executive, and then by the Society as a whole at its "for members only" meetings, the tracts were meticulously crafted. They were the major means of spreading socialist opinions, and, as stated in the Basis, the "spreading of Socialist opinion" was the goal of the Society.

In addition to the writing of tracts and the giving of lectures to the Fabian Society, members were encouraged to give lectures to any other group or organization, socialist or not, which would have them. In time, a

"Speakers' Bureau" was set up to facilitate this process in London, and special courses of lectures on socialism, political economy, or working class history were offered in various provincial towns by itinerant Fabian lecturers. "Book Boxes," that is, sets of books devoted to topics of general reform, economic theory, or socialist propaganda, were circulated to other organizations; they were miniature lending-libraries offered at no cost to the users. Fabians were also expected to join other societies in order to influence opinion along socialist lines, and they were encouraged to run for office in their local districts.

In 1888, the Executive settled upon a series of lectures for the fall, to be given by its members, on the "Basis and Prospects of Socialism." By this time, the members of the Committee had managed to steer the Society between the Scylla of anarchist exhortation and the Charybdis of Marxist revolutionary rhetoric to general agreement on the importance of political solutions and evolutionary reform. The lectures were published in the following year as Fabian Essays in Socialism, a slim volume which sold for six shillings. The first edition of 1,000 copies sold out within a month; a paperback version in the following year sold 25,000 copies. This surprised the seven essayists as much as it did the rest of the member-ship, which totaled less than 150. The Essays were dis-tinctly eclectic. Shaw's was concerned with the transfer of "rent" from the "appropriators" to the community as a whole, by means of the gradual transfer of rent and interest to the state.[17] Here the economic principles of Jevons and Ricardo were clearly in evidence. Webb's essay offered a Benthamite rationale for communal production; that is, it would increase the well-being of the greatest number.[18] Bland's essay, on the other hand, borrowing in part from Marx's historical determinism, stated that gradual evolution of the democratic process would produce the desired economic system, for "democracy holds socialism in its womb."[19] The Fabian blueprint for socialist reform was not only drawn from numerous sources, it was clearly more reassuring than the barricades or bombs being advocated by Marxist or anarchist revolutionaries.

The effect of the Essays, although not immediate, was to produce the first of what was to become periodic booms in the growth of the London-based Society. Their success also facilitated the development of provincial Fabian Societies in the North of England, twelve of them in 1890, seventy-four by 1893. These Societies were completely autonomous; there were no fees to be paid to the parent body, no program to adhere to other than an acceptance of the "Basis." The growth of Fabianism in the provinces was also stimulated by developments within and without the Society. A generous gift by a new member, Henry H. Hutchinson, financed a series of lectures in the North Country which helped to spread the gospel. The wave of trade unionism among industrial workers and their

growing interest in political activity, as well as the
increasing unresponsiveness of the Liberal Party to social
reform, created an excellent, if temporary, climate for the
growth of Fabian Societies.[20]

By 1892 membership in the London-based Fabian
Society had grown to 541, with another 340 members from
abroad or elsewhere in Britain who were affiliated directly
with the parent organization. While membership in the
provincial Fabian Societies declined rapidly after 1894,
the London Society continued to grow slowly until 1899 when
the number of London members, that is, those "members
within reach of London for purposes of evening meetings,"[21]
reached 861, and those residing outside of greater London
numbered 402. After 1900, membership in both categories
declined significantly, totaling 730 in 1904. In the
course of its first twenty years, the proportion of women
relative to men members remained fairly stable. In London,
women made up approximately 20 percent of the membership;
outside of London they comprised approximately 25 percent
of the total number of members.

II. The Fabians and the "Woman Question," 1884-1914

With regard to its record on women's issues, the
history of the Fabian Society falls readily into four
distinct periods: 1884 to 1889, 1890 to 1895, 1896 to
1905, and 1906 to 1914. Whether or not the Society took

much notice of the "woman question," whether it actively campaigned for feminist measures in a given period, depended not only on the number of women in the organization, but who those women were, how long they stayed, and how much support they gained from feminist pressure outside the Society. The Fabian approach to the "woman question" also reflected the confusion of aims among the women Fabians, as well as the interests of a mostly male leadership. Not surprisingly, the record of the Society was very mixed.

* * *

In the 1880's the Fabian Society, while small and insignificant, showed itself quite progressive on women's issues. Lectures were given to the membership on such topics as "The Economic Position of Women," in which the enrollment of women in trade unions and a "similar wage for similar work" were advocated, while the exclusion of women from any industrial jobs was censured.[22] The Society's second tract strongly recommended equal political rights between the sexes, and several thereafter called for "adult suffrage" in both parliamentary and municipal elections.[23] While the doings of the Society remain shrouded in partial darkness due to the lack of records, it is clear that in this period it was not yet dominated by males.[24] In fact, women were more prominent on the Executive than at any time prior to 1909.

Charlotte Wilson, the first woman on the Executive,

had also been one of the first students at Newnham College, Cambridge. Four or five years older than her Fabian colleagues, and extremely bright, she had little tolerance for other women, a taste for Marxist dialectics, and a passion for anarchy. She and her stockbroker husband lived in a "simplified" cottage, adorned with "aesthetic pots and pans" where she often played hostess to the Hampstead Historic Society, which she herself had helped found in 1884.[25] These fortnightly meetings dedicated at first to discussions of Marx's Das Kapital, and later to the works of other economic and political theorists, were attended by the most intellectual Fabians and a few of their counterparts in the Socialist League and the S.D.F. Within the Fabian Society, much was done to accommodate Mrs. Wilson's anarchist predilections, including the establishment of a separate Parliamentary League in 1886.[26] It proved unnecessary as Mrs. Wilson gave up her place on the Executive in 1887 in order to devote herself more fully to anarchism. She edited Freedom, the anarchist journal, and was instrumental in bringing Prince Kropotkin into close contact with his English colleagues. While Mrs. Wilson certainly was an "emancipated woman," her interests at this time were in securing less government for all, rather than the increased participation of women in government.

Annie Besant, who served on the Executive from 1885 to 1889 and was one of the seven essayists, was the Committee's first full-fledged feminist. Anxious to

improve the position of women on many fronts, Mrs. Besant
pushed for reforms far beyond the vision of most of her
colleagues. She provided a feminist perspective with a
flair for publicity and a penchant for action which was
unique among the early Fabians. Annie was never involved
with the organized women's movement; she was a feminist not
by design or affiliation, but in reaction to her own
circumstance and experience.

At a relatively early age she became aware of the
disadvantages of being a female. Her mother's widowhood
and resulting impoverishment, her brother's public school
education and her lack thereof, her strict Evangelical
upbringing which protected her from any experience of men
and landed her in an early and unwise marriage, all conspired to enlighten her. Marriage to the stern and unbend-
ing Reverend Frank Besant brought her much unhappiness; her
religious studies spawned religious doubt and further
alienation from her husband. The little money she earned
by writing, she found to her horror, belonged to him, not
to her. As Annie began to fight against the inequities
she encountered, their numbers increased. She left her
husband and discovered that legal separation was possible,
divorce and remarriage were not. She discovered, too, that
a lady's education left a lady unable to support herself,
and, after a lengthy court battle over her daughter, that
a father had a stronger right to his two children than did
the mother.[27]

Annie found a creed, a job, and a mentor in the National Secular Society. She adopted atheism, began to write for the National Reformer, and became Charles Bradlaugh's trusted ally in his campaign for free thought and radical reform. With him, Annie became involved in her first major feminist battle--one which earned her no plaudits from her feminist sisters. The fearless twosome published an "obscene pamphlet" by Dr. Knowlton which urged conjugal prudence on its readers and instructed them in the basics of feminine physiology and birth control. The argument was broached in neo-Malthusian rather than feminist terms. Yet in this pamphlet, and in another version which Annie published on her own in 1877, birth control devices such as the soluble pessary or the sponge were recommended because they offered "the enormous advantage of being entirely in the hands of the woman." In addition, she spelled out the harm done to women's bodies by too frequent pregnancies, while insisting that "celibacy is not natural to men or women" and that bodily needs, which exist even for women, "require their legitimate satisfaction."[28] Thus, in the space of a short pamphlet, Mrs. Besant managed to defy most Victorian conventions regarding female sexuality. In demanding reproductive rights and sexual satisfaction for women, Annie Besant was clearly a century ahead of her times; the highly publicized trial which followed publication of the Knowlton pamphlet was not even mentioned in the leading feminist journals of that period.[29]

When Annie joined the Fabian Society in January
1885, she was a decade older than most of her new associates, and brought with her that many years of crusading
experience on speakers' platforms and in editorial pages.
She quickly became one of the Society's most active and
effective speakers. Trained by combat in Bradlaugh's
political campaigns, Annie moved the Fabian Society, at
least temporarily, toward political activism. She herself
became increasingly involved in the rallies and marches
against unemployment which swept London in 1886-87, and
she was able to convince a few of her colleagues to participate with her. Mrs. Besant also owned and edited a
monthly magazine, Our Corner, which had been devoted to
secularism and science and now became a forum for the
discussion of socialist ideas as well. Between 1886 and
1888, when she ceased publication, Our Corner ran a regular
column, "The Fabian Society and Socialist Notes," which
provided space for Fabian propaganda and a running account
of happenings within the Society. Given the fact that
until Fabian News began publication in 1890, the organization had no journal of its own, Our Corner, like its editor,
was a useful adjunct to the Society.

In the pages of her magazine Mrs. Besant also waged
a continuing campaign on behalf of women's rights. Her
most subtle tactic involved raising the consciousness of
her readers with such articles as: "Some Advanced Women
of the Past,"[30] "Anti-Slavery Women,"[31] and flattering

commentaries on the lives and works of women authors. Many
of her articles were more directly didactic, however, such
as her review of Bebel's work on socialism and the "woman
question": <u>Women in the Past, Present and Future</u>. Here
Mrs. Besant thoroughly aired and applauded Bebel's arguments in favor of total equality between the sexes, easier
divorce for all, and an end to the double standard in
sexual morality.[32] In other articles, as in her lectures,
Mrs. Besant continually linked sexual equality and socialism. Believing that the "foundations of complete social
equality will be laid in the schools," she argued for a
"common education" to prepare all for "common work."[33]
Moreover, unlike many of her socialist colleagues, she
argued for "a similar wage for similar work," and insisted
that women must not be excluded from earning a living in
any occupation they chose. "If a woman may not earn her
living by selling her labour," she wrote, "she must earn
it by selling her body, and it makes comparatively little
difference, if she be forced to sell herself, whether the
sale is for life or for a term. Marriage for an establishment is as loathsome as sale for a night."[34] Few feminists
or socialists were prepared to state the case in such
strong terms.

Annie Besant's efforts on behalf of women were not
limited to articles and lectures. In June 1888, she helped
organize the "match-girls" working at Bryant and May
Company. Their strike led to a series of concessions

by the employers, a slight wage increase, and to the
formation of a Matchmakers' Union, of which Annie was
elected Honorable Secretary. Several of her Fabian
colleagues, particularly Shaw, Wallas, Olivier, and the
Reverend Stewart Headlam, were drawn into her program for
distributing funds to the striking women, but none of the
Fabians took to union organizing as she did in the following months, traveling around the country organizing women
weavers, shop assistants, gas workers, and the like.

Mrs. Besant's newfound enthusiasm for union organizing and the S.D.F. brand of socialism--she had become a
member in September 1888--did not last long. In May 1889,
she joined the Theosophical Society, at last finding a
creed she could embrace and a crusade she could, and did,
remain faithful to for the next forty years.[35] Annie's
adoption of Theosophy necessitated a retreat from several
of her positions on women's rights, and from many of her
socialist activities. Theosophical doctrine held that the
worst social evils followed from sexual or animal instincts.
She therefore ceased publication of The Law of Pouplation,
and refused to sell the copyright, depriving the public of
one of the few explicit and inexpensive manuals on birth
control, and one of the few well-reasoned arguments in
favor of feminine control over reproduction. The organized
feminist movement took no notice of the loss.

The Fabian Executive noted tersely that Mrs. Besant
had "gone to Theosophy,"[36] and, perhaps, breathed a

collective sigh of relief that this indefatigable activist
had left their inner council. The Executive was now free
to pursue its growing commitment to educating the populace
rather than organizing it, and could leave subjects like
reproductive rights to future generations. One wonders if
the younger men of the Executive had been so traumatized by
Mrs. Besant that they sought thereafter to contain any
similarly strong-minded women within their midst. Annie
Besant had no successor on the Executive.

* * *

By 1889 Shaw, Webb, Wallas, Olivier, and Bland were
in control of the Society, with Edward Pease about to take
over as the underpaid but meticulous General Secretary. In
the six years which followed, the Society continued to
attract intelligent, well-educated women, and to maintain a
feminist perspective. The women in the Society were not
always of one mind, however, as to the course of action a
feminist line dictated. Nor were they always able to
inspire male colleagues with their enthusiasm for feminist
reform.

In the early 1890's there was continuing pressure
from a good many women for more lectures on women, more
attention to the battle for women's suffrage, and greater
representation on the Fabian Executive. Mrs. C. Mallet, an
older woman who had joined the Society in 1886 and served
on the Executive from 1890-92, was one of the more out-
spoken feminists of this period. Her ties to the Liberal

Party, and consequent campaigning for a Liberal candidate
at the expense of his socialist opponent, did on one
occasion earn her the displeasure of her fellow Fabians,[37]
but her generous contributions to the cause more than
offset such indiscretions. Mrs. Mallet's interest in
promoting women's suffrage, and in protecting women from
the "deadly trades," led her to the lecture podium fairly
frequently, although a tract she wrote on the latter did
not pass Fabian muster and was not published. As a member
of the Fabian Women's Committee, a short-lived but vociferous group, she pressed, with some result, for the
addition of more women lecturers to the autumn lecture
schedule.[38] Her associate on the Executive, and in the
Women's Committee, Miss Grover, was at the same time
pressuring the Executive for a paragraph in the Fabian
News, and a resolution by the Executive, on behalf of
women's suffrage.[39] After much discussion, Miss Grover
obtained rather less than she wished. No resolution was
forthcoming, but an unenthusiastic note did appear in the
News stating that "a number of Fabians who are working for
the extension of the suffrage, . . . wish to get resolutions passed at council meetings of Liberal and Radical
Associations."[40]

A few months later, members of the Central Group, a
geographical subdivision of the Society, went so far as to
empower their Secretary, Miss B. Walter, to summon a
meeting of Fabian women to discuss the nomination of women

candidates for the Fabian Executive.[41] This move followed
the spring election which had produced only one woman on
the eight member Executive. (Both Miss Grover and Mrs.
Mallet had declined to run, Mrs. Mallet because of the
death of her husband early in the year.) In November 1892,
this same Central Group, now led by the staunch feminist
and champion chess player, Mrs. Fagan, listened to an
address on the Women's Guild of Co-operators and considered,
but did not carry through, the formation of a Women's Guild
of Fabians.

Yet in the midst of this feminist (and quasi-
separatist) enthusiasm, there remained a good many Fabian
women who believed that equality would be best achieved
by ignoring any differences between the sexes. Accordingly,
Miss Mary Lacey sent notice of a resolution to be moved at
the May (1892) meeting, which protested the discussion of
women candidates for the Executive: "As implied in the
Basis, the sex of its members is a matter beyond the
cognisance of the Society."[42] This was the same Mary
Lacey--one of two "lady lecturers" for the Cambridge
Extension Program--who protested strongly against her
own exclusion, for reasons of gender, from the Extension
lecturers' dinner. Far from being against women's rights,
or unconcerned with them, she wished to do whatever she
could "toward helping . . . the free and rational intercourse of the sexes."[43] Sexual equality she considered
"one of the principles that we are struggling for."[44]

The novelist Emma Broke, who served on the Executive between 1893 and 1896 and was an active member in the Society from its very beginnings, presented a similar argument and a similar resolution: "the prominent introduction into the Fabian Society of the Woman Question . . . is unnecessary; further . . . the selection of candidates for the Executive should have sole regard to the ability of the nominees . . . and be therefore without regard to sex."[45] While Miss Brooke considered herself "chiefly a student of the Woman Question,"[46] according to one of her fictional heroines, being a woman "is one of those facts that has to be looked well in the face and then forgotten."[47]

In spite of this dissension over how best to achieve sexual equality, a number of Fabian women continued to lecture to the Society, and to various other organizations, on a wide variety of women's topics. Speeches entitled "Women and Socialism," "Socialism and Women," and "Women Under Socialism" were great favorites, as were those more specifically directed at "Woman Suffrage," "The Citizenship of Women," and "The Emancipation of Women." During the same period, the Society maintained a cautiously feminist policy in its tracts. In three of them published between 1890 and 1895, the recommendation was for adult suffrage.[48] By including women's suffrage within the larger demand for adult suffrage, the Society solved the problem of the so-called propertied vote. If the vote were extended to all adults, there would be less risk to social programs than if the electorate were increased only by the enfranchisement of women on the same terms as men, that is, by propertied women.

On the local level, the Fabian Society was consistent in asking that women be eligible for all representative bodies.[49] In the two page tract, "Questions for School Board Candidates," the Society set forth its least cautious demands on behalf of women. It recommended that women be eligible as Inspectors of Schools, and that the School Board create a "crèche" or nursery school for every infant school. More importantly, it asked candidates to "urge a scale of payment for women teachers" which would be the same as that for men.[50] This was the first and, until 1914, the last time the Society supported equal wages for women. Interestingly enough, "The Unemployed," published two years later, called for "the gradual elimination of married women from factory occupations altogether."[51] Such a suggestion was as retrogressive on the "woman question" as the previously mentioned tract was progressive.

In all these tracts, however, the women's issue was treated as one of many items on a long list of reforms; one had to look closely to notice it was there. In 1893 Mrs. Fagan and J. F. Oakeshott moved that the Executive appoint a committee to prepare a tract devoted exclusively to the advocacy of civil and political rights for women.

The immediate outcome of their efforts was a heartrending letter by Emma Brooke protesting her exclusion--as a member eminently interested in the subject--from the committee which was in the course of being constituted. The flurry of letters which eventually rectified this error show George Bernard Shaw's reputed skill at tact and diplomacy to have been very real indeed.[52] Miss Brooke accepted a place on the committee with Oakeshott, G.B.S., Beatrice Webb, and Harriot Stanton Blatch; the names of Miss Bridgeman and R. A. Peddie, at their own requests, were added to the committee list in March 1894, as were those of Mrs. Mallet, Mrs. Brownlow, Mrs. Garrett, Sidney Olivier, and Edward Pease in the following June. This large and unwieldy group then proceeded to adopt a simple course: it approved a "sketch" for a tract drawn up by Mrs. Blatch, and thereupon adjourned to await further news.

Mrs. Blatch's credentials for her task were of the highest order. She was a strong feminist virtually from birth, if not by birthright. Her mother, Elizabeth Cady Stanton, convened the world's first women's rights convention at Seneca Falls, New York in 1848, and was the founder of the National Woman Suffrage Association twenty-one years later. When Harriot was born (January 1856), the sixth of the Stantons' seven children and their second daughter, her mother rejoiced "that a female is born into the world . . . [and] that no boy was sent in her stead."[53] Obviously, Harriot would face few of the difficulties Elizabeth Cady

had experienced as a child, repeatedly and unsuccessfully
trying to convince her father, after the death of his one
son, that little girls could be as bright and able as
little boys. While Harriot had to contend with frequent
separations from her parents--her mother off lecturing or
organizing for women's rights, her father, a New York state
legislator, living away from home for long periods of time--
she never felt demeaned or devalued because of her sex. As
the brighter, more precociously verbal of the two Stanton
girls, the one clearly destined to carry on her mother's
work, Harriot was "especially precious" to her mother.[54]

Harriot grew up in a home where each child was
allowed and expected to express his or her own opinion on
all the important issues of the day. Vassar, with its
apolitical student body, its conservative faculty, and the
major gaps in its curriculum, was not the stimulating
environment she had anticipated. Not one to acquiesce
to custom or constraint, Harriot pushed through a regulation that each member of the freshman class, of which she
was President, read a newspaper for twenty minutes a day
or pay a fine. Soon after, she formed a Democratic Club
to stir her non-voting classmates with enthusiasm for
Tilden. Later she started a debating club. Aside from
engaging in uphill battles against political apathy,
Harriot convinced one of her professors to teach a class
in political economy and another to work up a reading list
in economics for her, since no such course was taught. In

addition, she studied in the recognized disciplines of mathematics and astronomy.

Graduating in 1878, Harriot went on to study at the Boston School of Oratory. Shortly thereafter, she was called upon to help her mother and Susan B. Anthony in the editing of their History of Woman Suffrage. Harriot insisted that the American Woman Suffrage Association, rival organization to the National Woman Suffrage Association, founded and led by Mrs. Stanton and Miss Anthony, be included in the history. To her dismay, she herself was nominated to compile that chapter. Harriot Stanton thus did postgraduate work in "feminist studies" almost a century before the term had been coined or the courses developed.

At the age of twenty-six, Harriot married Henry Blatch, a tall gentleman of Tory background, residing in Basingstoke, England. Given that Mrs. Blatch later devoted something less than a page and a half of her memoirs to Mr. Blatch and the twenty years she spent with him in Basingstoke, before "breaking up [her] home there" and returning to America, one senses a certain lack of compatibility between them.[55] Their daughter Nora was another matter entirely. Educated according to her mother's precepts, that is, with a concentration on serious mathematics rather than frivolous novel-reading, Nora went on to become an engineer, and to work for "the Cause" alongside her mother.

While in England Mrs. Blatch placed herself under a "self-denying ordinance," refusing to run for public office, in order to demonstrate her continuing loyalty as an American citizen. She was, however, much involved with a number of suffrage societies, including the Woman's Local Government Society and the Women's Liberal Federation. Early on she had joined the Equal Franchise Committee, organized by Mrs. Jacob Bright, and devoted to new methods of advancing the suffrage. Mrs. Blatch considered herself and her friend and contemporary, Mrs. Emmeline Pankhurst, the "admiring neophytes" of the circle, too busy with young children to be much more than that. The Committee weakened as Mrs. Bright, like Annie Besant, became increasingly involved with Theosophy and left worldly concerns to others. The political methods and ideas suggested by the older suffragists, however, were not lost on Mrs. Blatch or Mrs. Pankhurst.

Harriot met Annie Besant often at the Brights, and just as often felt that Mrs. Besant was trying to win her over to Theosophy. Upon meeting Madame Blavatsky, the founder of the Theosophical Society, Harriot was so repelled by this "huge spider spinning a webb" for possible recruits, that even the remotest possibility of her conversion was ended. Accompanying Annie to her farewell speech to the Fabians, Harriot was much more impressed by the eloquence and clarity of her speech than with the wisdom of her newfound religion.[56]

By the time Harriot herself joined the Fabian
Society in February 1891, she was no stranger to the
speakers' platform or to the subject of women's rights.
She had become interested in the subject of working women
by then, and undertook an investigation of women's work
which formed the basis of her thesis for a Master's Degree
at Vassar, awarded in 1894. In February of that same year,
she made herself well known to the Fabian Society with a
lecture on "Collectivism and the Economic Freedom of
Women," and in the spring voting was elected to the
Executive.

If Mrs. Blatch's credentials were in perfect order
for the writing of a feminist tract, her patience, particularly with regard to the "over cautious" policies of Shaw
and Webb, and their unwillingness to try new experiments,
was not.[57] Her health, too, seems to have been uncharac-
teristically poor at this time. A lecture scheduled for
5 October 1894 in which she was to elaborate further on
the ideas in her "sketch" was cancelled due to illness.
The committee nonetheless agreed on a "rough draft" she
submitted, which was "to be amended" and published under
her name.[58] It then adjourned until after her next
scheduled lecture (7 February 1895), since part of her
revised tract was to be explained in that lecture. Alas,
that lecture was not to be. Moreover, Mrs. Blatch decided
she did not wish to amend her rough draft as suggested; in
fact, she "declined to alter her manuscript" at all.[59]

After arduous debate, it was decided that Shaw and Oakeshott would rework the political portions of her tract for Fabian publication. Mrs. Blatch thought otherwise; demanding her manuscript from her colleagues, she sent it off for publication in America. In the absence of a manuscript, the committee dissolved itself on 24 April 1896.

The offending portion of Mrs. Blatch's argument probably centered on her notion that women needed to specialize their functions, to end "the unfortunate union of cradle and frying pan."[60] Women should devote themselves either to raising children or keeping house, since not all do each task equally well. And, she argued, "associative housing" would allow some women to be paid for housework or child-raising, while those not so inclined could devote themselves to advancement in their chosen line of work. Although Mrs. Blatch had numerous supporters, most members of the Fabian Society were not ready for such radical feminist notions as "associative housing" or the payment of mothers and housewives--at least not in 1895.

After all this ado about nothing, the Society did manage to produce a tract concerned with one aspect of the "woman question," that is, protective legislation. Based on a lecture by Beatrice Webb, the tract argued in favor of extending the Factory Acts in order to protect women from overwork and unsanitary work conditions. On the surface a simple proposition, this issue too was fraught with pitfalls. Feminists devoted to equality between the

sexes did not see any merit in special legislation for
women, and argued forcefully against it. Mrs. Blatch, for
one, opposed the tract and demanded to see the manuscript
before it was published. Shaw requested Pease to send it,
to quiet her accusations: she "pours forth vials of
vitriol on me and insists that Mrs. Webb is wrong about
the Factory Acts and is bluffing the Society."[61] Despite
the objections of many Fabian women, the tract, "Women and
the Factory Acts," was published in 1896. This was Harriot
Blatch's second defeat and her last major battle in the
Fabian Society. She had retired from the Executive in
April 1895, after one term, and soon retired from active
membership in the Society. In 1902 she returned to America
to take part in the suffrage movement there.[62]

* * *

In the period which followed the Blatch affair,
particularly between 1897 and 1904, the Fabian Society
experienced a slump in membership, enthusiasm, and activity.
For much of this time foreign affairs were uppermost in
everyone's mind. What most divided the membership was the
vote on whether or not to declare the Society against the
South African War. When the Society voted against con-
demning the War, at least twenty members felt compelled
to resign, including the Pankhursts and Ramsey MacDonald.
The "woman question" all but disappeared from view. The
membership of the Society continued to elect an average
of two or three women to its fifteen member Executive each

term, but none emerged with the status or commitment of
an Annie Besant or Harriot Blatch. The few lectures to
be given by women (which were announced in the Executive
Minutes or the News) were cancelled, usually by the women
themselves, with depressing, but unexplained, regularity.
And lectures about women were as scarce as those given by
women. The same was true of tracts.

Only two tracts were published which dealt with the
"woman question"; together they demonstrate the Society's
ambivalence toward women's rights. On the one hand, "Women
as Councillors" (1900) objected to the ineligibility
of women, as a result of Lord Dunraven's exclusion clause,
for the newly created metropolitan borough councils. As
women had previously sat on vestries, the bodies which the
councils were designed to replace, their exclusion from the
latter was clearly "a deliberate step backwards in political
development."[63] On the other, "The London Education Act of
1903: How to Make the Best of It" strongly supported
transferring all educational functions from the London
School Board to the London County Council, in spite of
the fact that women were not eligible for the L.C.C.,
whereas they had served on the London School Board. The
one strong statement in favor of women's rights was
reserved for a footnote: "The great increase of the
educational work of the L.C.C. enormously reinforces the
argument in favor of allowing women to be elected as
councillors."[64]

The only issue which exercised the Executive in 1898 seems to have been whether or not to use the titles "Miss" and "Mrs." in connection with members' names in the Fabian News. The Executive announced its decision not to use such titles in May, only to rescind this judgment in June. The editors of the News, in the meantime, carefully refrained from sexist expressions in their wedding announcements: "A" and "B" "have married each other," they wrote, or "C" and "D" "have married." But, when a new set of Fabian Essays was being planned, the "woman question" was not among the topics to be included. In 1905 the Executive was still answering a request for active support of the Woman's Local Government Bill with a reply containing their "good wishes,"[65] and was responding to letters advancing woman suffrage by marking "noted" in the Executive Minutes.[66] In short, the Fabian Society's record on women's rights between 1897 and 1905 consisted of some bluster, much fluff, and little substance.

Interest in the "woman question" began to revive in 1905, although the positions adopted were of questionable merit from a feminist's point of view. In a tract advocating "The Abolition of Poor Law Guardians," posts for which women were eligible, the Society went beyond recommending the eligibility of women for the county and borough councils which were to take over the guardians' responsibilities. "The solution of the Woman Question" required not only the direct election of women to these councils, but the "co-option" of additional women to bring the total number to a minimum of five on each council.[67] "The Case for a Legal Minimum Wage" (July 1906) published a few months later also advocated the maintenance of different standards for the sexes. Here, however, the distinctions recommended were far more invidious. The minimum wage for women must be lower than that fixed for men, according to this tract, otherwise men will always be hired for their industrial superiority. A woman's wages should be sufficient to support herself, a man's to support a family, regardless of the individual's marital status.

* * *

In the course of 1906 various factors conspired to infuse the Society with a more feminist point of view. First, under the aegis of the Women's Social and Political Union, there was the growing strength and militance of the women's movement.[68] Second, the increasing interest in politics in general, and socialism in particular, inspired by the Liberal-Labor victories brought many new members and much new enthusiasm to the aging leadership and decreased numbers of the Fabian Society. Third, the "confused, tedious, ill-conceived and ineffectual campaign" of H. G. Wells "to turn the little Fabian Society" into an elitist governing class like the "Samurai" of his Utopian novel sparked an additional interest in the staid old Fabian.[69]

After ten years of neglect, the "woman question" was rediscovered. Wells, its new advocate, was more vociferous, more iconoclastic, than any of his predecessors in the Fabian. Concerned with the position of women in the family, Wells picked up where Mrs. Blatch had left off and went well beyond her proposals. Designating socialism as "a plan for the reconstruction of human life," he declared that it

> repudiates the private ownership of the head of the family as completely as it repudiates any other sort of private ownership. Socialism involves the responsible citizenship of women, their economic independence of men and all the personal freedom that follows. . . . Socialism is, in fact, the state family.[71]

With or without socialism, Wells claimed, "the family like capitalism is weakening of its own defects."[72] He described the feminine mind as offering a new source of "criticism against the individual family, . . . property of the once ascendant male," and suggested that "the discontent of women is a huge available force for socialism."[73] The practical equality of men and women in a civilized state, he argued, should be brought about by direct state payment to mothers for the children they bore and raised. Only in this way could women be spared, in the absence of a husband, the "monstrous absurdity . . . of discharging their supreme social function, bearing and rearing children, in their spare time as it were."[74]

Wells had joined the Fabian in 1903, a time when the number of lectures given and tracts sold was decreasing, and the one hundred or so active members always seemed to be giving lectures to the same one hundred or so active members. His "campaign" began in February 1906, with a lecture, "Faults of the Fabian," attacking the slow, gas and water brand of socialism of the Fabians, and its hidebound Executive. Wells's assault led to the establishment of a "Special Committee." Composed of ten members, chosen by Wells, himself, the purpose of the Committee was to issue a report suggesting possible reforms of the Society. Membership in the Fabian began to increase rapidly in the course of the nine month commotion which followed, attracted by the prospect of a confrontation between two such important literary lions of the left as Wells and Shaw.

The "Special Report" produced by Wells's "Special Committee" called for a variety of reforms. The Basis was to be altered to include the demand for the equal citizenship of men and women, and the substitution of public for private authority in the education and support of the young. The policy of permeation was to be abandoned. The structure of the Society was to be modified by the rejuvenation of group organizations, the transformation of the Executive into a Directorate of three, the expansion of commercial operations--including the publication of a major weekly--and the alteration of the mode of election of members.[75] Wells later described the process of reform: "Our seriousness was intense. We typed and printed and issued reports and replies and committee election appeals and personal statements, and my original intentions were buried at last beneath a steaming heap of hot secondary issues."[76]

The confrontation between the Special Committee and the Executive came to a head in December 1906 at two over-crowded members' meetings in Essex Hall. After a long and humorously malicious speech by Shaw on behalf of the Executive, the Special Committee's Report was defeated. Instead the Executive's Report, with its several conces-sions to the Special Committee's suggestions for reform, was endorsed. This outcome was as much a tribute to the membership's appreciation of the years of service of the "Old Gang" and to the effects of Shaw's eloquence as it was to Wells's ineptitude as a public speaker. Years later Wells candidly described his own performance as "speaking haltingly on the verge of the inaudible, addressing my tie through a cascade moustache that was no sort of help at all, correcting myself as though I were a manuscript under treatment," and as a series of "ill judged departures into parentheses."[77] Others were less flattering.

The major result of this "storm in the Fabian teacup"[78] was a change in the Fabian Basis, the first since its adoption in 1887. Rebellious female Fabians threatened to support Wells if a clause supporting equal rights for women was not inserted in the Basis. As mediator, Shaw was authorized only to offer the women "a tract on the subject."[79] After meeting with them, however, he returned and convinced his fellow Executors that they had no choice but to capitulate and add the innocuous phrase "including the establishment of equal citizenship for men and women" to that part of the Basis which called for "political changes" of all sorts.

Not surprisingly, given the nature of Wells's proposals, the percentage of women who joined the Society in the course of his "campaign" far exceeded that of men. Female membership doubled between 1906 and 1907, whereas male membership increased by only 30 percent. Thus, in 1907 women made up 33 percent of the London Membership, and 26 percent of the total membership of the Society. The percentage of women relative to men continued to climb until the War, reaching 43.4 percent of the 1,271 London members in 1913.[80] With the influx of new members, the need for a larger Executive was apparent; it was expanded in March 1907 to twenty-one seats. As one would expect, given the increase of women, many of them staunch feminists like Mrs. Pethick-Lawrence, the number of women on the Executive and the dynamism of their commitment to women's rights also increased.

Despite these changes the "Old Gang," which had both vanquished Wells and co-opted some of his ideas, remained in power for several more years. And it occasionally delivered some rather ambiguous views on the "woman question." Sidney Webb's tract (starting in 1907 tracts were signed by their authors, ending a twenty-three year policy of anonymity), "The Decline in the Birth Rate,"

is a case in point. Based in part on a survey of the
Fabian membership, Webb and his subcommittee found that a
decrease in family size was due to "deliberate volition"
in one-half to three-fourths of all families. Webb deplored
the declining birth rate, and the Irish and Jewish immigra-
tion he foresaw as a consequence.

To reverse this demographic trend, he proposed
altering "the economic incidence of child-bearing."[81] In
addition to calling for unlimited medical attendance for
mothers, a municipally-run scheme for the free distribution
of milk, the provision of free school lunches, and an
increase in the number of maintenance scholarships, Webb
advocated "the endowment of motherhood." By paying mothers
for raising their children, he hoped to put mothering on an
"honorable economic basis." He assured his readers that "to
the vast majority of women, and especially to those of fine
type, the rearing of children would be the most attractive
occupation, if it offered economic advantages equal to
those of school teaching or service in the post office."[82]
If motherhood were revered and honored by the state, it
would attract "the best and most patriotic citizens" and,
in so doing, the nation would "avoid race degeneration."[83]
Aside from the racist overtones of this Fabian tract,
several of its suggestions, including the endowment of
motherhood, were not only sensible, and in keeping with
Wells's earlier suggestions, but foreshadowed reforms of
the postwar welfare state. To his feminist associates,

however, Webb seemed to be making many of the right pleas,
for many of the wrong reasons.

* * *

In 1908, the tensions created by the Fabian old
guard's indifference to the "woman question" were both
eased and exacerbated by the formation of the Fabian
Women's Group. The Honorable Secretary no longer had to
record feminist requests for support with "courteously
acknowledged," in the Executive Minutes; he wrote instead,
"refer to Women's Group." The driving force, "the fount
and inspiration,"[84] behind this new group was an "old"
member, Mrs. Charlotte Wilson, returned to the fold after
years of anarchist activism. Her crusading experience, as
well as her early years on the Fabian Executive, added
significantly to her ability and credibility as a feminist
reformer. Mrs. Wilson was elected the first General
Secretary of the F.W.G., and remained so until ill health
forced her to resign in 1914. The two other women most
closely involved in the initial planning of the Group were
Mrs. George Bernard Shaw, who had been in the Society and
on the Executive for ten years, and Mrs. Pember Reeves.
Mrs. Reeves had become a member in February 1906, shortly
after settling in London with her husband, the Agent-
General for New Zealand. Her experience as a suffragist
in New Zealand, where women were granted the vote in 1893,
and as a political organizer of the newly enfranchised,
stood her in good stead. She gained immediate recognition

in the Society when she filled in as guest lecturer at a large Fabian meeting at Clifford's Hall in April 1906. She spoke without notes on her favorite topic, women's suffrage.[85] The following year she had been elected to the Executive, and it was she who negotiated with Shaw for the suffrage amendment to the Basis.

This little band of Fabian women resolved to form a group with two main objectives: to make equality in citizenship a prominent part of the Society's propaganda, as well as a reality in its internal organization, and to study women's economic status. The Group they formed was open to all women of the Fabian Society for the annual fee of one shilling, and to non-Fabian women at a somewhat higher rate. By the third meeting it had 159 members; within a few months that total was, and remained, over 200 members. The philosophy which infused the early work of the Group was a belief that "the difference between men and women in mental outlook," caused by differences in function, had been "artificially exaggerated and dis-torted by the subjection of women." Further, the "mental faculties of women are essentially similar to those of men, whilst the naturally distinctive mental outlook of each sex is equally valuable in social evolution."[86] Since the Fabian Society had "always implicitly conceded the principle of equality of opportunity between men and women," it was "meet and right that the Fabian should be the first Society to try . . . to define the intimate relation between the two most vital movements of the time, socialism and women's emancipation."[87]

In order to make the equality of Fabian men and women "a working reality," the Group immediately nominated three women candidates for the Executive, in addition to the four women who had served between 1907 and 1908 and were standing for re-election. Seven women on an Executive of twenty-one members would, they felt, more accurately reflect the increased proportion of women in the Society. To promote the citizenship of women in local government, F.W.G. members helped in local elections, worked to qualify themselves as municipal electors, and a few of them ran as candidates for local bodies. The major effort here was putting forward three Fabian women as possible candidates for the newly accessible London County Council in 1910. On the national level, the F.W.G. was single-minded in its support of women's suffrage; it was responsible for the first, and succeeding, Fabian contingents in the large suffrage demonstrations which began in June 1908. The Group sent resolutions protesting the treatment of suffrage prisoners, whose ranks included eleven of its own members. It prompted the Fabian Society to pass resolutions in support of women's suffrage bills, and to send them to the Prime Minister. And it pressured the two Fabian parliamentary candidates "to urge upon the electors the cause of Women's Suffrage"[88] by making their contributions to the Parliamentary Fund dependent upon such actions.

With regard to their investigations into economics,
the Women's Group first arranged a course of lectures on
the "Natural Disabilities of Women as Workers" to examine
what was known about those factors hindering women in the
workplace. A consensus was reached in favor of paid work
for married or single women not actively engaged in raising
children and of state assistance for mothers. The Group
discovered that "the greatest stumbling block" to reaching
more specific conclusions about the form women's "economic
independence" should take was that "women themselves have
not studied the question scientifically in their own
interests."[89] To this end, the next set of papers discussed was an historical series: "Women as Producers and
Consumers of the Past." This was followed by a series of
lectures on "The Present Economic Condition of Women" which
dealt with the lives of servants, actresses, clerks,
teachers, and the like. In the course of 1912, a subcommittee began to consider the issue of a minimum wage
and how it related to women. It began an investigation to
test the proposition that most women and girls worked only
to support themselves, and hence their wages should be
lower than men's. Such an inquiry had not taken place
prior to the publication of Fabian Tract 128, which advocated a disparity between the wages of men and women, based
on just that proposition.

The Fabian Women's Group was certainly not always
able to get its way on women's issues. It received "cordial

furtherance and support from the Fabian Executive,"[90] but
the various sets of Fabian Minutes are strewn with refusals
of F.W.G. requests that their summaries be distributed with
the Fabian News,[91] or that resolutions be forwarded,[92] or
circulars on behalf of their candidates be distributed with
their Annual Report,[93] as well as reprimands for printing
such resolutions without first consulting the Executive.
Yet as a result of the investigations and the continuing
pressure of the F.W.G., the publications of the Fabian
Society began to reflect more accurately the problems
and concerns of women, particularly after the Group began
a series of tracts under its own imprint, subject only to
final approval by the Fabian Executive.

In "The Working Life of Women," Miss B. L. Hutchins
argued that women were not necessarily less healthy as a
result of working, as long as the conditions of employment
were satisfactory. Moreover, it did not make sense to
discuss women's "true role" when working was a necessity
for so many. Nor did it make sense to discuss women's
greater physical disabilities, given the fact that there
were more male criminals and more male alcoholics than
females of that ilk. Women were handicapped by their
inferior economic position, she claimed, not by their
physical weakness.[94]

"Family Life on a Pound a Week," by Mrs. Reeves,
chronicled the results of her three year study of the
budgets and methods of survival adopted by families forced

to live on eighteen to twenty-four shillings a week.
Showing how impossible a task the wives were attempting,
she pressed for a national minimum wage, school feeding,
school clinics, and compulsory baby clinics.[95] In "Women
and Prisons," Helen Blagg and Charlotte Wilson discussed
the dreadful conditions women faced in prisons, and pointed
to the need for women officials as magistrates and as
governors of such institutions. To document their case,
the authors made use of firsthand information garnered
from a new type of inmate, imprisoned suffragettes.[96]

With the publication of "The Economic Foundations
of the Women's Movement," by Mabel Atkinson, the F.W.G.
went beyond a careful study of women's particular problems
to champion certain concepts antithetical to those formerly
endorsed in Fabian publications. Miss Atkinson charted the
course of women's economic history in the nineteenth
century, and of the women's movement which began in 1867.
The first generation of feminists were apt to be older,
unmarried women whose main concern was with greater freedom
and equal rights for women; they tended to de-emphasize the
differences between the sexes. But the second generation
of feminists were beginning to want "both" marriage and
work, and, for all but the "few exceptional women," working
on the same terms as men during child rearing was imprac-
tical. This, however, did not preclude women working after
their children were of school age, and certainly did not
dictate a blanket dismissal of married women from their

jobs.[97] This, of course, ran contrary to Fabian Tract 47 in which Mr. John Burns proposed just such a dismissal.

Recognizing the central problem of child raising, Miss Atkinson argued in favor of the endowment of mother-hood just as Mr. Henry Harben did in Tract 149. Unlike Mr. Harben, however, she did not predicate her support for this plan on the expectation that it would keep women at home. Instead, she recommended it as a means of allow-ing the wages between men and women to be equal, since men would no longer be solely responsible for supporting their children. Naturally, this espousal of equal wages contradicted the view expressed in Tract 128 in which Mr. Stephen Sanders supported unequal wages between the sexes. So too, Miss Atkinson supported the endowment of mothers because it would encourage marriage, by reducing its economic burden on men, but would not necessarily increase the number of children born to these marriages. Here Miss Atkinson parted company with Mr. Sidney Webb's view in Tract 131 wherein he recommended the endowment of motherhood as a means of increasing the declining English birth rate. She suggested instead, what modern studies have confirmed, that the economic independence of women leads to their having fewer children, not more.[98]

Perhaps what is most interesting about "The Economic Foundations of the Women's Movement" is how clearly it illustrates the difference between earlier tracts written by men and published by a Society which "has always favored

women suffrage,"[99] and those written by women and published
by a Society which was suddenly propelled by a well
organized minority fully committed to women's rights.
Indeed, the activities of the F.W.G. demonstrate both the
capriciousness and the paucity of previous Fabian efforts
on behalf of women.

III. Fabian Couples

In considering the Fabian Society's record with
regard to the "woman question" between 1884 and 1914,
however, it is not to the Fabian Women's Group one must
look. The Group's first, somewhat cautious, tract ("The
Working Life of Women") was not published until 1911.[100]
Miss Atkinson's far more dynamic and demanding tract
was issued in 1914. For the many years prior to these
publications, other forces were at work, other people were
in charge. In part, the Society's earlier behavior
reflected the fits and starts of the wider feminist movement, the disagreements among its own feminine members with
regard to women's issues, and the absence of long-term
feminine leadership within the Society, that is, of women
who remained active in the Society and actively interested
in feminism over a long period of time. More than this it
reflected the contradictory notions and prejudice of
the most influential members of the Society, most of
whom happened to be men.

The "Old Gang" dominated the Fabian Executive, and

by extension, the rest of the Society, almost from its inception. While other names are occasionally included under this rubric, none would disagree that its principal members were Sidney Webb, G.B.S., Graham Wallas, Sidney Olivier, Hubert Bland, and Edward Pease. Bland and Pease, founder members, were Treasurer and Secretary, respectively. In his twenty-six years as General Secretary, Edward Pease served primarily as an administrator, rather than a policy-maker. Bland, on the other hand, in his far less demanding job as Treasurer, was very much involved in the making of policy and propaganda for the Society. Shaw, Webb, Wallas, and Olivier all joined the Fabian in the course of 1885-86, all were friends, all hammered out their distinctive version of socialism at the fortnightly meetings of the Hampstead Historic. With Bland they comprised five of the seven authors responsible for <u>Fabian Essays</u>, the work which was so important to the "first blooming" of the Fabian.

Graham Wallas, a schoolmaster turned lecturer and author, was the first to leave the fold; he resigned from the Executive in 1897, fearing to compromise his position on the London School Board by active participation in a socialist society. His increasingly Liberal leanings led him to resign from the society entirely in 1904. Sidney Olivier, a high level civil servant in the Colonial Office, had to resign from the Executive in 1900 when he became Acting Governor of Jamaica. Thereafter, he spent significant amounts of time away from London, although he remained active in Fabian affairs whenever he was in town. Neither Mrs. Graham Wallas nor Mrs. Sidney Olivier showed much interest in the Fabian Society.

The most powerful and lasting influence on the Society was that of George Bernard Shaw and Sidney Webb. Until just before the First World War, they held sway over the Society by dint of their continuing interest, their diligent work on its behalf, and their singular abilities. The alliance they formed with regard to most issues was rarely to be balked, particularly when Hubert Bland was in agreement with them, that is, when he was not playing his role as the most persistent thorn in their Fabian flesh.

Perhaps it is not surprising that the wives of Webb, Shaw, and Bland were among the few women who were involved in the Fabian over an extended period. Each of them was important to the Society, each in her own way, and at different times. E. Nesbit Bland was most active in the formative years of the Society, Charlotte Shaw in the first decade of the twentieth century, and Beatrice Webb became fully involved in 1912. None of these women played as important a role as did her husband; yet all expressed interest--and, in Beatrice's case, exerted influence--in the Society even in the years they were not active.

In describing the strength of the Fabian Society, Sidney Webb maintained that its accomplishments were merely

the sum of its members' efforts. Few members were as
accomplished or as influential within the Society as
Webb and Shaw, and to a lesser extent Hubert Bland.
Certainly, no other couples of equal importance to the
Society emerged until the advent of G.D.H. and Margaret
Cole a generation later. To understand fully why the Fabian
response to the "woman question" was "lukewarm," one must
understand the views of these leading Fabians. On an issue
as emotionally charged as is women's rights, however, stated
opinions are not enough. Seeming indifference to women's
problems is as likely to represent a conflicted response to
the role of women, or to the relationship between the sexes,
as it is to represent ignorance of those problems or apathy
toward them.

     To clarify both the ideological response of these
six Fabians, and the experiences and attitudes which
informed those responses, I propose to examine not only
the tracts, essays, poems, plays, and books they wrote,
but their marriages as well. My assumption is that a
partner's real feelings about the rights and responsibilities
of each sex, and his or her own sexual identification, are
nowhere more apparent than in the conjugal relationship.
Thus, in discussing the biographies of these three Fabian
couples--the Shaws, the Blands, and the Webbs--I hope
to shed additional light on their views with regard to

the "woman question" and on the correspondence or
contradiction between their views and their life experiences.

Footnotes

[1]See Karl Marx and Frederick Engels, The Communist
Manifesto (New York: International Publishers, 1948),
pp. 26-28; Frederick Engels, The Origin of the Family,
Private Property, and the State (New York: International
Publishers, 1972); August Bebel, Women in the Past, Pre-
sent, and Future (London: Modern Press, 1885).

[2]Marx and Engels, Communist Manifesto, p. 27.

[3]See Sheila Rowbotham, Women, Resistance and
Revolution (New York: Pantheon Books, 1973); Sheila
Rowbotham, Hidden From History (New York: Random House,
1974); Elizabeth Wilson, Women and the Welfare State
(London: Tavistock Publications, 1977); Jean H. Quataert,
Reluctant Feminists in German Social Democracy, 1885-1917
(Princeton, N.J.: Princeton University Press, 1979);
Marilyn Boxer, "Socialism Meets Feminism in France 1879-
1813" (Ph.D. diss., University of California, Riverside,
1975); Mary-Alice Waters, "Feminism and the Marxist Movement," International Socialist Review 33, no. 9 (1972):
8-23.

[4]Quataert, Reluctant Feminists, pp. 234-35.

[5]Boxer, "Socialism Meets Feminism," p. 307.

[6]Rowbotham, Hidden from History, p. 90; Quataert,
Reluctant Feminists, p. 234; Boxer, "Socialism Meets
Feminism," p. 322.

[7]On British Socialism in the 1880's and 1890's,
see Chushichi Tsuzuki, H. M. Hyndman and British Socialism
(London: Oxford University Press, 1961); E. P. Thompson,
William Morris (New York: Pantheon Books, 1976); Robert E.
Dowse, Left in the Centre, the Independent Labour Party
1893-1940 (Evanston, Ill.: Northwestern University Press,
1966); Laurence Thompson, The Enthusiasts: A Biography of
John and Katharine Bruce Glasier (London: Gollancz,
1971); R. C. K. Ensor, ed., Modern Socialism (London:
Harper and Brothers, 1904); Helen M. Lynd, England in
the Eighteen-Eighties: Toward a Social Basis for Freedom
(London: Oxford University Press, 1945); Eric J. Hobsbawm,
ed., Labour's Turning Point, 1880-1900 (Cranbury, N.J.:
Associated University Presses, 1974); Max Beer, A History
of British Socialism (London: Allen and Unwin, 1953).

[8]Eric J. Hobsbawm, Labouring Men: Studies in the
History of Labour (London: Weidenfeld and Nicolson,
1964), pp. 250-71. On the Fabian Society, see also

Edward R. Pease, The History of the Fabian Society (New York: Barnes and Noble, 1963); Anne Fremantle, This Little Band of Prophets (New York: New American Library, 1959); Margaret Cole, The Story of Fabian Socialism (Stanford, Ca.: Stanford University Press, 1961); Margaret Cole, ed., The Webbs and Their Work (London: Frederick Muller, 1949); A. M. McBriar, Fabian Socialism and English Politics 1884-1918 (Cambridge: Cambridge University Press, 1962); for the most recent treatment, see Norman and Jeanne MacKenzie, The Fabians (New York: Simon and Schuster, 1977).

[9]Cole, Story of Fabian Socialism, pp. 127-28.

[10]For diverse considerations of the "woman question," see Simone De Beauvoir, The Second Sex, trans. H. M. Parshley (New York: Alfred A. Knopf, 1953); J. A. and Olive Banks, Feminism and Family Planning in Victorian England (Liverpool: Liverpool University Press, 1964); Juliet Mitchell, Women's Estate (New York: Random House, 1971); Michelle Rosaldo and Louise Lamphere, eds., Women, Culture, and Society (Stanford, Ca.: Stanford University Press, 1974); Martha Vicinus, ed., Suffer and Be Still, Women in the Victorian Age (Bloomington: Indiana University Press, 1972); Renate Bridenthal and Claudia Koonz, eds., Becoming Visible, Women in European History (Boston: Houghton Mifflin, 1977); Patricia Hollis, Women in Public: The Women's Movement 1850-1900 (London: George Allen and Unwin, 1979). On the psychological aspects of the "woman question," see Sigmund Freud, The Standard Edition of the Complete Psychological Works of Sigmund Freud, trans. and ed. James Strachey (London: Hogarth Press, 1953-74), vol. 19, Some Psychical Consequences of the Anatomical Distinction Between the Sexes (1925), pp. 248-60; vol. 21, Female Sexuality (1931), pp. 225-46; vol. 22, Femininity (1933), pp. 112-35. See also, Melanie Klein, "Early Stages of the Oedipus Conflict" (1928), in her Love, Guilt and Reparation, and Other Works, 1925-45 (London: Hogarth Press, 1975), pp. 186-98; Karen Horney, Feminine Psychology (New York: W. W. Norton, 1967); Jean Baker Miller, ed., Psychoanalysis and Women (Harmondsworth, Middlesex: Penguin Books, 1973); Jean Strouse, ed., Women and Analysis (New York: Grossman Publishers, 1974); Eleanor E. Maccoby and Carol Nagy Jacklin, The Psychology of Sex Differences (Stanford, Ca.: Stanford University Press, 1974); Patrick C. Lee and Robert S. Stewart, eds., Sex Differences: Cultural and Developmental Dimensions (New York: Urizen Books, 1976); Juanita H. Williams, The Psychology of Women (New York: W. W. Norton, 1977); Nancy Chodorow, The Reproduction of Mothering: Psychoanalysis and the Sociology of Gender (Berkeley: University of California Press, 1978).

[11]Pease, History of the Fabian Society, p. 31.

[12]Edith Lees, Attainment (London: Alston Rivers, 1909), p. 263.

[13]George Bernard Shaw, Essays in Fabian Socialism (London: Constable and Company, 1932), pp. 132-34.

[14]"Fabian Basis" in Hobsbawm, ed., Labour's Turning Point, p. 55.

[15]S. G. Hobson, Pilgrim to the Left (London: Edward Arnold, 1938), p. 139.

[16]Edward Pease gave up the stock exchange in 1886 because it conflicted with his socialist principles. Between 1886 and 1889 he was living in Newcastle, working as a cabinet maker. Pease was induced to return to London and take up the secretaryship of the Society in 1890.

[17]George Bernard Shaw, "The Economic Basis of Socialism," in Fabian Essays in Socialism, ed. George Bernard Shaw (London: Walter Scott, 1908), pp. 173-201.

[18]Sidney Webb, "The Historic Basis of Socialism," ibid., pp. 30-36.

[19]Hubert Bland, "The Outlook," ibid., p. 214.

[20]The Independent Labour Party had its origins in the same impulse toward collectivist solutions to the economic problems of the early 1890's, and many provincial Fabians were instrumental in the development of local I.L.P. branches in 1893-94. But the I.L.P. was preponderantly working-class; its ranks included many more trade unionists than middle-class intellectuals. More important, it was an activist party dedicated to the election of labor representatives to Parliament, and its existence made local Fabian Societies superfluous. By the end of 1894, eleven of them had joined with corresponding branches of the I.L.P. and had ceased to function. By 1900, there were only four provincial Fabian Societies in existence, with a total membership of 153, although this number increased considerably with the rise in popularity of the Fabians after 1906.

[21]Fabian Society, Annual Report (London: Fabian Society, 1909), p. 12.

[22]Annie Besant, Lecture to Fabian Society, December 3, 1886, reprinted in Our Corner 10 (August 1887): 95-99.

[23]George Bernard Shaw, "A Manifesto" (1884),
Fabian Tract No. 2, reprinted in Pease, History of the
Fabian Society, pp. 41-43; see also "The True Radical
Program," Fabian Tract No. 6 (London: Fabian Society,
1888); "Facts for Londoners," Fabian Tract No. 8 (London:
Fabian Society, 1889).

[24]The Annual Report, a summary of the year's work;
Fabian News, a monthly newsletter; and Edward Pease's
"Executive Minutes" were all begun in 1890.

[25]E. Nesbit Bland to Ada Breakell, 1885, in Doris
Langley Moore, E. Nesbit, a Biography (New York: Chilton
Books, 1966), pp. 85-86.

[26]Hubert Bland to G. B. Shaw, 25 September 1886,
Shaw Papers, M.S. 50557, British Library.

[27]Annie Besant, "Autobiographical Sketches,"
Our Corner 3 and 4 (January-December 1884); 5 (January-
June 1885).

[28]Annie Besant, The Law of Population: Its Consequences, and Its Bearing upon Human Conduct and Morals
(London: Freethought, 1889), p. 32.

[29]J. A. Banks, Feminism and Family Planning in
Victorian England (Liverpool: Liverpool University Press,
1964), p. 97.

[30]"Some Advanced Women of the Past," Our Corner
4, 280-84.

[31]"Anti-Slavery Women," Our Corner 6, 167.

[32]Annie Besant, "Women in the Past, Present and
Future," review of Women in the Past, Present and Future,
by August Bebel, in Our Corner 6 (August 1885): 94-98.

[33]Annie Besant, "Modern Socialism," Our Corner 7
(1886): 263.

[34]Ibid.

[35]The Theosophical Society was founded in America
in 1875 by Madame Blavatsky and Colonel Olcott to achieve
universal brotherhood and to investigate the unexplained
laws of nature and the psychical powers latent in man.
According to their dictates, "man is a spiritual intelligence, . . . born and reborn . . . evolving slowly into the
ideal man." He is not the product of matter, but is
encased in it, and his intelligence and will are creative

forces which manifest themselves in "thought forms" which
persist after his death and shape the new person he is
to be. Annie Besant, An Autobiography (London: T. Fisher
Unwin, 1893), pp. 352 and 241.

[36]Membership List, "Fabian Minutes" (1890), Fabian
Papers, Nuffield College, Oxford.

[37]"Fabian Minutes," January 1892.

[38]Ibid., June 1891.

[39]Ibid., 7 July 1891.

[40]Fabian News 1, no. 6 (August 1891).

[41]Periodically the members of the Fabian Society
split up into geographical groups, which met for purposes
of increasing local political activity and intellectual
contact. They were fairly unstable constellations which
came and went irregularly.

[42]Fabian News 2, no. 3 (May 1892).

[43]Mary Lacey to Graham Wallas, 6 January 1893,
Wallas Collection, British Library of Political and Economic Science.

[44]Ibid., 8 January 1893.

[45]Fabian News 2, no. 3 (May 1892).

[46]Joseph Edwards, ed., The Labour Annual (1895;
reprint ed., Brighton, Sussex: Harvester Press, 1971),
p. 163.

[47]Emma Brooke, Transition (Philadelphia: J. B.
Lippencott, 1895), p. 286.

[48]See "The Workers' Political Program," Fabian
Tract No. 11 (London: Fabian Society, 1890); "The New
Reform Bill," Fabian Tract No. 14 (London: Fabian Society,
1891); "Questions for Parliamentary Candidates," Fabian
Tract No. 24 (London: Fabian Society, 1891).

[49]See "Questions for Town Councillors," Fabian
Tract No. 27 (London: Fabian Society, 1891); "Questions
for County Councillors," Fabian Tract No. 28 (London:
Fabian Society, 1891).

[50]"Questions for School Board Candidates," Fabian
Tract No. 25 (London: Fabian Society, 1891).

[51]"The Unemployed," Fabian Tract No. 47 (London: Fabian Society, 1893).

[52]Emma Brooke to Edward Pease, 9 March 1894, 16 March 1894, 18 March 1894, and 22 March 1894, Fabian Papers, Box A6, Nuffield College, Oxford.

[53]Elizabeth Cady Stanton to Elizabeth Smith Miller, 24 January 1856, cited in Harriot Stanton Blatch and Alma Lutz, Challenging Years, the Memoirs of Harriot Stanton Blatch (New York: G. P. Putnam's Sons, 1940); Westport, Conn.: Hyperion Press, 1976), p. 3.

[54]Alma Lutz, Created Equal, a Biography of Elizabeth Cady Stanton (New York: John Day, 1940), p. 259.

[55]Blatch, Challenging Years, p. 85.

[56]Ibid., pp. 73-74.

[57]Ibid., pp. 84-85.

[58]"Fabian Minutes," 5 October 1894.

[59]Ibid., 25 January 1895.

[60]Harriot Stanton Blatch, "Specialization of Function in Women," Guntons Magazine 10 (May 1896): 352.

[61]G. B. Shaw to E. Pease, 28 January 1896, Fabian Papers, Nuffield College, Oxford.

[62]In America Harriot Stanton Blatch took up the suffrage cause in earnest. The Equality League of Self-Supporting Women which she founded in 1907 (it became the Women's Political Union [W.P.U.] in 1910) was a strong force in the campaign for suffrage in New York state. Eager to finish the work her mother had begun, Harriot employed new methods for the old battle. Her organization included working-class women and younger women, several still at university, and it stressed influencing those in power, rather than educating and organizing those already converted. The cross-fertilization which had gone on between the English and American suffrage movements since Elizabeth Cady Stanton's first trip to England in 1840 was nowhere more apparent than in the policies of, and the interaction between, Mrs. Pankhurst's W.S.P.U. and Mrs. Blatch's W.P.U.

[63]"Women As Councillors," Fabian Tract No. 93 (London: Fabian Society, 1900).

[64]"The London Education Act, How to Make the Best of It," Fabian Tract No. 117 (London: Fabian Society, 1904), p. 4.

[65]"Fabian Minutes," March 1905.

[66]Ibid., December 1905.

[67]According to "The Abolition of Poor Law Guardians," there was a minimum of five women on the council in only 64 of 645 unions. It stated further that "co-option is only an alternative form of democratic government," a necessary one when democracy itself fails to produce sound representative government. "The Abolition of Poor Law Guardians," Fabian Tract No. 126 (London: Fabian Society, 1906), p. 15.

[68]On the subject of women's suffrage, see Helen Blackburn, Women's Suffrage (1902; reprint ed., New York: Source Book Press, 1970); Millicent Garrett Fawcett, What I Remember (1925; reprint ed., Westport, Conn.: Hyperion Press, 1976); E. Sylvia Pankhurst, The Suffragette Movement (London: Longmans, Green, 1931); Emmeline Pethick-Lawrence, My Part in a Changing World (London: Victor Gollancz, 1938); Ray Strachey, The Cause (Port Washington, N.Y.: Kennikat Press, 1969); Constance Rover, Women's Suffrage and Party Politics in Britain, 1866-1914 (London: Routledge and Kegan Paul, 1967); Marian Ramelson, The Petticoat Rebellion (London: Lawrence and Wishart, 1967); David Mitchell, The Fighting Pankhursts (New York: Macmillan, 1967); David Mitchell, Queen Christabel (London: MacDonald and James, 1977); Andrew Rosen, Rise up, Women!: The Militant Campaign of the Women's Social and Political Union, 1903-14 (London: Routledge and Kegan Paul, 1974); David Morgan, Suffragists and Liberals (Oxford: Blackwell, 1975). For a most useful text on the American Suffrage Movement, see Aileen S. Kraditor, The Ideas of the Woman Suffrage Movement, 1890-1920 (New York: Columbia University Press, 1965).

[69]H. G. Wells, Experiment in Autobiography (New York: Macmillan, 1934), p. 564.

[70]H. G. Wells, "Socialism and the Middle Classes," in his Socialism and the Family (Boston: Ball, 1908), p. 6.

[71]Ibid., p. 30.

[72]Ibid., p. 40.

[73]Ibid., p. 36.

[74] Ibid., p. 59.

[75] "Report of the Special Committee," 1906, Fabian Papers, Box B5/2, Nuffield College, Oxford.

[76] H. G. Wells, Autobiography, p. 565.

[77] Ibid.

[78] Ibid., p. 564.

[79] "Fabian Minutes," 30 November 1906.

[80] Fabian Society, Annual Report (1890-1914).

[81] Sidney Webb, "The Decline in the Birth Rate," Fabian Tract No. 131 (London: Fabian Society, 1907), p. 17.

[82] Ibid., p. 19.

[83] Ibid.

[84] Edith Morley, ed., Women Workers in Seven Professions (London: George Routledge and Sons, 1914), p. v.

[85] Keith Sinclair, William Pember Reeves (Oxford: Clarendon Press, 1965), p. 313.

[86] "Three Years' Work of the Women's Group" (London: Fabian Society, 1911), pp. 1-2.

[87] Ibid.

[88] Ibid., pp. 6-7.

[89] Ibid., p. 12.

[90] "Extracts from the Report for 1908," Fabian News (March 1909).

[91] "Publishing Committee Minutes," September 1909.

[92] "Finance and General Purposes Committee Minutes," October 1909.

[93] "Publishing Committee Minutes," March 1911.

[94] Mrs. B. L. Hutchins, "The Working Life of Women," Fabian Tract No. 157, Fabian Women's Group Series No. 1 (London: Fabian Society, 1911).

[95]Mrs. Pember Reeves, "Family Life on a £ a Week," Fabian Tract No. 162, F.W.G. Series No. 2 (London: Fabian Society, 1912).

[96]Helen Blagg and Charlotte Wilson, "Women and Prisons," Fabian Tract No. 163, F.W.G. Series No. 3 (London: Fabian Society, 1912).

[97]Mabel Atkinson, "The Economic Foundations of the Women's Movement," Fabian Tract No. 175, F.W.G. Series No. 4 (London: Fabian Society, 1914).

[98]See Ronald Fletcher, The Family and Marriage in Britain (Baltimore: Penguin Books, 1962), p. 116.

[99]"Fabian Minutes," 23 February 1892.

[100]In "The Working Life of Women," Miss Hutchins seems to be leading up to a demand for equal wages between the sexes, but she does not overtly suggest such a reform.

Chapter 2

THE GEORGE BERNARD SHAWS

The most famous, and the most emphatically feminist,
of the early Fabians was George Bernard Shaw. His wife,
Charlotte Payne-Townshend, a latecomer to the Fabian fold
and to the feminist movement, was, nonetheless, active in
both and a true believer in the feminist cause. As a
revolutionary dramatist intent on peaceful revolutions,
Shaw insisted on rephrasing and expanding the "woman
question" to allow for a myriad of diverse answers. His
suggestions often involved changes in the very nature of
society and, at times, went well beyond the demands being
made by the most ardent feminists. Charlotte Shaw, every
inch the Victorian lady, supported the more conventional
reforms of the women's movement, while believing as strongly
as he in the need for revolutionary changes in the existing
relationships between the sexes.

The Shaws might have created a marriage which
managed to translate feminist ideology into practice.
Instead, their marriage provides an interesting example of
the discrepancies which so often exist between the theories
we preach and the routines we practice. Their relationship
suited them both, most of the time; insofar as Charlotte's
careful ministrations extended the productivity of the

"writing machine" Shaw considered himself, it benefited generations of Shaw's reading public as well. On the subject of nontraditional and mutually rewarding relationships between the sexes, however, one must look to Shaw's writings and not to their union for edification.

I. The Quintessence of Shavian Feminism

"Men no longer need special political privileges to protect them against women, and . . . the sexes should henceforth enjoy equal political rights."[1] Thus read George Bernard Shaw's demand for the political emancipation of women in his first publication on behalf of the Fabian Society--Tract 2, "A Manifesto," published in 1884. In the course of the next thirty years, Shaw remained steadfast in this view of the relative strength of the sexes. He was far less resolute in his support for women's political rights.

As one might expect of a public figure with as much to say as he had on the subject of women and their political rights and wrongs, Shaw was often inconsistent on such matters. To a certain extent, his inconstancy as a woman-suffragist was related to changes in his thinking, over time, about the value of the democratic process or the benefits to be gained from any extension of the suffrage. As a Fabian, the erosion of his faith in what a socialist organization could accomplish or what a socialist state might achieve also affected his view of the "woman question." In 1885, for example, he talked optimistically of socialism as "a principle on which to judge all measures and a hope for the future of civilization."[2] In this context, Shaw viewed the extension of women's rights as an issue on which socialists would naturally take a stand, and as one of the goals toward which socialists were striving. A decade later, however, he had decided that socialism was merely a series of practical installments of economic reform, and socialists could not be expected to hold any particular views on issues such as women's rights.[3]

Several years of espousing doctrines which seemed to have no hope of being implemented, and of seeing lesser reforms yield little of the hoped for results, certainly contributed to Shaw's diminishing expectations. Beyond this, one finds an ambivalence in Shaw's attitudes toward women which complicated, and often made contradictory, his responses to the "woman question," regardless of his sentiments on democracy or socialism. Thus, in 1889 when Shaw was concerned with democracy as a means of evolving the Social Democratic state, he claimed--in his second contribution to Fabian Essays--that "the outlawry of women, monstrous as it is, is not a question of class privilege," and was not, therefore, a crucial issue. What was needed, inter alia, "to complete the foundation of the democratic state," was "manhood suffrage."[4] After the elections of 1895, and the complete defeat of labor

candidates amidst a Conservative victory, Shaw stated that
as a socialist he <u>was</u> <u>not</u> concerned with democracy; therefore he could not be bothered about the enfranchisement of
women. He told the Fabian Society at the end of that year
that

> just at present the extension of the franchise from
> the Collectivist point of view is not very pressing,
> because . . . the working class has already got
> more votes than it knows how to use. . . . But
> the educated and intelligent woman is still dis-
> enfranchised on the grounds that the majority of
> women are fools whilst the majority of men are
> let loose with votes in their hands at every elec-
> tion. This, however, is a matter of Enlightenment
> rather than study or investigation: it is a waste
> of time to argue about it.[5]

He stated the case against democracy more vitupera-
tively a few years later in his "Preface" to <u>Man and</u>
<u>Superman</u>, lampooning it as "the last refuge of cheap
misgovernment,"[6] and railing against the fact that "the
aristocracy has come back to power by the votes of the
'swinish multitude.'"[7] If democracy was, as he suggested,
like some men's plays, "it reads well but it doesn't play
well,"[8] why bother to enlarge the franchise?

Despite his lack of enthusiasm for extending the
suffrage, Shaw's role in the Fabian Society, until the turn
of the century, was a positive one on the issue of women's
political rights. Of the few tracts published in support
of votes for women, on any level, Shaw had penned three of
them. His first and most enthusiastic salvo, Tract 2, has
already been discussed. His second, Tract 70, "Report on
Fabian Policy," was composed of resolutions recommended by

the Fabian Society for the International Socialist Workers'
and Trade Unionists' Congress in London in 1896. The
Fabian program called for: "complete equality in all
political rights and duties," equal pay for equal work,
and equal opportunities for educational and technical
training for men and women, along with a series of other
moderate, non-revolutionary reforms. Interestingly enough,
in contrast to other pronouncements by Shaw, specifically
his contribution to Fabian Essays, the "Report" stated,
"Democracy as understood by the Fabian Society . . . makes
no political distinction between men and women." Because
of the very nature of the tract, that is, as a report to
a Socialist Congress, its proposals cannot be solely
attributed to Shaw. Unlike the process followed in the
writing of most tracts, especially those by Shaw, each
resolution therein had been discussed by the members
of the Executive beforehand. Shaw acted more as amanuensis
to the Executive and the twenty Fabian delegates to the
Congress than as sole creator of the tract.[9]

However, Tract 93, "Women as Councillors," written
by Shaw, was pure Shaw; it used several of the arguments
for giving women the vote on local matters that he had used
elsewhere. This brief tract was a protest against the
"deliberate step backwards in political development" which
the Dunraven Exclusion Act of June 1899 represented. The
Act kept women from sitting on the newly created metropolitan borough councils in spite of the fact that these

councils were replacing vestries to which women had been elected since 1894. The major point stressed by the tract was that the new councils would have to do work that could not be done by men, such as interacting with women inspectors employed under the Public Health Act to inspect workshops and sanitary accommodations or seeing to the provision of public lavatories for women. Shaw's own six year experience as a vestryman for St. Pancras is very much apparent in this tract, especially in the distinction he draws between the need for women's involvement on issues which concern them, a point he felt was being stressed sufficiently by many others, and his own point that there was a good deal of work that could not be done at all without women there to do it.

The "woman question," however, was not merely a matter of political rights. If Shaw could not be classified as an overly enthusiastic or consistent suffragist, his ability to understand and delineate the common humanity that bridged the gap between the sexes was, at times, remarkable. In the first decade of the Society's history, Shaw was the most persuasive enunciator of this broader feminist perspective. His lecture, "The Quintessence of Ibsenism," delivered to the Fabian in 1891, is a case in point.

Praising the Norwegian playwright, and depicting him as far more of a feminist than in fact he was, Shaw also expounded one of the most convincing arguments for the emancipation of women since Mill's <u>The Subjection of</u>

<u>Women</u>:

> Our society, being directly dominated by men,
> comes to regard Woman, not as an end in herself
> like Man, but solely as a means of ministering
> to his appetite. The ideal wife is one who does
> everything that the ideal husband likes and nothing
> else. Now to treat a person as a means instead
> of an end is to deny that person's right to live. [10]

What makes such a situation at all viable for a woman is

that "the self respect she has lost as a wife she regains

as a mother,"[11] but this solution is extremely limited:

> It depends upon the accident of the woman having
> some natural vocation for domestic management and
> the care of children. . . . Hence arises the
> idealist illusion that a vocation for domestic
> management and the care of children is natural
> to women, and that women who lack them are not
> women at all. . . . But it is not true. The
> domestic career is no more natural to all women
> than the military career is natural to all men.
> . . . If we have come to think that the nursery
> and the kitchen are the natural sphere of a woman,
> we have done so exactly as English children come
> to think that a cage is the natural sphere of a
> parrot--because they have never seen one anywhere
> else.[12]

As the decade of the 90's wore on, Shaw began

to address himself less often to the "woman question" in

any of its guises. After writing Tract 93 for the Society

in 1899, he remained relatively quiet on the subject of

women's rights for several years. By this time, Shaw had

little if any faith left in the democratic state, or in

socialist solutions to society's ills. He had become

thoroughly disenchanted by the ineptitude of socialists,

the inapplicability of socialism, and the inability of

the "multitude" to understand their own interests. But,

he was not about to drop a doctrine he has espoused for fifteen years; in fact, he remained a professed socialist and a Fabian throughout his long life. Writing to Sidney Webb in 1901 about their mutual wish to back Lord Rosebery and the Liberal Imperialists, Shaw warned:

> We shall have to be very careful to avoid any appearance of going back on our socialism. Nothing is more unpopular in England than hauling down a flag, even if it has become a flagrantly impossible flag. . . . Politically then, we are committed for life to socialism and any appearance of backing out of it would leave us less influence than Hyndman or Hardie.[13]

Thus, Shaw retained his cloak of socialism by virtue of stitching the garment as he went along, making it fit Imperialist doctrines, then high tariffs, as well as the Conservative Education Bills of 1902 and 1903, and even National Socialism, briefly, in the early 1930's, and Stalinism thereafter.

* * *

The doctrine that Shaw embraced after the turn of the century and which was to infuse his plays to a far greater extent than had socialism, was Vitalism, or Creative Evolution. Here Shaw was strongly influenced by the theories of Samuel Butler and Henri Bergson. From Butler, Shaw borrowed an anti-Darwinian conception of evolution which posited that the strongest individuals in each species, including the species Homo sapiens, "will" themselves to change and pass these changes, à la Lamarck, on to to their offspring. Shaw used Bergson's notion of an élan vital to expand further Butler's emphasis on will, and assumed the existence of "a mysterious drive toward greater power over our circumstances" as the motivation for change in the individual and in the universe.[14]

Vitalism and socialism were not incompatible, however; in Man and Superman Shaw deftly combined the two. "We must either breed political capacity or be ruined by democracy," he claimed in its "Preface."[15] Since "equality is essential to good breeding and equality, as economists know, is incompatible with property," the urgent need is to do away with property and marriage, both of which interfere with the process of selective breeding, and to separate child-bearing from marriage and domesticity.[16] Socialism was, at best, a partial solution to society's ills; the socialization of the breeding process was far more important.

A partial explanation for Shaw's changing views between 1891 and 1903 was his growing awareness, in the interim, of the problems of a declining birth rate in Britain and of the large number of undernourished, undereducated, often retarded citizens that the recruiting efforts for the South African War had uncovered. Under these circumstances, motherhood became a far more important issue for Shaw than woman's suffrage or her emancipation, in the same way that he was to view, in later years, the smooth functioning of the state as more important than, and in conflict with, the rights of the individual. Thus,

Shaw placed himself in a minority position in both the feminist and the socialist movements. His increasing iconoclasm refused to be confined by the narrow restraints of mere political or economic reform. Instead he wished to transform marriage, family life, and parenthood in the interests of breeding a better race.

The one point on which Shaw was completely consistent, from his earliest works to his last, was that women were far more powerful than they were usually portrayed. Julia Craven, in The Philanderer, aggressively pursued Leonard Charteris using every feminine--and not so feminine--wile to land him. She never succeeded since Charteris was as amoral and cunning as she, and equally as intent upon not being caught as she was to catch him. Written in 1893 when "the discussion about Ibsenism, the 'New Woman,' and the like, was at its height,"[17] the play pays homage to Ibsen while wildly spoofing his followers. All the major characters belong to the Ibsen Club and are pledged, if males, to act always in an "unmanly" fashion and, if females, to conduct themselves in as "unwomanly" a manner as possible--disbarment being the penalty for "improper" behavior. The characters spout Ibsen-like slogans at each other: marriage is a "degraded bargain,"[18] "a woman belongs to herself and to nobody else,"[19] or "advanced people form charming friendships: conventional people marry."[20] Few, however, save Charteris, the philanderer, and Grace Tranfield, the woman

who spurns him, are able to abide by such sentiments. For
Julia, "advanced views were merely a fashion picked up and
followed like any other fashion, without understanding or
meaning a word of them."[21]

Yet, if Julia was, at heart, a "womanly" woman and
not nearly as bright as the philandering Ibsenian philosopher she chased, she was hardly a weak and passive maid
waiting to be swept off her trembling toes by a gallant
knight. She is a forceful presence with whom to be
reckoned, carefully. And Charteris--sounding a note off
his creator's bow--passively complains that he had "never
taken the initiative and persecuted women with advances"
as they had persecuted him.[22]

In Candida (1895), Shaw dealt with notions of
power within the family and pointed to the authority
wielded by women in their traditional domain. By dint of
describing the confusion that ensued when the weak and
vacillating young Marchbanks fell in love with Candida,
the wife of the much respected Reverend James Morell, Shaw
deftly unmasked the actual power structure of the Morell
family, and put the lie to the myth of patriarchical
power. Yet his real intention was not at first obvious
to London audiences and reviewers. As he complained to
his friend, William Archer, everybody likes Candida and
thinks it "vindicates every wife and mother and every
suburban home."[23] What he had intended instead was that
it show "how important the woman's part in the arrangement

is," without at all meaning to "justify the arrangement."[24]

By 1903, equipped with his Vitalist philosophy and
a knowledge of the Universal plan, Shaw was no longer
content merely to depict the heretofore unsuspected power
of women. In Man and Superman, an updated version of the
story of Don Juan, he demonstrated that the victor in the
battle of the sexes is almost always the woman. She is
the one who hunts her quarry to "carry on Nature's most
urgent work."[25] Unlike Julia Craven, Ann Whitehead gets
her man, Jack Tanner, even though she has to chase him
across Europe and has to put up with his self-delusions,
his philosophical meanderings, and his poet's "selfless-
ness." Her purpose is to obtain the brightest, most
worthy of men to father her children, and no deception
is too devious for her to employ to obtain her objective.
In following her sexual instinct Ann, alias "Everywoman,"
will accomplish what mere socialist reformers will not be
able to do, that is, breed a better specimen of man. Ann
is as strong a female character as Shaw ever placed on the
stage. Yet, unlike her predecessor, Vivie Warren, who
longed for her actuarial tables and her cigar,[26] Ann is
a strong woman cast in the most traditional of roles.
Vivie Warren was clearly "a man in petticoats,"[27] while
Ann belongs to a distinctly different sex with biologically
set goals that run counter to those of men.

Shaw's new eugenic slant recognized the active role
women play in the battle of the sexes and denigrated man's

baseness for placing the necessary work of building the
nation upon women and then disparaging both the task and
its tender. In Shaw's view, man sought revenge for his
hopeless failure to give birth by speaking of woman's
sphere with condescension, "as if the kitchen and the
nursery were less important than the office in the city."[28]
And it is difficult to argue with this interpretation.
Yet, for all his support of women's work, the portrait
he paints of Ann is far from sympathetic; rather it is
downright predatory. When he discusses the unscrupulous-
ness with which "woman pursues her purpose" in the "Preface" to the play, he notes that "the wildest hominist or
feminist farce is insipid after the most commonplace 'slice
of life.' The pretense that women do not take the initiative is part of the farce. Why, the whole world is strewn
with snares, traps, gins, and pitfalls for the capture of
men by women."[29]

Major Barbara of the Salvation Army was another
strong female, created by Shaw in 1905.[30] She too served
the Life Force courageously, but she followed her spiritual
rather than her sexual instincts. Barbara, like Ann,
married an artist-philosopher, but Barbara's instinctual
goal was to effect a combination of thought, power, and
spirituality in order to reform the world, as Ann had
applied herself to the creation of the gene pool necessary
to produce "Supermen."

The more involved Shaw became with eugenics and

vital economy in his plays, the greater the chasm between the sexes seemed to be. Although in later years he claimed to have been so successful in depicting women because he had "always assumed that a woman is a person exactly like myself," that "a woman is really only a man in petticoats,"[31] Shaw was sounding at this time as if the differences between the sexes were as vast as they were irreconcilable. This was particularly so when he stated in the "Preface" to Man and Superman:

> The ordinary man's main business is to get the means to keep up the position and habits of a gentleman, and the ordinary woman's business is to get married . . . on the whole, this is a sensible and satisfactory foundation for society. Money means nourishment and marriage means children; and that men should put nourishment first, and women children first is, broadly speaking, the law of nature.[32]

One wonders when reading about this "law of nature" if such a doctrine really had been suggested by the same author who wrote "The Quintessence of Ibsenism" twelve years earlier.

Shaw never lost his enthusiasm for, or his belief in, Creative Evolution and the Life Force. The plays he wrote after Man and Superman and Major Barbara, however, were not as overtly involved as these plays had been with the actual process of breeding a better race. Instead, they examined similar issues from a sociological, rather than an evolutionary, point of view. Nonetheless, Shaw's views on marriage, motherhood, and family life, as expounded in the plays that followed, were as unorthodox as his notions of Creative Evolution had been. Moreover, his

demands or suggestions on behalf of women and their well-
being usually went well beyond that which most bourgeois
feminists could countenance. His outspokenness on matters
of social engineering often proved as annoying or dis-
comfiting to suffragists as his reticence on suffrage
reform.

Marriage as legalized prostitution had been a
recurring theme in his work since The Irrational Knot,
written in 1880, in which Susanna, an intelligent and
independent actress, declined all matrimonial offers,
refusing to be bought "in the regular way," preferring
instead to support herself and live her life autonomously.
Mrs. Warren made similar statements about the meaning of
the marital contract when defending her own choice of
"profession" to her daughter Vivie. In 1908 Shaw wrote
Getting Married, his definitive statement on marriage, in
which he described and discussed a multitude of views and
types of marriages. In his customarily long-winded "Preface" to the play, he set forth his own views. Deploring
the "central horror of the dependence of women on men,"
he claimed: "At present it reduces the difference between
marriage and prostitution to the difference between trade
unionism and unorganized casual labor."[33] His solutions
were twofold. First, he called for the economic independence of women, suggesting that the newly founded Labor
Exchanges should function for both sexes, finding work for
unemployed wives and mothers and "new places in the world

for women."[34] Second, he felt that the worthless institution of marriage might be salvaged by easing the divorce
laws. At a time when most feminist reformers were anxious
to equalize them, making it possible for women, too, to
obtain a divorce on the grounds of adultery, Shaw suggested
instead that anyone should be able to obtain a divorce
merely because he or she desired to do so.

Unlike his female counterparts, the fact that
making divorce easily obtainable might result in the
breaking up of many families did not trouble Shaw in the
least. Like his evolutionary mentor, Samual Butler, he
claimed: "The family ideal is a humbug and a nuisance."[35]
The generations are so different they cannot live together
in harmony. Loving parents, especially loving mothers,
merely suffocate their offspring: "A wife entirely preoccupied with her affection for her husband, a mother
entirely preoccupied with her affection for her children,
may be all very well in a book . . . but in actual life
she is a nuisance."[36]

Blithly willing to do away with the nuclear family
and to dethrone mothers, thereby far outdistancing most
female reformers of the Edwardian era, Shaw was concerned,
however, with England's falling birth rate. The decline
in population was, he decided with questionable logic,
ample proof that the institution of marriage was not
working. Even with economic readjustments, such as payments to mothers, the population would not maintain itself

in the face of the evolutionary development of an increasingly urban civilization which "is a sterilizing process
as far as numbers go."[37] The possibility of divorce
was absolutely necessary in order to induce people to
marry at all, especially once the economic independence
of women had been accomplished, but even this was not
enough.

Given that the number of adult women far exceeded
the number of adult men, a great many women who would like
to have children would not be able to find husbands.
Others, like Lesbia Grantham in Getting Married, felt
that "if I am to be a mother, I really cannot have a
man bothering me to be a wife at the same time."[38] Shaw
suggested, therefore, that women should have the right to
bear children without the necessity of having husbands,
and legitimacy should be conferred upon all children
regardless of the legal status of the union by which
they were conceived.

In wishing to separate child-bearing and marriage,
Shaw not only outdistanced Edwardian feminists, but set
the argument central to the position of most modern radical
feminists, that is, that complete control over their
reproductive function is essential to the self-determination
of women. According to Shaw, "the right to bear a child,
perhaps the most sacred of all women's rights, is not one
that should have any conditions attached to it."[39] But
his concern for the well-being of the state is apparent

in the exception he makes to this "right": "except in the
interests of race welfare."[40] Thus his argument takes on a
eugenic slant, and one wonders whether he was as concerned
with the welfare and self-determination of women as he was
with their capacity as breeders for the state:

> I see a good deal of first rate maternal abil-
> ity and sagacity spending itself on bees and poultry
> and village schools and cottage hospitals; and I
> find myself repeatedly asking myself why this valu-
> able strain in the national breed should be
> sterilized. Unfortunately, the very women whom
> we should tempt to become mothers for the good
> of the race are the very last people to press their
> services on their country in that way.[41]

As Shaw was waxing poetic over the necessity of
easing sexual restrictions on women, the majority of
Edwardian suffragists were espousing purity not promiscuity
as their goal, and this with ever-increasing ferocity as
the battle for the vote became more militant. They viewed
greater sexual freedom as merely an extension of male
domination or as further confirmation of their role as
sexual object. As one feminist who detested the "new
morality" asked, "How can we possibly be Freewomen if, like
the majority of men, we become the slaves of our lower
appetites?"[42]

Considering the enthusiasm Shaw expressed for
rearranging old notions of sexuality and domesticity, one
would expect a corresponding ingenuity with regard to the
altering or expansion of the role of fathers. He did, in
fact, recommend "supplementary fathers" as a useful antidote to the stuffiness of small middle class families, that

is, extra men who lived with or frequently visited a family
and provided a stimulating and educational atmosphere for
the children by means of the intellectual discussions and
arguments they generated.[43] He made no suggestion, however, that fathers, supplementary or otherwise, were to
take a greater role in the raising of children, that they
might, for example, change diapers or wipe noses.

Shaw's notion of "supplementary fathers" is similar
to that of "Sunday husbands," an idea he first found in
Shakespeare and a role which he, himself, often played in
his younger years in the homes of his friends.[44] According
to this concept, it is the wife, and often the husband, who
benefit from the wit and intellect of a masculine Sunday
supplement. The absence of intellectually stimulating
supplementary mothers, or Sunday wives, or of domesticated
fathers in Shaw's lexicon is of a piece with the conservative twist in Shaw's Vitalist philosophy in the first
decade of the twentieth century. He questioned the existence of traditions and institutions, yet seemed to accept
as given the differences between the sexes and their
biologically determined roles. Despairing of many of the
old solutions and pursuing his visions of Vitalism and the
Life Force, he seems to have settled into a rather conservative, but peculiarly Shavian, version of "anatomy is
destiny."

Yet, even in his most hostile periods, Shaw continued to be of some service to the feminist cause. His

portrayals of women were not necessarily sympathetic, as
we have seen, but his major women characters were always
drawn against the prevailing stereotype, not from it. As
one essayist has suggested, Shaw's greatest service to the
emancipation of women may have been his depiction of
strong-willed and accomplished women.[45] He banished
two major stereotypes of women from his plays. First,
he showed that successful women, such as Vivie Warren,
Lina Szczepanowska, or Lesbia Grantham, who sought satisfaction and success outside the family, need not be fussy,
unattractive old maids. Second, he portrayed women, such
as Ann Whitehead and Candida, who were content with the
more limited roles society prescribed for them, as intelligent, strong-minded, and competent rather than inane and
inadequate.

Particularly with regard to the second group
of women, Shaw seems to have recognized quite early what
historians have begun to see only recently: that the
pedestal upon which Victorian women had been placed was,
for some, a bastion of power from which to proceed.[46] If
the conventions that surrounded her perch, that is, that
woman was weak, incompetent and passive, were nonsense,
the power which she wielded, emanating in part from her
strength within the family, was nonetheless real. Shaw
occasionally pinpointed the connection between woman's
moral power within the family and that power which she had
channeled and would continue to channel into the battle for

moral reforms and women's rights. "Give women the vote, and in five years there will be a crushing tax on bachelors," he warned in 1903.[47] "The political emancipation of women is likely to lead to a comparatively stringent enforcement by law of sexual morality (that is why so many of us dread it)," he admitted five years later.[48]

By this time the women's movement had begun to revive, and Shaw was continually called upon as a man of advanced opinions and as an orator of note to aid in its full recovery. As a partisan of the "New Drama" which was influenced by Ibsen, infused with feminism, and inspired by actresses whose independence and income had long outdistanced their non-thespian sisters, Shaw was surrounded by feminist actresses who expected him to support their cause. His response was positive; he supported the women's movement, but neither effusively nor often. His lack of enthusiasm for democracy, as we have seen, would not have predisposed him otherwise, since the women's movement was quintessentially a concern with the parliamentary vote for women.

To blandishments from feminists who thought he ought to be more militant in their cause, he replied that he was not a woman, he already had the vote and, therefore, cared little for the suffrage,[49] or that he had always found that men speaking on behalf of women--"between petticoats"--looked "so horribly ignominious and did it so very much worse than the women," that his "personal vanity" would not permit him to come forward. Moreover, unlike J. S. Mill who stressed that men must come forward to help women win their rights, Shaw believed "that women are hardier than men" and they needed no "affectation of magnanimity and protection" from men.[50] If pressed further, Shaw's standard answer for his lack of enthusiasm was that his efforts would do very little toward securing the vote for women and, more important, the vote, once achieved, would do very little to alter the position of women or the conditions of the world. Echoing his sallies against democracy in other contexts, he wrote to one feminist: "You have only to consider how little use the vote has been to the men, or indeed to the women in the case of the Municipal Franchise, to foresee how bitterly the results of the suffrage will disappoint those who are at present expecting so much from it."[51]

Yet, in his more sympathetic moments Shaw, himself, supplied the antidote for such negativism. Women must have the vote, not because they would usher in the Millenium on their way to the ballot box, but because it is the only way to make sure that government suits them: "You give a man a vote, not because you believe he is a very politically able person, but because you believe he has enough intelligence to know when he is uncomfortable."[52]

Letting the populace vote to make sure they were "comfortable" was a consistent thread in Shaw's arguments in favor of women's suffrage; it was the major theme in the

one play he wrote on the subject. <u>Press Cuttings</u>, which
he drafted in 1909 while motoring through Algeria, was a
rather frantic farce in which Shaw cast his satiric net
so far and wide, few individuals or institutions escaped.
The play depicts the gradual conversion of General
Mitchener, who is beseiged in the War Office by militant
suffragettes, to the suffragist point of view. He is
converted not by suffragist logic but by the willful
behavior of two staunch anti-suffragists. Mrs. Banger
does not want the vote because she thinks it is irrelevant;
women being the stronger sex must be given power, that is,
the right to military service, not mere ballots. Lady
Corinthia, being charming and graceful, knows that men
are ever ruled by talents such as she possesses and feels
that only if men are completely in power can women, such
as herself, continue to rule the country. Both women
disdain the vote and covet power, knowing full well the
distance between the two.

In the denouement, in reaction to Mrs. Banger's
energetic methods--she sits on General Sandstone's head to
get him to allow women in the army--and Lady Corinthia's
absolute dismissal of the "dowdies" in the feminine population, General Mitchener finally sees the light. He realizes
that the "woman question" is "a question of dowdies"; take
care of them and the rest will take care of themselves.
"How do you know when the shoe pinches your washerwoman?"
he asks. "How are you to know when you haven't made her

comfortable unless she has a vote? Do you want her to come
and break your windows?"[53] And just for good measure, he
asks Mrs. Farrell, his charwoman--the only person in the
War Office who can understand and obey orders--to marry
him.

In the course of the play, Shaw manages to lampoon
not only democracy, the military, and the General Staff,
but Balfour and Asquith, the suffragettes and the anti-
suffragists, and high society and class snobbishness as
well; which is to say, it is a standard Shaw performance.
However, on one point he is quite serious; that is, that
women must have a say in the passage of laws which regulate
them. It is not a grand faith in the principles of democracy or in the political wisdom of females that moves
Shaw, but memories of his years as vestryman and his
long struggle to get free lavatories for the poor women
of St. Pancras.

His argument, then, is not based on the similarities
between the sexes and the consequent right of women to
vote, but on the grounds of expediency due to differences
between the sexes. Shaw's position, at this time, represents a shift similar to the one which had taken place in
the American suffrage movement at the end of the nineteenth
century, and it represents for Shaw, as it did for the
American suffragists, both a declining faith in democracy
itself and a new recognition of the enlarged housekeeping
powers of the state.[54] The peculiarly Shavian twist to

this argument, that women should be allowed to make the laws now that laws are being made on matters which concern them, is that without women voters and lawmakers some of the laws that should be passed for women's benefit will not be made at all, for only women know what makes them "comfortable."

Shaw's shift in his dramatic portrayals of women at the beginning of the century to an emphasis on the disparity of their roles and aims from those of men, can be seen to precede and to complement this new reasoning. But his basic distrust of democracy could be reconciled with support for women's rights and the differences between the sexes in quite a different way. If, instead of concentrating on the suffrage, "they would demand that, vote or no vote, every public authority in this country, including the Houses of Parliament, should contain a considerable proportion of women, no matter how selected or elected, the question would take on a new seriousness."[55] Not democratic voting procedures, he suggested, but real representation was the issue; women must be elected or placed on law-making bodies at all levels to see to problems men would never understand or even deign to consider.

Emphasizing the differences between the sexes even more strongly, Shaw also suggested that women were necessary at all meetings of elected officials because they raised the moral tone of the gathering. The guffaws and innuendos that erupted whenever questions pertaining to

women arose, whether in a vestry meeting or on the floor of
the House had thoroughly convinced him that "only in the
presence of women will men behave decently."[56] The solution he proffered was the co-option of women on to all
elective bodies, a favored method of the Fabian Society
whenever dealing with the problem of the underrepresenta-
tion of women on school boards, or city councils, or the
like. Thus, when moved to expound upon matters of suffrage,
which was not very often, Shaw asked more, not less, than
most suffrage leaders were asking, predicting, rightly,
that equal opportunity at the ballot box would not yield
equal representation on the borough council or in the
Commons.

*　*　*

In summing up Shaw's views on woman suffrage, and
the "woman question" in general, one funds it extremely
difficult to place him in the mainstream of either feminist
or socialist thought. In some instances he was simply too
realistic about the vagaries of human nature and the
limitations enforced by conventional society to be contented
with the limited reforms ardently sought by his contemporaries. At other times, it seems as if his own peculiar
attitudes and feelings about women interfered with his
reformer's zeal in matters concerning the fairer sex.
What is clear is that Shaw's need to destroy the conventions and conformity of the society in which he lived far
outweighed his allegiance to any body of rationalist

belief. He was more committed to the restructuring of
society and the relationships between the sexes than he
was to the nitty-gritty details of equality. Thus, he was
an errant socialist and an unpredictable feminist. His
complicated attitudes toward women and society were a
melange of his own making, and the roots of his iconoclasm
reached far deeper than his conversion to socialism or his
adherence to an organized set of feminist principles.

II. G.B.S.: The Apprenticeship of a Critic at Large

What emerges from any brief sketch of the early
years of George Bernard Shaw is how well his family con-
stellation had equipped him for his role as late Victorian
idol-breaker and aberrant feminist. Born in Dublin in
1856 of Protestant parents, he was the only son of a
younger son. His father, George Carr Shaw, was a civil
servant turned not very successful corn merchant. The
family belonged to the class of the "shabby gentile,"[57]
too poor to send George Bernard to public school and
university and too proud to send him to board schools.

From his father, G.B.S. claimed to have inherited
his comic sense. The elder Shaw reacted against all that
was venerable: "The more sacred an idea or a situation was
by convention, the more irresistible was it to him as the
jumping-off place for a plunge into laughter."[58] One
suspects the younger Shaw's need to laugh was also a

by-product of his relationship to his father, and his
father's constant state of inebriation. It "was so humil-
iating that it would have been unendurable if we had not
taken refuge in laughter. It had to be either a family
tragedy or a family joke."[59] The younger Shaw, a lifelong
teetotaler, was careful not to repeat his father's mis-
takes. Instead, as he wrote years after his father's
death, "I worked as my father drank."[60] The disillusion
G.B.S. experienced at age three or four, when he first
discovered that his supposedly teetotaling father was,
in fact, "a hypocrite and a dipsomaniac, was so sudden
and violent that it must have left its mark."[61]

His father, then, was not likely to instill young
George Bernard with a high regard for the infallibility of
the male sex or, by extension, for masculine systems of
authority. Nor did he and the rest of the Shaw clan,
several of whom were quite original in their displays of
eccentric behavior, instill in G.B.S. veneration for
the family in general, or his in particular: "The family,
far from being a school of reverence for me was rather a
mine from which I could dig highly amusing material without
the trouble of inventing a single incident."[62]

Shaw's mother, Elizabeth Gurley, was the daughter
of a widowed country gentleman. She had been raised by
her great aunt in the strictest fashion, a fact and a
fashion which she greatly resented and which she did not
repeat in the raising of her own three children. The

combination of a cold and austere upbringing and a very
disappointing marriage, which deprived her of social
status and social contacts, did little to bring out the
maternal side of Mrs. Shaw. According to her son, "she
did not hate anybody, nor love anybody"; for the most
part she left the care of her children to the servants
who were few in number and incompetent in their duties.[63]
She was "neither a mother, nor a wife, and could be classed
only as a Bohemian anarchist with lady-like habits."[64]
As a mother, she was "the worst in the world . . . fond
of animals and flowers, but not of human beings."[65] "The
specific maternal passion awoke in her a little for my
younger sister, who died at twenty; but it did not move
her until she lost her, nor then noticeably. She did not
concern herself much about us."[66]

Mrs. Shaw's lack of maternal feeling fostered in
her son a multitude of conflicting attitudes toward her
and her sex, and a great many compensatory mechanisms as
well. "Her almost complete neglect" had left him awkward
and shy in his youth.[67] As an adult, however, he saw to
it that the speaker's platform and the stage brought
him all the attention he had missed:

> I first caught the ear of the British public
> on a cart in Hyde Park, to the blaring of brass
> bands, and this not at all as a reluctant sacrifice
> of my instinct of privacy to political necessity,
> but because, like all dramatists and mimes of
> genuine vocation, I am a natural-born mountebank.
> . . . The cart and trumpet for me.[68]

Mrs. Shaw's salvation was music. Possessed of a
pure mezzosoprano voice, she was carefully trained by
George John Vandalear Lee, an orchestral conductor and
heterodox music teacher. She brought most of Dublin's
amateur musicians into their home to rehearse for operas
and oratorios and filled the house with music and interesting people. The latter, being mostly Roman Catholics, even
caused the young George Bernard to doubt that God really
was "a Protestant and a wholesaler" as his father's family
had led him to believe.[69]

Mrs. Shaw's relationship to her music teacher was
rather unusual. When George Bernard was four or five,
Lee moved into the household, and the menage a trois--
plus children--functioned relatively harmoniously until
Lee moved to London several years later. What kind of non-
professional relationship existed between Mrs. Shaw and
Lee is not clear. Beatrice Webb commented in her diary
many years later on the resemblance between Lee and G.B.S.,
and speculated on Shaw's paternity.[70] But Shaw's subsequent biographers and he, himself, have never suggested
any such link, painting the relationship between Lee and
Mrs. Shaw as mostly professional and platonic. There
seems to have been no particular affection between Lee
and G.B.S., but one recognizes in the role Lee played in
the Shaw household the origins of the concepts of "supplementary fathers" and "Sunday husbands" that Shaw recommended in a few of his prefaces and plays. One wonders,

however, why Shaw's enthusiasm for these ideas never
took into account the effect on the "supplemented" male
that he himself noted in his own family: "Lee's . . .
mesmeric energy and enterprise reduced my father to nullity
in the house. . . . When . . . we all deserted him, he
must have found himself much happier."[71]

The desertion of the elder Mr. Shaw took place in
two stages, beginning in 1872, when Mrs. Shaw initiated the
family exodus to London. She left Dublin to launch her
eldest daughter Lucy as a prima dona and herself as a
teacher of music, leaving the male members of the family
behind. Young Shaw was by then a junior clerk, soon to
be a reasonably well-paid cashier, in an exclusive estate
office. His formal education had ended at age fifteen;
his far more important autodidactic education continued
apace. To make up for the absence of music in the house,
once his mother had left, he taught himself to play the
piano, beginning in characteristic fashion with the complicated overture to "Don Giovanni." He continued to frequent
Dublin's National Gallery and the theatre and the opera
whenever he could, gaining an education, as he later
claimed, in both sentiment and the arts. (Shaw's education
in sentiment appears to have been incomplete, judging from
the passionately intellectual but emotionally bloodless
plays he was to create.) His education in the arts stood
him in good stead after he had followed his mother and
sister to London in 1876. His career as a critic of the

arts began in 1885 when he became art critic for The World.
By 1888, as "Corno di Bassetto," he was doing a column on
music for The Star, and by 1895 he rounded out his critical
endeavors with theatre reviews for The Saturday Review.

Perhaps not inappropriately, Shaw had turned
art critic and social critic, or Fabian, at about the
same time. The assumption of both callings, however,
followed several years of apprenticeship in London during
which time he earned almost no income at all. He lived
frugally with his mother and sister Lucy on Mrs. Shaw's
earnings, plus a pound a week subsidy from George Carr
Shaw who remained in Dublin. First they occupied a semi-
detached villa at West Brompton, but they soon moved to a
more interesting location for the unemployed son. Thirty-
seven Fitzroy Street was a short walk from the British
Museum, the university of a good many self-taught scholars.
Having decided to become an author, Shaw resolutely set
himself to fill five quarto pages a day with the ink of
his successive, but never successful, novels. Between
1879 and 1883 he wrote five of them, each in turn rejected
by each of the numerous publishers to whom they were sent.
At the same time, owing to a good many hours spent under
the vaulted dome of the Reading Room at the British Museum,
he taught himself musical counterpoint, shorthand, and
French, and then went on to social and economic theory.

He became a public speaker with the same dogged
determination that he filled up blank pages, haunting the

numerous literary and debating societies of London and
forcing himself to participate in the discussions until
he had lost his nervousness. Upon hearing a lecture in
1884 by the American, Henry George, on land nationalization
and the single tax, Shaw became convinced of the centrality
of economics to all the major problems confounding society.
He then descended upon the Democratic (later Social-
Democratic) Federation, only to be chastised by its founder,
Henry Mayers Hyndman, for not having read Marx. This duly
accomplished, with the British Museum's copy of the French
translation by Deville, he applied to the Federation for
membership. He withdrew his application, however, when he
discovered the newly founded Fabian Society, in which
he "recognized a more appropriate milieu as a body of
educated middle-class intelligentsia: my own class in
fact."[72]

During the period of his self-styled "apprenticeship," Shaw's relationship to his older sister loomed
large. Lucy was an attractive soprano, a professional
singer and actress, who married late in life and then only
briefly. She made her debut on the London stage in 1879
and, it has been suggested, provided the personna for
several of the actresses and singers in Shaw's works. She
also gained for her impecunious and provincial brother an
occasional entrance into London's musical society in
his early years there. Shaw's gratitude toward her for
such services seems mixed at best; she regarded him as an

unredeemed financial burden on the family's finances.[73]

The brother and sister in The Irrational Knot, Shaw's second novel, come closest to portraying their relationship, and Shaw's feelings for his sister. The fictional relations between the two alternate between indifference and involvement, but the interactions are almost always stormy and resentful. The characterization of the sister Susanna, alias Lalage Virtue, an actress in the opera bouffe, is both complimentary and highly critical. She is shown as an independent and intelligent woman, able to earn her own way; yet at the end of the novel she dies a rather pitiful drunkard. The destructive drinking of the fictional sister did not correlate with the drinking habits of Shaw's factual sister and was not necessary on artistic grounds. Rather, it seems to represent Shaw's ambivalence toward his sister and, by extension, toward strong-willed, cynical women in general. Once brother and sister no longer occupied the same house, the two rarely met, and neither seemed to miss the meeting. One of Shaw's few nonfictional representations of Lucy was this brief summation of her character and her relations with men, which he delivered some time after her death in 1920: "Her heart, if she had one, was quite unbreakable and the hearts she broke, not at all lethally by the way, were innumerable."[74]

While Shaw's attitude toward women was influenced by his feelings for his sister, his relationship to his mother was central in this regard. Of primary importance was the fact that in Shaw's family his mother was by far the stronger, more dominant character. It was his mother with whom Shaw identified, rather than his alcoholic, "nullified" father. He shared and greatly benefited from her interest in music. But Mrs. Shaw's ability to remove herself and her children from the stagnation of genteel poverty in Dublin, that is, her power both to create life and to alter its circumstances was even more significant for her young son. Whatever his subsequent attitudes toward women might be, he would never be able to view them as the "weaker sex."

To a certain extent, Shaw's involvement in the arts allowed him to work through some of his residual conflicts with his mother, and to satisfy his wish to identify with her and her procreativity, displacing such needs on to an intellectual plane. If "Shakespeare was like Mother's milk" to him as he claimed,[75] his own plays may have sufficed as his form of creation. More than one of his female characters alludes to the envy men feel for women's ability to bear children. "What do men want?" asks Mrs. Hushabye in Heartbreak House. "Why are they not satisfied? Why do they envy us the pain with which we bring them into the world, and make strange dangers and torments for themselves to be even with us?"[76] In contrast, for the enlightened Shaw, getting "even" resulted in a sizable increase in the quality and quantity of English drama.

Yet, as successful and impressive as were Shaw's defenses against his "devil of a childhood"[77] and his unloving mother, as one would expect, difficulties did arise for him in several aspects of his relationships to others, especially to women and to women's causes. He lived with his mother for all but four of his first forty-three years with little friction or affection, and did battle against sexual inequities to a far greater extent than most males of his time. However, as previously noted, he tended to be somewhat inconsistent in his support of women's causes, inconsistent in his beliefs on the differences between the sexes, and so intent upon reversing the stereotypical notions of femininity that he often created equally stereotypical characters in the opposite extreme, depicting females as predatory and frightening in their strong-mindedness and overt sexuality.

Shaw's relations with women reflected the difficulties he had with sexuality as a result of his ambivalence toward his mother. He was a virgin until the age of twenty-nine when he was initiated by Jenny Patterson, a friend and music student of his mother's and fifteen years his senior. For the next fourteen years "there was always some lady";[78] in fact there were often several women with whom he was involved. But as Bertha Newcombe, a Fabian artist, wrote with reference to her five year relationship with Shaw, he remained

> by preference a passionless man. . . . He seemed
> to have no wish for and even to fear passion, though
> he admitted its power and pleasure. . . . Frequent
> talking . . . of marriage . . . of his dislike of
> the sexual relation and so on, would create an
> atmosphere of lovemaking without any need for
> caresses or endearments.[79]

Shaw claimed he "was never duped by sex as a

basis for permanent relations, nor dreamt of marriage in

connection with it." He "put everything else before it and

never refused or broke an engagement to speak on Socialism

to pass a gallant evening."[80] In his later plays, espe-

cially in Back to Methusela, Shaw tried to remove sexuality

from the process of procreation entirely.

But for all his protestations on the unimportance

of sex and the sex relation, he spent the decade before the

First World War writing plays that discussed little else.

While the "social question" and the "woman question"

occupied much of England, Shaw seemed at times to be

reducing them both to the lowest common denominator.

Beatrice Webb worried in her Diary of 1910 over Shaw's

exclusive concern with the "sex question." She felt that

he harped on sex and "the insignificance of the female for

any other purpose but sex attraction with tiresome itera-

tion."[81] A careful reading of his discursive plays of that

time will not sustain Beatrice's criticism, but then

Overruled (1912), "a clinical study of how polygamy actually

occurs among quite ordinary people"[82] or "how and why

married couples are unfaithful,"[83] had not yet been written.

In the "Preface" to this play, Shaw not only suggests the

"inevitability" of polygamous behavior, he once again attempts to disabuse his reading public of its monstrously exaggerated notions "of the power and continuity of sexual passion."[84]

Shaw's own difficulties with sex were often manifested in the series of intense relationships, both professional and romantic, he maintained with various actresses. Peters has suggested that Shaw identified with the actress as an outsider, as he himself had been in his early years in London.[85] The roots of these relationships, however, could be traced to his earliest psychological needs which were merely accentuated by his later social deprivations. Ellen Terry, especially, seemed to play the role of surrogate mother for Shaw. They corresponded regularly for five years before their first meeting in 1900. Shaw's letters of that period are startling in their intimacy and frequency, and they give his maternal casting of the famous actress, eight years his senior, an incestuous taint. They also indicate the difficulties Shaw had in his liaisons with other women and his methods for dealing with his difficulties.

In a particularly revealing letter in 1896, he advises her to "use" him for her own benefit, explaining that "all his love affairs end tragically" because the women cannot use him: "Everything real in life is based on need: just so far as you need me I have you tightly in my arms. Beyond that I am only a luxury, and for luxuries

love and hate are the same passion."[86] After giving her
the news of the current state of his love affairs, including the one involving the "Irish lady with the light green
eyes and the million of money" whom he had gotten "to
like so much that it would be superfluous to fall in love
with her," he dismisses the "others":

> And finally there is Ellen, to whom I vow that
> I will try hard not to spoil my high regard, my
> worthy respect, my deep tenderness, by any of those
> philandering follies which make me so ridiculous,
> so troublesome, so vulgar with women. I swear it.
> Only do as you have hitherto done with so wise
> an instinct: keep out of my reach.[87]

In this letter Shaw's desire to be needed might be
viewed as a reversal of his own needs in relation to
women. More important, the split he creates between
"love" and "liking" reflects a suspicion of "love" as
being tainted by sexuality and therefore less perfect
than "liking." His solution is clear: he resolves his
problem of needing woman as mother and wanting her as
sexual object by writing of his passion rather than acting
on it. "I love you soulfully and bodyfully, properly and
improperly, everyway that a woman can be loved," he wrote
to a woman he had never met.[88]

For those women with whom he did become physically
involved, he claimed:

> My pockets are always full of the small change
> of lovemaking; but it is magic money, not real
> money . . . love is only diversion and recreation
> for me. . . . It is also, alas! why I act the
> lover so diabolically well that even the women
> who are clever enough to understand that such a

person as myself might exist, can't bring themselves
to believe that I am that person. My impulses are
so prettily played.[89]

Either his "impulses" were "played" or they were blocked

entirely, and the emotional short circuit that accompanied

the procedure rendered him a difficult and often heartless

lover who indulged, according to Beatrice Webb, in "all

sorts of rather cruel philanderings with all sorts of odd

females."[90]

Shaw had stated that being a socialist did not

determine what side of an issue, such as equality for

women, one would support. His social life demonstrated

that being a male feminist did not determine how sincere

that male would be in his relationships with women. "The

sex relation is not a personal relation," he remonstrated,

it tells nothing of the person.[91] In his own case, one

could argue, his relations with the opposite sex showed his

intense uneasiness about loving the same person with whom

he had sex, and demonstrated the long shadow cast by his

most unmaternal mother. In the epilogue to Pygmalion

(1912) Shaw explains Professor Higgins's indifference to

Eliza's charms on the basis of his attachment to his lovely

and cultivated mother. He then speculates that the exis-

tence of a good many similarly intelligent and attractive

old maids and bachelors makes one suspect "that the dis-

entanglement of sex from the associations with which it is

so commonly confused, a disentanglement which persons of

genius achieve by sheer intellectual analysis, is sometimes produced or aided by parental fascination."[92] Shaw leaves out, however, the price that often needs to be paid for such a "disentanglement," and the fact that in many cases, others are made to pay it.

III. Charlotte Payne-Townshend: The Instruction of a Reluctant Bride

One wonders how Shaw could have ever found a woman whose conception of herself and her sex coincided with his "advanced views" on women, yet whose actions would not exacerbate his fears of strong, predatory females. Where could he possibly discover a woman who might be able to provide him with the maternal care and affection he sought, without causing him to violate the incest taboos such care evoked? Find her he did, although not until they were both in their forties and could establish a relation-ship cleared of "all such illusions as love interest, happiness interest and all the rest of the vulgarities of marriage."[93] Charlotte Payne-Townshend seems to have been in training for such a relationship from the time she was a young girl; judging from the relative success of her forty year marriage to Shaw, her preparation seems to have been more than adequate.

Charlotte Payne-Townshend's commonplace books, which she began to keep at the age of twenty, offer the clearest intimation of the kind of young woman she was,

the views she held, and the woman she was becoming. The
books were filled with bits and pieces of wisdom from her
readings, interspersed with brief essays of her own on
topics of importance to her. Immersing herself in a
haphazard study of history, literature, and religion,
Charlotte tried to make sense of her world and put meaning
into her life. What emerges from the views expressed in
her books are a series of unresolved contradictions, both
within her own thinking, and between the principles she
expressed and her own actions. She seemed to vacillate
between a fascination with the "other worldly path" that
leads to "the Divine"[94] and a delight in the tangible
exploits of the very worldly. Similarly, she oscillated
between her praise of nature as the font of all that
is good and wise, the source of inspiration for "the
lonely thinker," far more important "than intercourse
with men, however exalted, or systems of human philosophy,
however plausible,"[95] and her own passion for picking up
bits and pieces of intellectual wisdom from the books she
read.

Perhaps the strongest contradiction, however, was
that between the values she expressed most often in her
writings (the improtance of "attainment and achievement,"
or of "work and earnest purpose" and the "ennobling powers
of work")[96] and her own attendance at a continuing round
of parties and balls. Whether Charlotte felt any frustra-
tion at not being allowed to do any "ennobling" work is

difficult to ascertain. She did serve a brief stint as her father's secretary when he was trying to get a permit for a branch railroad between Rosscarbery and Cork. Their efforts were unsuccessful, but they pleased her sufficiently to cause her to make the same effort, on her own, several years later. Too, Charlotte took a course in first-aid, despite protests from her mother, but it ultimately led to nothing.

Aware, no doubt, of the conflict between the work ethic she praised and the absence of work in her daily routine, at twenty-seven Charlotte announced to a new commonplace book that she was committing herself to something far more doable for someone in her position, that is, "self-cultivation." Quoting Wilberforce on the importance of resolution and purpose, she affirmed: "If we are but fixed, resolute, bent on self-improvement, we shall find means enough to it."[97] Then, after having written little for a few years, she plunged again into literature and history, plundering the works of French, German, American and English authors for words of wisdom. The astonishing array of sources quoted in her commonplace book, without the benefit of any systematic means of organization, are a sharp contrast to the diaries of her contemporary, Beatrice Webb, another autodidact brought up in polite society. Beatrice's long extracts from histor- ical and philosophical sources and her essays on social and political questions bear witness to her evolving methodology and system of thought. In contrast, Charlotte's efforts were more likely to take the form of historical tables, briefly noting who ruled where and when, than to follow carefully a particular explanation of a set of historical events. Similarly, the wisdom she extracted from a given author usually consisted of a brief quotation on any one of a number of topics. The extent to which a given argument can readily be understood from a two line quotation suggests the inefficacy of Charlotte's methods and the limited degree to which they served her purpose.

While Charlotte was presumably unaware of anything so outlandish as middle class socialists in the 1880's, she shared with several Fabian contemporaries an interest in the occult and a concomitant concern with religion, either how to replace it or how to make it fit the changing needs of society. The one belief that informed her conception of history was that religious eras were better than irreligious ones. Times of irreligion, she felt, "were infinitely more michievous than where the religion--be it ever so corrupt--continues in some measure to influence and hold the hearts of men."[98] In her writings Charlotte was just as likely to quote Samuel Smiles on sloth as St. Matthew, but her quest for religious understanding and peace is always apparent. Even her voluminous quotations from drama and poetry, of which she was particularly fond, were often concerned with the nature of the soul or of moral force. The answer she seemed to be seeking was:

how to express her religiosity, while living in the world, and how to use it to ease some of the conflicts within her life and her nature.

Whatever the conflicts Charlotte suffered, the outward circumstances of her family's life were completely conventional. She was born in the county Cork in 1857, into a wealthy Protestant family of the landed class. First from their estate in Derry, then moving into ever more sophisticated and cosmopolitan levels of society, in Cork, in Dublin, and finally, in Charlotte's twentieth year, in London, the Payne-Townshends participated in the activities of the socially ambitious well-to-do. They spent the autumn in the country, riding and hunting. They spent the winter traveling, preferrably in the Mediterranean, and the spring season in London, taking carriage rides in the park to see and be seen in the mornings, paying social calls and leaving cards in the afternoons, and going to dinner parties and the theatre in the evenings.

Unfortunately, not all of the members of the Payne-Townshend family were equally enthralled by the glories of London or the Mediterranean. Charlotte's father, Horace Payne-Townshend, was the eldest son of an old Anglo-Irish family. While he was a shrewd businessman, who made a good deal of money investing the rents from his lands in various banks, utility companies, and railways, he detested living in the city and loathed society life. He longed to be back at Derry, managing his country estate

and administering local affairs.[99] He was a "well-educated
and well-read" man, a barrister by profession, and he was
"a marvel of patience with his wife." But he "led a most
unhappy life . . . having been separated from his home
and interests, and constantly snubbed and corrected" by
his overbearing wife.[100] According to Charlotte, he was
often ill in his later years, and he died, at a relatively
young age, of "pure unhappiness."[101]

Charlotte thought of herself as being in many
ways like her father, and like him she was much troubled
by their way of life and by the corrosive effects of her
mother's "domineering strain" and her hysterical temper.[102]
Yet, there were many aspects of their social life Charlotte
enjoyed, hunting and riding chief among them. Her correspondence includes more than one letter purportedly from
a horse asking when she would return to ride it,[103] and
her Diary notes the death of her horse Kudos as a particular tragedy. Another of Charlotte's favorite pastimes was
traveling. Considering the absence of airplanes and
high-speed trains, some of her itineraries were quite
remarkable. A trip she took with her father, one of
several they took together when Charlotte was in her
twenties, included seven French and ten Spanish cities
visited in the course of seven weeks.[104] In her adult
years Charlotte's constant answer to any problem was that
a "change of air" or a month abroad was needed. One
suspects that continual motion eased the conflicts she

experienced in her family and within herself.

Charlotte's mother, Mary Susanna Kirby, had been born in Shropshire, England into a middle-class family. Having married into the gentry, she was determined to enjoy her new status in society, but only in the most sophisticated of settings. She hated the backwoods of Ireland and had initiated and insisted upon each successive move of the Payne-Townshend family. Similarly, she had cajoled her husband into adding an "H" to their surname to add to the distinction of their lineage.

Mrs. Payne-Townshend brooked no interference with her plans or her ambitions. If anyone in her family denied her wishes, she argued, wept, screamed, and stormed until she had her way. Clearly, she was the dominant figure in the family; she was the one Charlotte held responsible for her own "perfectly hellish childhood and youth."[105] Being the older of their two daughters, Charlotte often found herself standing between her raging, tyrannical mother and her "gentle and affectionate" father, acting as a "kind of buffer" between them. Her younger sister, Sissy, took after "another branch of the family, and got through it best."[106] She enjoyed the social whirl and her part in it. She married at the appropriate age, an appropriate young man (Hugh Cecil Cholmondeley, a Captain in the Rifle Brigade) and raised one appropriate daughter, Cecily, to do much the same as she had done.

Unlike her sister, Charlotte was sorely troubled by

the relationship between her parents and the corrosive
effects of her mother's temper. And unlike her sister,
she sought solace, from what seemed to her an intolerable
situation, in intellectual pursuits. Retreating into her
father's large library, she read widely, if unselectively,
among its many volumes. Unfortunately the schooling she
received, being a proper, young, Victorian lady, did little
to direct her efforts. She had the usual run of not
very competent governesses who taught her languages and
music and a smattering of literature and history and
trained her for nothing but the intricacies of genteel
social life and the art of attracting a suitable mate.
Thus, her reading reflected an attempt to escape from
a milieu which did not suit her, but it did little to
instill in her the intellectual training or the work
habits necessary to effect a break from such a milieu.

*　*　*

Charlotte's views on the subject of women's rights
were slow to develop and were not always clearly defined.
She had first considered the problem of women and their
special needs while in her teens, but at that time she
saw the issue of the different roles of the sexes in
strictly romantic terms. In a segment she translated
from her favorite novelist, Theophile Gautier, she quoted
his view of women approvingly, without the slightest trace
of irony or anger: "Women always fancy men who can put
their thoughts into actions . . . obliged by their education and their social position to be silent and to wait,

women naturally prefer those who will come to them and speak out."[107]

At the age of twenty, Charlotte was still formulating women's role in terms of their relationship to men, but she fashioned out of this relationship both an historical standard for judging the level of civilization of a given era and a means of assessing Shakespeare's talents--a considerable feat for the most learned investigator. Based on her reading of Schiller she decided that "a man or a nation is great in exact proportion to their appreciation of the dignity of women."[108] Using Macaulay as her source that Shakespeare's life occurred during "a low state of civilization," which is to say an irreligious era, and formulating the belief that in such a "low state" the "position of women is one of degradation and contempt," she postulated that when there is depreciation of women there will be degradation of love. She then concluded that this accounts for the fact that the plots of Shakespeare's plays "in no way turn upon the almost universal subject of love."[109] Her explanation for this was that the dramatist's greatness lay in his ability to depict human characters, not heroes or heroines, and somehow his "great dramatic insight . . . told him instinctively that upon the paltry and miserable idea of love presented to him by his era could never be hung mighty thoughts and daring deeds."[110]

There is much to be derived from Charlotte's

theory. First, one is grateful that she gave up writing dramatic criticism after one attempt. Second, she felt she lived at a time when women were respected: "Of love as we conceive it today, in its essence, intellectual and spiritual love, the age of Shakespeare had no glimpse."[111] Third, she viewed woman's role as important, but secondary, and as yet saw no need to enlarge it. Man looks to a woman, she wrote, "for sympathy, for counsel, for encouragement; where the man was but a master . . . the woman could never make his intellect her own and herself the beacon to light him to great acts."[112] Fourth, she was contemptuous of "animal love" and praised in its stead "ideal love," which is "of the spirit and of the soul" and involves two people "attracted by the purity, dignity, and power of each other's intellect."[113]

As Charlotte reached her mid-twenties, she seemed to be increasingly disenchanted with the place of women in society. Miss Stewart, the heroine of her one extended and untitled fictional attempt, chastises the dandified Sir John on this score, while at a social gathering of "their set":

> Indeed you ought to enjoy yourselves, you gentle-
> men . . . seeing society is altogether constituted
> and arranged for the furtherance of your pleasures.
> . . . The young men . . . are the only people
> considered on all hands. The rest of society groups
> itself round them as it were--exists, in short, that
> they may take their pleasure in it.[114]

The issue of women's rights is addressed only tangentially in the course of a later diatribe by Miss

Stewart on the necessity of democracy. She informs Lady
Jane that "the great unwashed are on the winning side
now and that is the side we poor women must always be
found upon; it is our only chance."[115] But she does not
bother to disclose how they are to place themselves on
such a side, nor why it is important for them to do so.
No doubt, the author had reference to the expected Reform
Bill of 1884 and the hopes it generated of votes for
women. But her expressed concern is the need for the
"infusion of new blood and brains" into effete society
by men of business, literature and science, rather than
with specific reforms for women. She sounds more the
Saint-Simonian radical of an earlier period than a firm
supporter of women's rights.

By this point Charlotte was no longer certain that
women were held in high regard. She had begun to see that
a problem existed, but she had not thought it through.
Her activities did not include membership in any of the
fledgling women's organizations dedicated to the vote or
education for women, but she did know that the role of an
undereducated, weak, and dependent female was unacceptable
to her. Her difficulty lay in sorting out what it meant to
be a strong woman, whether or not strength was to be
interpreted only through one's relationship to a man.
At twenty-seven she was still inclined to add to her
commonplace books such proverbs as: "The counsel of a
woman is not worth much, but the man who has never taken

it is worth nothing."[116] Yet she, herself, had decided not
to marry; by that time, she had refused at least three
offers of marriage. She assured one suitor that she could
not marry because she was unable "to stick to one person
for long,"[117] and she assured herself that, instead of
falling prey to the expected routine of marriage and
maternity, she would accomplish something worthwhile
with her life.

In 1885, Charlotte's father died and her sister
married leaving Charlotte and her mother alone to face
their perpetual round of hotels, house parties, and horse
shows together. Whether Charlotte, in fact, had any
alternatives open to her, other than dancing in attendance
upon a mother she hated, is open to speculation. Clearly,
she perceived she had none. Her "fearful streak of conscience and sense of duty," her feeling that she owed her
mother "respect and devotion . . . and must defer to
her as representing properly constituted authority,"[118]
did not help to strengthen Charlotte's earlier resolve to
be independent and to do something with her life. With
each passing year she felt more and more hemmed in and
"longed for freedom."[119] Yet until her mother's death in
1891, their routine continued. Years later, writing of
that death she noted: "It is really awful to think how
glad I was. I sometimes wonder whether my constant longing for her death had anything to do with killing her."[120]

Charlotte's feelings toward other members of her

sex were not as hostile, yet she much preferred the company
of men to that of women. How directly her negative feelings for her mother were reflected in this preference is
difficult to determine. Given the paucity of educational
opportunities and professional training and experience
open to women at the time and the consequent likelihood
that more learned discussion would be found in the presence
of men than of women, Charlotte's predilection was shared
by a good many of her intellectual female contemporaries.
It was with men that Charlotte corresponded on matters
political or philosophical, and it was to men that
Charlotte usually looked for guidance. In the years
immediately following her mother's death, two men in
particular were important to Charlotte in this regard.

Charlotte had known General Clery casually for
several years. Now that she was thirty-seven years old
and was finally independent, with a sizable inheritance
to support her, a flat of her own in Piccadilly, and the
family estate at Derry for periodical retreats, she found
she was still dissatisfied with her life. It was to Clery
she wrote asking if he thought she would "be good as a
worker of charity," for she wanted very much to be of
service to others.[121] Although his answer was negative,
his personal interest in her was clear, and Charlotte
responded to it, as was her wont, by leaving England for
an extended trip to India. Upon her return, no further
mention was made of charity work, but the relationship

between the two progressed to the point of a great many letters, a few passionate kisses, and a proposal of marriage which she eventually refused.

What she wanted, she wrote to him after much anguish and soul-searching, was "to be free, free, free!"[122] and, if possible, to do some useful work in her lifetime. As the two year relationship between them ended, Charlotte's problem was to determine how to make the best use of her freedom in the interests of this long-range goal. Whatever the novelty of her intent, however, her immediate solution was a customary one--a change of scene. In January 1894 she sailed for Egypt, planning to visit friends in Italy in the spring.

In Rome Charlotte met a Swedish physician, Dr. Axel Munthe, who ministered to the medical needs of both wealthy cosmopolitans in Rome and to the very poor. After he had prescribed Valerium for Charlotte's nerves and listened to her complaints of ill health, the doctor-patient relationship altered considerably. They had numerous tête-a-têtes, and, for the first time, Charlotte was sufficiently smitten to play the pursuer, rather than the pursued. Accustomed to the attentions of his wealthy female patients, Dr. Munthe proved an elusive companion, but they carried on a desultory correspondence for a few months from various corners of the globe. In one letter in which he informed her that he never wrote to anyone, he mentioned his project for a dispensary for the poor in

Rome from which he might freely dispense medical services
and medicines to the needy. Naturally, it would cost a
good deal of money: "If ever you decide to do good in
grand style, let me know and I shall put you on the right
track."[123]

In how grand a style Charlotte ultimately decided
to "do good" is not clear. However, the relationship
ended soon thereafter, and she sustained a badly broken
heart and a strongly awakened social conscience. With
memories of the abject poverty he had shown her in Rome
and his example before her, Charlotte felt even more
keenly the need to do something useful with herself and
her wealth. She began to mull over the idea of giving up
all she owned to the poor, not only in hopes of lessening
their poverty, but as a protest against the degradation in
which they were forced to live. Charlotte continued to
entertain the notion of "suffering as protest" for some
time,[124] just as she continued to suffer over the absence
of Dr. Munthe.

Charlotte's attraction to personal suffering as the
ultimate protest, and as a solution both to her own grief
and to the plight of the Roman poor, smacks of martyrdom
and masochism. It was, moreover, in keeping with views
she had expressed at an earlier date that suffering was
"ennobling"[125]--an idea with which she had comforted a
rejected suitor--and with her romantic attachment to the
Middle Ages and its "worship of sorrow."[126] She had,

after all, grown up in a situation conducive to masochism.
Like so many Victorian women, the number of outlets open to
her were extremely limited. Charlotte suffered additionally
from being bright enough to be aware of those limitations,
humorless enough not to enjoy certain aspects of the
limitations, and enraged enough by her tyrannical mother
not to be able to allow herself those outlets open to
women of her class. She would not marry; she would not
have children.

Charlotte's decision not to marry General Clery or
her previous suitors had been tantamount to a decision to
remain celibate and, one suspects, was decided upon, at
least partially, to obviate her sexual fears, fears which
later became patently clear in her relationship to Shaw.
Renouncing sexuality was not without residual conflict,
however, and Dr. Munthe's presence had exacerbated that
conflict. The sexual tension thus created, as well as
the more conscious distress she experienced over her
wealth in the presence of poverty, were alleviated, to
some extent, by her masochistic fantasies of suffering.
In addition, Charlotte took refuge in a myriad of aches
and illnesses, as she did throughout her life, and she
traveled extensively--as much to escape inner turmoil as
to enjoy external changes of scene. Her war of independence
with her mother, and fears of her own anger and her sexuality, however, were very difficult problems to avoid. The
consequences that followed from Charlotte's conflicts and

her masochistic defenses against them were to cast a
shadow over much of her life. A lack of "adequate
aggressiveness," often seen to accompany masochistic
behavior, [127] was manifested in Charlotte's repeated
attempts to begin something--to write, to become a charity
worker, to take up medicine or sociology--which always came
to naught.

* * *

While Charlotte did not ultimately give all her
fortune to the destitute population of Rome, or adopt a
hair shirt, she was convinced that "self-cultivation" was
not a sufficient occupation. She made inquiry about
admission to medical school, but found her woefully defi-
cient background in science ruled out any such possibility.
Her disappointment was alleviated by a trip to Rome that
spring and by the occasional company of a new set of
friends. Charlotte had met the Webbs in 1895 and found
them "very interesting" and a welcome change from her
society acquaintances. Moreover, her one rebellious act,
thus far, had been refusing to marry; she was ready, at
this point, for a more positive kind of rebellion. She
joined the Fabian Society in 1896, not the first
conscience-stricken person of wealth to be attracted to
its pacific and intellectualized brand of socialism.

Charlotte's political beliefs had been vaguely
Gladstonian in the 1880's. She was sure then that "the
great unwashed are on the winning side," and that democracy

was a necessary evil that need not be feared, for "dregs
are dregs and though you stir them ever so much they
must go to the bottom again."[128] Drawing comfort and a
faintly democratic message from the social Darwinian
ideas of the time, she averred that "those who are best
and wisest and most fit to govern will infallibly come to
the surface by a sort of 'survival of the fittest.'"[129]
In addition, she had always been sympathetic to the plight
of Irish peasants and fully in favor of land reforms in
Ireland as well as democratic reforms in Britain, a considerable concession to reform for the daughter of a
wealthy Irish landowner. Aside from Irish matters, however, she had never been particularly interested in politics. Having absolutely no knowledge of the "dismal
science," she was not drawn to socialism by a careful
study of society and its ills. For Charlotte, Fabianism
offered a set of principles she could borrow, without
necessarily understanding them, a purpose she could endorse,
on humanitarian rather than theoretical grounds, and a
means of channeling her money into causes that she considered worthy.

She decided to give "her time and her money to
trying to make things more even between the 'Haves' and
the 'Have nots.'"[130] High on her list of priorities,
reflecting the influence of the Webbs, was the London
School of Economics and the study of sociology. As she
wrote enthusiastically to a friend,

> what I hope to do is this: with all my power,
> physical, financial, and intellectual, to study
> sociology . . . and to help and encourage others
> cleverer than myself to study it. If I only make
> the way one little bit easier for the students
> who are with me and come after me, or if by my
> failures and mistakes I only show them what to
> avoid--that will be reason enough for me to devote
> my life to it.[131]

The financial "power" she offered the L.S.E. was considera-

ble: £1,000 to its library fund, an endowment of a woman's

scholarship, and an additional £300 yearly in the form of

rent for the flat above the school in its building on

Adelphi Terrace.

Charlotte's interest in medicine, too, was chan-

neled along Fabian lines. Instead of pursuing medicine

directly, she would study ways to improve the study of

medicine:

> I go, several times a week, to the London School
> of Medicine for Women. I have taken up Anatomy
> and Physiology, but not only because I am deeply
> interested in those subjects. My principal object
> is to get to know the students and teachers there
> and all the people connected with the School. I
> think medicine the finest of all professions and
> I would like to help women to get into it, and
> to be a credit to it when they do get in. . . .
> I propose to watch and notice and get to know the
> School and its inhabitants well, and thus, if it
> seems desirable, to found a scholarship there which
> would help at least one woman every year to get
> along. I have also thought about helping them
> with the building fund of the new college they
> hope to start soon.[132]

Her heightened interest in the "woman question"

also reflected the influence of her Fabian friends. For

Charlotte, the Fabian Society represented a blend of

socialist solutions and of expanding expectations for

women, and her close association with the Webbs and the
L.S.E. seemed, at first, to offer her a means of helping
to accomplish important work and of achieving a goal of
her own. The Webbs, on the other hand, thought of Charlotte
as "sweet tempered and sympathetic" and very generous. "It
was on account of her generosity to our cause . . . that
I first made friends with her," Beatrice candidly admitted
to her diary the following year.[133] With the intention of
introducing her to more of their Fabian friends and cement-
ing the mutually rewarding relationship, the Webbs suggested that Charlotte rent a summer home with them in
Dorking, in the fall of 1896.

Thinking "she would do very well for Graham Wallas,"
Beatrice was surprised to discover that "Wallas bored her
with his morality and learning" and that she was "an
'original' with considerable charm and certain volcanic
tendencies" who was attractive to, and attracted by
G.B.S.[134] She, too, had mastered the bicycle, and the
two of them spent their time "scouring the country together
and sitting up late at night." Beatrice surmised that she
was in love with "the brilliant philanderer" and that he
was quite taken, "in his cold sort of way," with her.[135]

Beatrice considered Charlotte attractive and well
dressed, "a large graceful woman with masses of chocolate
brown hair, pleasant grey eyes, matte complexion which
sometimes looks muddy, at other times forms a picturesquely
pale background to her brilliant hair and bright eyes.

. . . [I]n her flowing white evening robe she approaches
beauty. At moments she is plain."[136] According to Shaw,
whose powers of observation were heightened by the engagement of his feelings, her eyes were anything but grey.
She was "the green-eyed one . . . a ladylike person at whom
nobody would ever look twice, so perfectly does she fit in
her place. . . . Perfectly placid and proper and pleasant.
. . . And takes it all off like a mask when she selects
you for that intimacy, which she does in the most cold-
blooded way."[137] A year later, Shaw thought her "a restful
person, plain, green-eyed, very ladylike, completely
demoralized by contact with my ideas, forty, with nice
rooms on a solid basis of £4,000 a year, independent and
unencumbered, and not so very plain either when you are
in her confidence."[138]

Charlotte was not only "demoralized," she often
felt compelled to bring back her hair shirt. As G.B.S.
complained to Ellen Terry, he was in a

> ridiculous difficulty with Miss P-T. She insists
> on coming to my lectures on Sundays in all sorts
> of holes and corners . . . these experiences make
> her very unhappy. . . . [I]t appears that my
> demagogic denunciations of the idle rich--my
> demands for taxation of unearned incomes--lacerate
> her conscience; for she has great possessions.
> What am I to do: she won't stay away; and I can't
> talk Primrose League. Was there ever such a situa-
> tion?[139]

The old difficulty of staying with a project
plagued Charlotte as well. She was sufficiently disci-
plined and humane to continue to finance causes and

organizations she had conscientiously decided warranted such sums. She was not, however, sufficiently motivated to pursue any particular work of her own. Beatrice Webb noted in the spring of 1897 that Shaw

> finds it pleasant to be with her in her luxurious surroundings, he has been studying her . . . dissecting the rich woman brought up without training and drifting at the beck of impulse. . . . He has been flattered by her devotion and absorption in him; he is kindly and has a catlike preference for those persons to whom he is accustomed. . . . But ominous signs that he is tired of watching . . . and he is annoyed by her lack of purpose and utter incapacity for work. If she would set to--and do even the smallest and least considerable task of intellectual work--I believe she could retain his interest and perhaps develop his feeling for her.[140]

At the same time, Beatrice was angry with Shaw for causing Charlotte pain, and was worried over the "blank haggard look"[141] she would see in Charlotte's eyes when the relationship was not going well:

> She is always restless and sometimes unhappy-- too anxious to be with him. . . . He is sometimes bored, but he is getting to feel her a necessary part of his "entourage" and would, I think, object to her breaking away from the relationship. He persuades himself that by keeping her occupied he is doing her good.[142]

Shaw was keeping Charlotte "occupied" as his official secretary to whom he dictated his articles and plays. He also kept her busy, and possibly confused, reading his steady barrage of letters in which lines such as "Keep me deep in your heart; write me two lines whenever you love me"[143] alternated with such admonitions as "Don't fall in love: be your own, not mine or anyone else's."[144]

Contrary to Beatrice's view, Shaw seemed equally ambivalent about his wish that Charlotte become an independent worker, rather than an appendage of him. In one letter he chastised her for being away and abandoning his work: "Do you forsake all your duties, even those of secretary? . . . Must I go back to writing my own articles and wasting half hours between the sentences with long trains of reflection?"[145] In another, angry over her long absence, he dismissed her in favor of his old friend and amanuensis, Mrs. Salt, and wrote: "There is clearly no future for you as a secretary . . . you must get your own work, your own, own, own work. Do you hear?"[146]

The work they had jointly decided upon for Charlotte was well suited to her preference for Rome in the spring. She was to collect data on the Roman municipal system and prepare it as a text for students at the L.S.E. Shortly after her departure, however, Shaw's health began to fail. From an abscess on his instep he developed necrosis of the bone which refused to heal and forced him to hop about on one foot and endure a great deal of pain. Worried about his continuing decline, Charlotte returned from Rome.

Charlotte's first decision was to take him away from the unhealthy disorder of the rooms he shared with his mother, and to nurse him properly. She intended to rent a home in the country where he might benefit from sea air and solitude, in addition to her careful ministrations. But, he wrote to the Webbs, "to have let her do

this in any other character than that of my wife would have
involved our whole circle and its interests in a senseless
scandal."[147] Moreover, their relationship had finally got
beyond its

> inevitable preliminary character of a love affair.
> She had at last got beyond that corrupt personal
> interest in me, just as the [recent success of]
> Devil's Disciple had relieved me of the appearance
> of a pecuniary interest in her. The thing being
> thus cleared of all such illusions as love
> interest, happiness interest and all the rest
> of the vulgarities of marriage.[148]

They were married on June 1, 1898 at the West Strand
Registry Office.

IV. The Shaws: An Unconsummated Union

The relationship between the Shaws was, on the
whole, a beneficial one for both parties. A pragmatic, if
highly conventional, arrangement evolved which allowed
G.B.S. to work productively and prodigiously without
undermining his health while doing so, as he had in the
past. How well such a relationship served Charlotte's
needs is another matter.

While Shaw's suggestions to Charlotte about what
she ought to do with her life seemed to vary considerably,
what he needed of Charlotte was fairly straightforward:
"somebody to waste my time and keep my brain quiet until
5."[149] Thus, he lamented before their marriage, when
Charlotte's sister's visits or her travels interfered
with his schedule: "Where am I to spend my evenings?"[150]

or "It is most inconvenient to have Adelphi Terrace shut up, I have nowhere to go, nobody to talk to."[151] Rather than a scientific investigator, he required someone to listen to him, to take care of him, to mother him. All the better that he also found an "ally in repression."[152]

In Shaw's letters to Charlotte his epistolary passion was frequently apparent; he threatened to "crush in all your ribs with an embrace"[153] when they met again, or bemoaned her absence, finding it "frightful not to be able to kiss your secretary occasionally."[154] In Charlotte, however, Shaw had met his match--a woman far more repressed than he. Her usual proposal "to part at the church door, so to speak," if they were to travel together was, he claimed, enough to whiten his hair.[155] On one occasion his advances elicited a sufficient rebuke from Charlotte that he was forced to apologize: "You shall not be worried into any more headaches. I am now a perfect gentleman."[156]

Even such reserve on Charlotte's part, however, was not enough to calm the sexual fears of either. For Shaw, "fragility is the only endurable condition."[157] He wrote her in April of 1898, when his health had temporarily improved: "Curse this cycling and country air: It revives my brute strength and brings unrest. I want a woman and a sound sleep. I am never happy except when I am worked to desperation in London and can eat only a little. . . . What people call health--appetite, weight,

beefiness--is a mistake."[158] Fragility was just what he
achieved in the first months after their marriage. In the
event that he was not fragile enough at this point he
managed to break his left arm, in a fall down the stairs,
sprain his good ankle in a bicycle tumble and sprain the
ankle of his injured leg twice in the ensuing months.

Judging from this propensity for accidents, Shaw
may have needed some help to comply with Charlotte's
resolution that their marriage could only take place if
it were to remain unconsummated. In his old age, he
expressed some regret that their marriage had been fruit-
less, and felt he ought to have been "firmer" with
Charlotte about sexual relations.[159] Yet it seems doubtful
that she would have yielded on this point. Contraceptive
methods were sufficiently well known that Charlotte's wish
not to bear children need not have been a critical factor
in this decision. I would suggest, instead, that the
relationships within her own family had made sex seem
extremely dangerous to Charlotte.

Possibly, equating sexuality with her mother
and her mother's destructiveness toward her father--who
died "of pure unhappiness"--she feared to reenact such a
scenario. Her somewhat excessive love for her father, her
pleasure in siding with him, traveling with him, and
sharing his interests, did not make matters any simpler
for her. She had not planned to marry because she wanted
to remain free of familial bonds which she had found so

painful. She would not have sex, once she had married in spite of her own injunction, because she felt the need to protect her husband, as she would have liked to protect her father, from the destructiveness of the female sex and from her own incestuous wishes.

Charlotte's fear of her sexual impulses had been apparent in her previous romances and in the string of minor ailments that accompanied her through the years. She feared such impulses just as she feared her rages against her mother. If Shaw handled his rage and confusion over early injustices he had suffered by placing himself on permanent exhibition, Charlotte handled hers by staying out of the limelight, lest any of the impulses she carefully smothered might be revealed. Thus, it was not only a lack of training or tenacity that kept Charlotte from completing projects or making a greater personal contribution to the causes and organizations in which she became involved, but an excess of repression, as well, which contaminated many seemingly unrelated areas of her life.

* * *

According to Shaw, in "The Quintessence of Ibsenism" Charlotte found "gospel, salvation, freedom, emancipation, self-respect and so on," months before she ever met the author.[160] Hyperbole aside, Shaw's influence on his wife was unmistakeable, nor is it surprising given Charlotte's propensity to look to men for guidance. The question is: did Charlotte's relationship to Shaw after they were married allow room for her own development, and did it foster feminist activities on her part or hinder them?

Despite the early return from her fact-finding trip to Rome, Charlotte had brought back a massive collection of documents. By Shaw's account, he suggested that she immediately get to work, but she, seeing dimly "that the accomplishment of such a magnum opus would be indeed the conquest of a profession for herself and consequent salvation," got no further than "arranging her material."[161] Instead, Charlotte devoted her energies and affections to the care and tending of G.B.S. in his invalid state. This seemed to give sufficient purpose to her life and to provide her with all the accomplishment she required.

At first glance, Charlotte would seem to have been an important member of the Fabian Society. She was elected to the Executive Committee a few months before her marriage, and she continued to be reelected and to serve for seventeen years--the only woman in the Society, before the First World War, to hold office for such a long period of time. Moreover, in the first decade of her tenure, Charlotte was usually one of only two or three women to sit on the Executive. Despite the length of her incumbency, however, it is difficult to detect her imprint on the Fabian program. While her attendance at Executive and Publishing Committee meetings was regular, except when she was out of London, there is no record of any speech given by Charlotte to the Society, either in its private or public meetings.

The ever cautious Secretary, Edward Pease, wrote
to Shaw questioning the advisability of Charlotte's remaining on the Executive after her marriage, implying that she
would be merely another vote for her husband. Shaw was
adamant, however, and had his way:

> I have always repudiated the theory that man
> and wife on the Executive means two votes for the
> man (or woman). If I thought that Mrs. Shaw would
> vote against her view of the interest of the Society
> out of duty to me I should institute divorce pro-
> ceedings forthwith. I often urged Mrs. Bland to
> come on the Executive when she was an active member;
> and I am strongly of opinion that Mrs. Webb would,
> at a later period, have been extremely useful on
> the Committee. I therefore flatly refuse to resign;
> and unless I offer myself along with my wife as
> a sacrifice to superstition the Executive cannot
> in decency accept her resignation--should she fancy
> herself bound to resign. I am open to argument
> on the subject; but that is my view at present.[162]

Shaw's assurances to the contrary, Pease was on the mark
with his line of questioning. But her vote was not so
much a second vote for Shaw as it was another vote for the
Webb-Shaw faction. For Charlotte, the Fabian Society was
G.B.S., Webb, Olivier, and Wallas; it did not exist apart
from them. She rarely attended the public meetings of
the Society except when one of the "Old Gang" was lecturing
or a row was impending and votes were important.[163] Her
opinion of the rest of the Society was not always flattering. A few months after assuming her place on the Executive she wrote to the Webbs, off on their year long trip
to America, of Shaw's injury-wracked convalescence and of
the business of the Fabian Society:

> I expect the Executive meetings are a funny
> contrast to what they used to be when G.B.S. and
> Sidney were there. I find them slow--slow! I
> am perfectly out of patience with the Fabians
> (strictly between ourselves): from my point of
> view it now consists of a parcel of boys and old
> women thinking they are making history, and really
> making themselves ridiculous. Possibly, this may
> be an exaggeration.[164]

Clearly, after her initial burst of enthusiasm,

Charlotte's socialism lay lightly on her mind. She worried

less and less over what to do with her life, or how to

make the "haves" and the "have-nots" more equal, and

concerned herself instead with the care and protection

of G.B.S. As Shaw's strength returned, the energies of

both were increasingly diverted to the theatre and to

Shaw's growing fame as a dramatist. Beatrice Webb noted,

by 1906 "the smart world [was] tumbling over one another

in the worship of G.B.S."; he was "the adored one of

the smartest and most cynical set of English Society."[165]

Fabianism became just another interest of her husband

which had to be balanced against the temporal require-

ments of his work and his physical well-being.

Years before, Charlotte had written in her common-

place book that a man's work, not his words, was important.

Talk wastes one's efforts, she felt, for "mental power

. . . is a finite thing," and there is much danger that

it will be "frittered away" in conversation.[166] Charlotte

never changed her views, and she conceived her role and

her responsibilities to her husband in this light. Thus,

Beatrice Webb complained that Charlotte tended to draw

Shaw away from her and Sidney "and other Fabians in order
not to waste his intellectual force in talk and argument."[167] That Charlotte also seemed to prefer the
company of people of her own class often entered into
such decisions.

If Charlotte's enthusiasm for Fabians and Fabianism
often flagged, she continued in her financial support of
the L.S.E. As one of the five Hutchinson Trustees,
Charlotte also continued to support Sidney Webb in his
efforts to use the trust money for the school and its
library or for Fabian educational lectures on social and
political subjects, as he saw fit. Her interest in the
"woman question" was usually less faltering than her
socialism, and on occasion she extracted some consideration
of women's issues from Sidney in return for her support.
In one of the many personal letters he sent her soliciting
additional contributions, he noted the school's intention
to take on an apprentice to train as a librarian, pointing
out what he knew she would appreciate, the benefits to
women's technical education achieved "in that small way."[168]

Charlotte's philanthropic decisions on how to
distribute her wealth were almost totally her own, although
one doubts that her husband's influence was completely
limited, as he protested, to "an earnest endeavor to
dissuade her from giving it."[169] Insofar as most of the
organizations in which Charlotte was involved as committee
or Executive member were devoted to interests she shared

with or derived from her husband, his talents and input
loomed large in the background of her contributions. If
a play were to be read and considered for production by
the Stage Society, Charlotte's view could be counted upon
to reflect Shaw's. As he wrote to a fellow dramatist,
concerned about his play, "I shall read it this afternoon
and fortify C. with my opinion for the S.S. [Stage Society]
Committee on Wednesday."[170]

On matters Fabian, as Pease had predicted, Shaw was
especially prone to "fortify" Charlotte with his opinions.
In the Wells episode, the last major battle within the
Society in which he took part wholeheartedly, Shaw's
handiwork is unmistakable in most of Charlotte's decisions.
Their respective roles in the episode are illuminating, not
only in this regard, but in terms of the ways they worked
and how they responded to personal attack. Aside from his
part as chief speechmaker for the Executive, Shaw played
his customary one as tactician and mediator. Charlotte's
role was less public than Shaw's. She was a member of
Wells's Special Committee, one of three representatives
from the Executive. As a feminist Charlotte might have
been expected to endorse Wells's views, yet she did not
sign her own committee's report. Even before Wells offered
the amendment censuring the Executive which would have made
agreement with his position impossible for her, she had
refused to sign. Charlotte's reasons for disavowing the
document were fairly straightforward; her loyalties lay

with the Executive and far outweighed her inclination to
support the feminist reforms in the Report. The letter to
Wells in which she expressed her dissent, however, provides
an interesting example of Shaw's willingness to "fortify"
Charlotte's opinions with his own, and it illustrates some
of the differences between the oddly matched couple.

Explaining her lack of support, she wrote to Wells
in September 1906: "Try to realize that I believe in the
Executive, that I approve of the work of the Executive, that
I have sat on the Executive for years and that everything
that belittles its work belittles me, every shortcoming
found in it is a shortcoming in me."[171] The letter which
Wells received, however, read:

> Try to realize that I am the accomplice of
> the Executive, that I am married to the Executive,
> and that I am the Executive, and that I really
> believe in the Executive and approve of it and
> am in a state of continual astonishment at all
> it has done with its means. If I had to choose
> between the Committee and the Executive to form
> the Society, in the future, I shouldn't think
> twice about backing the Executive.[172]

Similarly, Charlotte stated her refusal to comply in these
terms: "I don't know what the other members of the Executive will do, . . . as for me--no, Mr. Wells, no."[173] But
the corrected version was: "What I will do I cannot
say until the report has been discussed--what I won't do
is quite certain: I won't sign."[174] The olive branch
which Charlotte extended at the end of the letter, "Come
and see me and have a chat about it,"[175] was reworded to
read: "G.B.S. has a scientific play nearly finished which

he would like to read to you. If only there were any
chance of its being finished I should propose a Folkstone
week-end; but it has only reached the end of the third act
and there are to be five."[176]

The decision not to sign the document was clearly
Charlotte's; the form of her refusal, however, was pure
G.B.S. His participation in its composition was as obvious
in the tone of the remarks as it was in the presence of
his correcting pencil on the rough draft of her letter.
The disparity between Charlotte's original letter and
G.B.S.'s amended edition was not, however, merely a question of tone or prose style; it reflects a very basic
difference in their respective ways of perceiving themselves and the external world. Charlotte's reply was
immediately personal; the attack on the Executive was
a threat to her integrity and to the essence of her personality. G.B.S., the man who received sixty rejection
slips for his first five novels and kept on writing,
ignored the personal connection, defended the actions
of the Executive, and then took the offensive. Her approach
was emotional but direct; his was impersonal, humorously
aggressive, and somewhat devious. Ironically, Wells
answered by return post that it was she who had "betrayed"
him, rather than the reverse, and wondered somewhat wistfully, "Isn't Shaw on my side?"[177]

Charlotte had not supported Wells, nor had she
signed the "Special Report," but she was sympathetic to

many of his ideas and was impressed by the Report's agenda
for reform. Heretofore, Charlotte's presence on the
Executive had been discernible by occasional announcements
in the Minutes or in the Fabian News of her financial
gifts to the Society for lectures, tracts, research,
book boxes, and the like, and by her steady but highly
inconspicuous work on various committees. Following
the Wells episode, Charlotte became a more visible member.
She urged, for example, that Wells's article on marriage
be printed as a Fabian tract. (This suggestion was voted
down by an Executive Committee whose views did not encom-
pass the breakdown of the family as part of their socialist
ideology.)[178] She also suggested the formation of new
groups within the Society, and the publication of more
propaganda tracts and of elementary tracts on socialism,
recommendations which had appeared in the "Special Report,"
and which were greeted favorably. Her proposal for a
series of "What I Believe" lectures resulted in a highly
successful sequence of lectures given by Fabian lumi-
naries.[179]

It was not merely Charlotte's involvement with the
Special Committee that had spurred her on to greater
interest in the Fabian. The Society itself had experienced
a change in the aftermath of the Wells furor, and, amidst
the growing volubility of the women's movement, it had
begun to take a renewed interest in the "woman question"
and to chart a more feminist course. Charlotte had never

attempted to lead the Society in such a direction; her
interest in the Fabian had been too fitful; her disinclina-
tion to lead had been too strong. Yet she was quick to
follow the lead of those who did.

When Mrs. Wilson, newly returned to the Society,
determined to organize a Fabian Women's Group in 1908,
Charlotte was willing and anxious to help her do so.
She, along with Mrs. Reeves, joined Mrs. Wilson in setting
up objectives for the group and arranging meetings.
Charlotte became a member of its Executive Committee
and was closely identified with much of its work for the
next five years. She wrote the "Preface" for the Group's
tract on the National Insurance Bill of 1911 which protested
against the Bill's unfairness to women and against the
contributory aspects of the state-aided insurance, a
criticism that was generally in keeping with the Fabian
bias against contributory plans in any welfare undertaking.
As a member of the Women's Group Studies Committee, she
summarized, for private publication, the letters received
by the Group on the six papers they had presented in their
first lecture series. While she remained on the Fabian
Executive, Charlotte's efforts for the Society were involved
primarily with the Women's Group or as an intermediary
between the two Executive Committees.

Like so many women drawn into public life by
a concern for the problems of others, Charlotte had
increasingly begun to be concerned with issues that

touched her more directly. From the American abolitionists
turned suffragists in the middle of the nineteenth century,
to their descendants in the civil rights movement a century
later who turned to radical feminism,[180] the basic desire
to set one's own house in order and one's own problems
straight, once one has gotten into the business of ordering
houses and setting problems straight, provides a recurring
pattern. For Charlotte, the women's movement promised
redress of personal grievances rather than a search for
solutions to the problems of others. Thus, once the
movement had gained sufficient momentum to offer her
a choice of platforms, she invariably channeled her efforts
along feminist rather than socialist lines.

Then too, Charlotte had never been one to enjoy
people who were not of her own class, unless they were
redeemed by talent or intellect. From the time she and
G.B.S. had married, despite his abstemious habits, they
had always lived in great comfort and luxury with servants
in attendance and travel a constant diversion. Charlotte
gave and accepted invitations, the few that G.B.S. would
allow, to renowned artists, philosophers and composers,
and to dukes and duchesses as well. Feminist activities
and committees were more likely to keep her in the kind of
company she preferred. The New Independent Party, which
began its brief existence for the purpose of representing
women's interests in local government and electing more
women candidates to the metropolitan borough councils and

the London County Council, was a case in point. Charlotte
was among the two duchesses and four countesses and
assorted other noteworthy women who were elected to its
Council at the inaugural meeting in December 1913.[181]

By this time, Charlotte was nominally a socialist;
she was truly a feminist. Her class affiliation, to say
nothing of her basic snobbishness, made it less than
likely that she would be frightened by the notion of
giving women the vote on the basis of the existing property
qualification. Despite her husband's lack of enthusiasm
for suffrage solutions, she was very much in favor of
giving women the vote. She marched in all the major
suffrage processions, occasionally with G.B.S. at her
side, and in 1911 when the Government announced its intention of bringing forth a Manhood Suffrage Bill, in the
midst of the truce that accompanied negotiations over the
Conciliation Bill, Charlotte felt impelled to write a long
emotional letter to the Times, her first, in protest.

In arguing against the new Government Bill Charlotte
was not concerned with what society suffered from women's
disenfranchisement. She protested, instead, against
the "intolerable insult of being . . . dismissed . . .
as creatures of another and inferior species." As long
as there was a whole class of men excluded from the vote,
she declared, the argument could be made that the criteria
for exclusion was incapacity and irresponsibility, not sex.
"Now it is proposed to throw away this last rag of decency

. . . the vilest male wretch . . . shall have a vote, and
the noblest woman in England shall not have one because
she is a female." Obviously, for Charlotte, issues of
sex were far more important by now than those of class.
Her age and her dignity, however, precluded recommending
W.S.P.U. tactics. "It is no use jostling policemen," she
warned; one must continue to work toward passage of the
Conciliation Bill or, failing that solution, for an amendment to the Manhood Suffrage Bill.[182]

Apart from her work with the Fabian Women's Group,
whose efforts were usually geared to the problems faced by
women of the working class, Charlotte's endeavors were
likely to involve issues which spoke to her own concerns.
Having never worked, she was not particularly sensitive
to the difficulties of a wage differential between the
sexes; having no children, but several servants, she was
unaware of the need for child-care, or for communal organization of household tasks, to free working women from some
of their chores. She did, however, understand at first
hand the need for the vote, for access to governing boards,
for better education and more professional training opportunities, and for reform of the laws and customs governing
both marriage and divorce. As a feminist Charlotte was
back to worrying over problems of her own class.

In 1907 she wrote to the Divorce Law Reform Union,
of which she was a contributing member, demanding to
know why there were no women on their Board of Directors

and suggesting that their mailing list include the names of
many more women. Charlotte believed as firmly in divorce
as did G.B.S., having been brought up by as ill-matched
a pair of parents as had he. She also believed in the
importance of birth control and, in later years, gave
generously in support of birth control clinics. While the
latter were beneficial primarily for women of the working
class, the issue of birth control had been shorn of its
connection with the left by the 1930's when Charlotte
became involved with it. Campaigning for free access to
birth control information was, by then, largely a liberal,
middle-class cause, many of whose adherents were motivated
by eugenic or neo-Malthusian concerns.[183] Whether
Charlotte understood its importance, as have later day
feminists, as a political issue, that is, as a means of
assuring sexual self-determination for women, is not
clear. One can be certain, however, that she was not
recommending her own solution, celibacy, as the method of
choice for achieving control over one's sexuality.

When in 1910, in support of the suffragist campaign,
Mrs. Jacob Bright asked all propertied women to refuse to
disclose their incomes to their husbands for declaration
to the Inland Revenue, Charlotte's immediate compliance
with this request caused a well publicized stir. In his
subsequent negotiations with the Inland Review Office, Shaw
argued, in truth, that his wife had always kept her own
bank accounts and transacted her own business interests,

that he knew nothing of her finances, and she on no account
would tell him about them. He stated he could not, therefore, include her income in his returns; she would have to
be consulted on her own income, as she desired, and be
taxed accordingly. In the stand-off that ensued, Shaw
was ultimately spared imprisonment on tax evasion by
the passage of an act which enabled husbands and wives
to make separate tax returns.[184] Charlotte, as a woman
of independent income married to a very famous man, had
secured a victory of sorts for the financial independence
of women with property.

        Being married to a famous man, however, had done
little to encourage Charlotte in her own literary endeavors.
Her previous attempts had always trailed off incompletely
in half-filled notebooks, and they continued to do so
after her marriage. Yet, enveloped as she was in Shaw's
world of manuscripts and publishers and theatrical productions, Charlotte did become involved in the publication and
presentation of a few works, not her own, which appealed to
her rising feminist consciousness.

        In 1904 Charlotte read and translated Maternité,
a feminist play by Eugene Brieux. She was so impressed
with the French playwright that she bought the American
and English publication rights for the translations of two
other plays of his and tried to publish them in England.
No publisher would do so, however, because of their con-
troversial nature. While she was on the Executive

Committee of the Stage Society she had persuaded the
Society to do a production of Maternité, but the censor
had refused to license the play. By 1911, after Brieux
had been made a member of the French Academy, Charlotte
was able to find a publisher for her Three Plays by Brieux.
The book contained another translation of hers, Woman
on Her Own, and a "Preface" by G.B.S.

Charlotte's translation of Woman on Her Own was
used at the inaugural performance in December 1913 of
the Women's Theatre. The Actresses' Franchise League
which sponsored the theatre was a committee of ninety
women whose purpose was to present the women's point of
view, provide an outlet for activities of women members
of the theatrical profession, and forward the cause of
women's enfranchisement. The play at the Coronet Theatre
was successful on a small scale and was much appreciated
by the mostly feminine audience which cheered Brieux's
message that it is impossible for a noble self-respecting
woman to make her way in the world because of the wicked-
ness and selfishness of men.[185] The battle lines drawn
by Brieux were clearly of a sexual nature and made little
allowance for differences between classes. The protagonist
in the play, Thérese, was cheated out of her inheritance
by her lawyer, deceived by her lover, and foiled in her
attempts to organize women workers by the anger of their
male counterparts over the influx of cheap feminine
labor.[186]

Charlotte saw to the publication of another Brieux
play in 1914, Damaged Goods, which also contained a "Preface" by G.B.S. and a "Forward" by herself. This one dealt
with the problem of venereal disease and its effects on the
innocent. It was extremely topical given the general
interest in the subject raised by the findings of the
Royal Society of Medicine and the subsequent appointment
of a Royal Commission on venereal disease by Mr. Asquith.
Feminists, particularly those of the W.S.P.U., were
extremely interested in the disease, seeing it as one
more problem foisted on innocent women and children by
men. The solution advocated by the more extreme members
of the W.S.P.U. was complete sexual abstinence; Charlotte's
more moderate view was that the medical aspects of the
problem had to be recognized and dealt with publicly,
rather than allowing the problem to fester quietly and
bring harm to innocent victims.[187]

*   *   *

In the midst of her involvement with Brieux's
works, Charlotte began to have problems of her own, of an
entirely different sort. Her marriage to Shaw, which
had seemed to work well for the better part of a decade,
was beginning to show signs of strain; the compromises
they had devised appeared to be unraveling. Charlotte's
persistent traveling, and her insistence that Shaw accompany
her, had become increasingly irritating to G.B.S. Writing
to his friend Granville-Barker in the summer of 1908, Shaw

complained of the inconvenience, the boredom, and the exhaustion he experienced as the couple swept across Europe and North Africa, Charlotte maintaining all the while that the trip would provide him with a much needed rest from his overly taxing writing schedule.[188] For her part, Charlotte felt, and no doubt suffered from, Shaw's growing impatience with her historical-theological meanderings. Rarely would he let her get through a discussion of this sort without interrupting, correcting, or dismissing her.[189]

In the aftermath of a particularly difficult tour of the continent in 1911, Shaw flatly refused to go to Rome with Charlotte the following spring. Writing of his decision to Beatrice Webb, he suggested that all spouses, including the Webbs, should take time off from each other occasionally--a preventative measure to keep relationships from stultifying.[190] Perhaps more to the point, and far more revealing of Shaw's inner feelings, was the play he had been working on that year, Overruled, the play devoted to the inevitability of adultery. The outward circumstances of his life could hardly have provided better evidence of the importance of this theme to Shaw.

After fourteen years of fidelity, G.B.S. had lost his head to Mrs. Patrick Campbell, the beautiful and headstrong actress, then enjoying a great vogue in London. The relationship had begun in mock seriousness with Shaw

pursuing and flattering Mrs. Campbell, as was his wont with
actresses whom he wanted to star in his plays. Shaw had
written _Pygmalion_ with her in mind for the role of Eliza.
While it took two years before the production made it
to the stage of His Majesty's Theatre in April 1914, both
the play and the actress were enormously successful--Shaw's
largest box office success to date. Charlotte spent
the better part of that two year period in great distress
over Shaw's apparent obsession with "Mrs. Pat."[191] That
the obsession was common knowledge, although never openly
acknowledged to Charlotte, added to her anguish; as Beatrice
Webb complained after seeing Shaw, he could speak of little
else but the perfections of "Mrs. Pat."[192]

Neither socialism, nor feminism, nor public involvement of any kind was sufficient to alleviate the emptiness
and pain that Charlotte experienced. She had always been
religious in her own anarchistic way, and it was to religion that she turned at this point in her life. The
comforts of religious belief have drawn many an activist
away from public questions, particularly at middle age.
Annie Besant had given up a multitude of isms and ideologies for Theosophy several years before, and Christabel
Pankhurst, turned Seventh Day Adventist, preached the coming
of the Millenium, as fervently as she had campaigned for
women's suffrage, when she emigrated to America after the
First World War. So too, Charlotte Shaw began to devote
her time and energy to "The Teaching" of Dr. James Porter

Mills, an amalgam of Christian Science and Eastern
mysticism.

For Charlotte this meant a final decision to focus
her energies on her own well-being. "The Teaching" made
a virtue of health and happiness and relieved her, at
least intellectually, of the need to suffer for others.
Thus, Charlotte had progressed from her wish to "suffer
as protest," to a desire to alleviate the sufferings of
the working class through socialism, to a greater activity
in redressing the wrongs of her own sex, to committing
herself to her own well-being.

In 1914, Charlotte gathered the assorted teachings
of Dr. Mills and had them published in a small book called
Knowledge Is the Door. Charlotte's editing did not do
much to alter Mills's densely unintelligible prose, but
she enthusiastically sent hundreds of copies of the book
to her friends and acquaintances. Few were as ascerbic
in their "thanks" as Roger Fry, who commented he would "be
very sorry to think that a man who writes so badly has
really got into close communion with the ultimate nature
of things."[193] In contrast, Theosophists in several
countries were most willing to overlook the prose and
were anxious to review the book or to exchange notes
with Charlotte.

Clearly, Charlotte herself was much comforted
by her "little book"; she seemed to be more at peace with
herself, happier, and healthier than she had been for

several years.[194]   Like so many of her generation,
Charlotte had long tried to reconcile her need for a
religious faith with the intellectual barriers to that
faith which rationalist dogmas and scientific data presented.   Charlotte's quest was hampered further, however,
by the unhappiness of the milieu in which her religious
views had been formed.   Her family life had been such that
she required a faith that was uncontaminated by any parental
endorsements, untarnished by associations with her
Protestant past.   Dr. Mills's "Teachings" provided just
such a system of beliefs.   She retained a lifelong attachment to it, as well as a lasting interest in mystical
theologies of all kinds.

In 1915 Charlotte finally left the Fabian Executive,
as G.B.S. had done in 1911.   Her input had not been significant for most of her tenure; her absence created little
change.   Only the Webbs and Edward Pease of the "Old Gang"
remained on board to see the Society through the upheavals
of war and internal division.

Shaw's infatuation with "Mrs. Pat" had ended in
1914, just after Pygmalion opened, when she contracted
a safe, successful marriage to another admirer.   Shaw was
much shaken by her defection, but once the affair was over
the comfortable relationship between the Shaws resumed and
continued relatively undisturbed by such volcanic attrac-
tions.   According to one friend who knew them in later
years, "their affection for each other was transparent,

and it increased and deepened as they grew older."[195]
According to another, "they mix[ed] like bacon and eggs."[196]
On most social and political issues they agreed; Mussolini's
invasion of Abyssinia, of which Shaw highly approved, was
a noticeable exception. And Charlotte was not at all fond
of some of the "odd" young socialists to be met at the
Fabian Summer School; she tended to stay at home, while
G.B.S. continued to enjoy his occasional links with the
Society. Similarly, she did not share his great admiration
for the Soviet experiment and declined to take the trip
to Russia with him in 1931.[197]

Certainly they both agreed that clearly demarcated
spheres of endeavor for men and women were foolish, that
the roles of the sexes should be completely flexible. Yet
in their marriage they practiced a clear-cut, traditional
division of labor. Charlotte managed the house, the
servants, social engagements, travel arrangements, and
the care and well-being of G.B.S. He saw to the camera,
the car, and his work. She managed him so that he managed
to work, comfortably and prodigiously. As time went on
G.B.S. deferred to Charlotte increasingly; he accepted her
wish to travel with better grace, he went to bed at eleven
as she insisted, and sang to her at night as she wished.
She "hovered about him like a guardian angel" dispensing
typed copies of the lists of foods he would or would not
eat to the chefs of the boats or hotels in which they
stayed, and warded off journalists and photographers

whenever she could.[198]

Maternal in her wifely ministrations, Charlotte seemed not to have missed having children. Shaw claimed that an author's books were his children, and his wife had "quite trouble enough nursing him through his confinements without having any of her own."[199] This was certainly the case in the first years of their marriage when the question of children might have been considered. But Charlotte's decision had been made years before, and had influenced her wish not to marry when she was a young woman. Thinking back on how and why she had arrived at her wish to remain childless, she wrote: "I don't believe, as far as I can remember, that I was born with a dislike of children-- perhaps I was. But, anyway, my own home life made me firmly resolve never to be the mother of a child who might suffer as I had suffered. . . . As I grew older, I saw many, and better, reasons for sticking to my resolution."[200] Whether or not her decision to remain childless was more a function of her abhorrence of sexual relations than of her abhorrence of children is not clear. One suspects that the two aversions were strongly felt, each in its own right. With the children of others, even those of her one niece of whom she was quite fond, Charlotte was extremely reserved, as she was with most adults. Babies, she thought, were "disgusting little things" and she wanted nothing to do with them.[201]

Yet, as she grew older, she developed close

relationships with a few of the younger authors in their
acquaintance and treated them in what can only be described
as a most maternal fashion. This was especially so with
T. E. Lawrence. He introduced himself to the Shaws in
1922, diffidently asking G.B.S. to read his first manuscript, The Seven Pillars of Wisdom, and to tell him
if it deserved to be printed or burned. Lawrence venerated
Shaw and wrote to Charlotte at first because he felt less
constrained in writing to her than to the "great man."
A close relationship, however, soon developed between
the young airman and Charlotte. They shared a mutual
passion for literature and music, and an antipathy for
physical passion of any sort. Of Irish descent, they
also shared a concern for Ireland and a vast sympathy
for the plight of the new Republic and its rebellious
offspring. Wherever he was posted, Charlotte sent him
letters, records, books (including the "little book" on
the teachings of Dr. Mills), chocolates, fine teas, and
other delicacies. She proofread both The Seven Pillars of
Wisdom manuscript and The Mint for him, and kept after
G.B.S. to read and correct the texts of Lawrence's works
and to do what he could to smooth the path to publication.

Lawrence's death in a motorcycle accident in
1935 was a great sorrow to both the Shaws, but especially
so for Charlotte. He had been the perfect son for her.
Having arrived on the scene full grown, his existence had
required neither sexual relations nor dirty diapers. His

growing pains, encountered elsewhere, had not involved her in painful remembrances of her own past. And his continued affection never necessitated daily contact or a fixed abode, neither of which her obsession with travel would have allowed.

Charlotte Payne-Townshend Shaw achieved in her long life--she died in her eighty-sixth year--her own particular emancipation. Having refrained from sexual contact she had assured herself of never becoming a sexual object for anyone; having had no children, she was relieved of the encumbering burdens they entailed; having inherited great wealth and managing her own finances very effec-tively, she had maintained her economic independence. Yet for all her independence, she remained, in the vocabulary of Simone De Beauvoir, the ultimate "other," a woman who defined herself through the man she married.[202] She had married a very particular man, a man whose talents and tenacity far exceeded her own; those of us who have enjoyed his plays may be grateful that she took him in hand before he managed to end his brief career as a drama-tist by overwork and malnutrition. Nonetheless, inherent in her choice was a decision to serve rather than to exist in her own right. She had been so properly social-ized, which, for a woman of her class and time, often meant so improperly educated, that she could not see herself as subject, as a prime mover in an organization or as author of her own works.

Still more, as she wrote to T. E. Lawrence in the one extended, self-revelatory statement she ever committed to paper, the difficulties of her childhood, the conflicts in her family, and especially her hatred of her overbearing social climbing mother had "warped my character and spoiled my life and my health and my mind."[203] "It really couldn't happen now," she wrote rather optimistically in 1927; "girls have emancipated themselves and expect to go out into the world and live their lives as boys do. And yet, how burning a question, this of the exaction of parents, remains."[204]

Footnotes

[1] George Bernard Shaw, "A Manifesto," Fabian Tract
No. 2, reprinted in Edward R. Pease, The History of the
Fabian Society (New York: Barnes and Noble, 1963), pp.
41-43.

[2] George Bernard Shaw, "The Practical Politics of
Socialism" [Lecture Notes], George Bernard Shaw Papers,
M.S. 50700, 1885, British Library.

[3] George Bernard Shaw, "What It Is To Be a Fabian,"
The Young Man, April 1896, pp. 113-16.

[4] George Bernard Shaw, "The Transition to Social
Democracy," in Fabian Essays in Socialism, ed. G. B.
Shaw (London: Walter Scott, 1908), p. 47.

[5] George Bernard Shaw, "The Political Situation"
[Lecture Notes], Shaw Papers, MS 50684, October 1895.

[6] Bernard Shaw, Prefaces (London: Constable,
1934), p. 158.

[7] Ibid., p. 159.

[8] Bernard Shaw, Misalliance, in Selected Plays of
Bernard Shaw, vol. 4 (New York: Dodd, Mead, 1957), p. 131.

[9] See "Fabian Minutes," 14 February and 28 February
1896.

[10] Bernard Shaw, "The Quintessence of Ibsenism,"
in Selected Non-dramatic Writings of Bernard Shaw, ed.
Dan H. Laurence (Boston: Houghton Mifflin, 1965), p. 227.

[11] Ibid., p. 228.

[12] Ibid., pp. 228-29.

[13] G. B. Shaw to Sidney Webb, 30 July 1901, Passfield
Papers, Box II, 4a, British Library of Political and
Economic Science.

[14] Bernard Shaw, "What Is My Religious Faith?" in
his Sixteen Self Sketches (New York: Dodd, Mead, 1949),
pp. 125-28.

[15] Shaw, Prefaces, p. 159.

[16]B. Shaw, "The Revolutionist's Handbook," ibid., p. 170.

[17]Bernard Shaw, The Philanderer, in The Collected Works of Bernard Shaw, vol. 7 (1898; reprint ed., New York: William H. Wise, 1930), xiii.

[18]Ibid., p. 77.

[19]Ibid., p. 73.

[20]Ibid., p. 80.

[21]Ibid., p. 78.

[22]Ibid., p. 74.

[23]G. B. Shaw to William Archer, 27 January 1900, Shaw Papers, M.S. 45296, No. 83.

[24]Ibid.

[25]B. Shaw, "Man and Superman," in his Prefaces, p. 156.

[26]Bernard Shaw, Mrs. Warren's Profession, in Selected Plays of Bernard Shaw, vol. 3 (1898; reprint ed., New York: Dodd, Mead, 1948), pp. 1-122.

[27]Bernard Shaw, "Woman-Man in Petticoats" (1927), in Platform and Pulpit, ed. Dan H. Laurence (New York: Hill and Wang, 1961), p. 174.

[28]Shaw, "Man and Superman," p. 156.

[29]Ibid.

[30]Shaw insisted, in the "Preface" to Major Barbara, that his unconventional, somewhat hostile view of women had not been derived from foreign philosophers like Schopenhauer, Strindberg, or Nietzsche: "As a matter of fact I hardly noticed Schopenhauer's disparagements of women when they came under my notice later on, so thoroughly had [Belfort] Bax familiarized me with the homoist attitude, and forced me to recognize the extent to which public opinion, and consequently legislation and jurisprudence, is corrupted by feminist sentiment." B. Shaw, "Major Barbara," in his Prefaces, p. 117.

[31]Shaw, "Woman-Man in Petticoats," p. 174.

[32]Shaw, Prefaces, p. 154.

[33] B. Shaw, "Getting Married," ibid., p. 23.

[34] Ibid., p. 33.

[35] B. Shaw, "Misalliance," ibid., p. 93.

[36] Shaw, "Getting Married," p. 9.

[37] Ibid., p. 15.

[38] B. Shaw, Getting Married, in Selected Plays, vol. 4, p. 403.

[39] Shaw, "Getting Married," p. 18.

[40] Ibid.

[41] Ibid.

[42] Kathlyn Oliver, [editorial] The Freewoman (1912), cited in Sheila Rowbotham, A New World For Women: Stella Browne--Socialist Feminist (London: Pluto Press, 1977), p. 11.

[43] Shaw, Misalliance, pp. 125-30.

[44] Shaw, Getting Married, p. 415; "To Frank Harris on Sex in Biography," in B. Shaw, Self Sketches, p. 178.

[45] Gladys M. Crane, "Shaw and Women's Lib," in Fabian Feminist, ed. Rodelle Weintraub (University Park: Pennsylvania State University Press, 1977), pp. 175-84.

[46] See Aileen S. Kraditor, The Ideas of the Woman Suffrage Movement, 1890-1920 (New York: Columbia University Press, 1965); Carl N. Degler, At Odds: Women and the Family in America from the Revolution to the Present (New York: Oxford University Press, 1980).

[47] Shaw, "Man and Superman," p. 156.

[48] Shaw, "Getting Married," p. 27.

[49] "G.B.S. and a Suffragist: An Intimate Interview by Maud Churton Brady," London Tribune, 12 March 1906, in Fabian Feminist, p. 237.

[50] B. Shaw, "Forcible Feeding," New Statesman, 12 April 1913, ibid., pp. 228-35.

[51] B. Shaw to Ethel Smyth, 25 June 1914, cited in Barbara Bellow Watson, A Shavian Guide to the Intelligent

Woman (New York: W. W. Norton, 1964), pp. 194-95.

[52]B. Shaw, "Why All Women Are Peculiarly Fitted to be Good Voters," New York American, 21 April 1907, in Fabian Feminist, p. 249.

[53]Bernard Shaw, Press Cuttings, in his Translations and Tomfooleries (New York: Brentano's, 1926), p. 186.

[54]Kraditor, Ideas of Woman Suffrage Movement, pp. 44-68.

[55]G. B. Shaw to E. Smyth, 25 June 1914.

[56]Shaw, Self Sketches, p. 202.

[57]B. Shaw, "Immaturity," in his Prefaces, p. 627.

[58]Ibid., p. 634.

[59]Ibid., p. 636.

[60]B. Shaw, "To Frank Harris," in his Self Sketches, p. 177.

[61]B. Shaw, "My Mother and Her Relatives," ibid., p. 28.

[62]Shaw, "Immaturity," p. 637.

[63]Shaw, "My Mother and Her Relatives, p. 29.

[64]Ibid., p. 30.

[65]B. Shaw, quoted in Hesketh Pearson, Bernard Shaw: His Life and His Personality (London: Methuen, 1961), p. 435.

[66]Shaw, "My Mother and Her Relatives," p. 29.

[67]B. Shaw, "London Music," quoted in Daniel Dervin, Bernard Shaw: A Psychological Study (London: Associated University Presses, 1975), pp. 30-41.

[68]B. Shaw, "Preface to Three Plays for Puritans," in his Prefaces, pp. 712-13.

[69]B. Shaw, "In the Days of My Youth," in his Self Sketches, pp. 75-78.

[70]Beatrice Webb diary, April 1911, Passfield Papers, British Library of Political and Economic Science.

[71]B. Shaw, "Biographers' Blunders Corrected," in his Self Sketches, p. 147.

[72]B. Shaw, "How I Became a Public Speaker," in his Self Sketches, p. 97.

[73]Margot Peters, Bernard Shaw and the Actresses (New York: Doubleday, 1980), pp. 12-14.

[74]B. Shaw, quoted in Pearson, Bernard Shaw, p. 380.

[75]Bernard Shaw, quoted in Archibald Henderson, George Bernard Shaw: Man of the Century (New York: Appleton-Century-Crofts, 1956), p. 30.

[76]Bernard Shaw, Heartbreak House in his Selected Plays of Bernard Shaw, vol. 1 (New York: Dodd, Mead, 1948), p. 529.

[77]B. Shaw, quoted in Pearson, Bernard Shaw, p. 22.

[78]Shaw, "To Frank Harris," p. 177.

[79]Bertha Newcombe to Ashley Dukes (n.d.), reprinted in Janet Dunbar, Mrs. G.B.S.: A Portrait (New York: Harper and Row, 1963), pp. 117-18.

[80]Shaw, "To Frank Harris," p. 178.

[81]Webb Diary, 1910.

[82]B. Shaw, "Overruled," in his Prefaces, p. 106.

[83]Ibid., p. 113.

[84]Ibid., p. 108.

[85]Peters, Bernard Shaw and the Actresses, p. xi.

[86]B. Shaw to Ellen Terry, 12 October 1896, in Bernard Shaw: Collected Letters 1874-1897, ed. Dan H. Laurence (London: Max Reinhardt, 1965), p. 676.

[87]Ibid., p. 677.

[88]B. Shaw to E. Terry, 8 September 1897, ibid., p. 803.

[89]Ibid., pp. 801-02.

[90]Webb Diary, 12 July 1913.

[91]Shaw, "To Frank Harris," p. 175.

[92]B. Shaw, Pygmalion, in Selected Plays, vol. 1, p. 283.

[93]B. Shaw to Beatrice Webb, 21 June 1898, Passfield Papers.

[94]Charlotte Payne-Townshend, "The Nightingale and the Poet" [unpublished essay], Charlotte Shaw Papers, ADD MS 56521, 1877, British Library.

[95]Charlotte Payne-Townshend, Untitled Short Story, C. Shaw Papers, ADD MS 56524, No. 28 (n.d.).

[96]Charlotte Payne-Townshend, "Happiness," C. Shaw Papers, ADD MS 56521, 6 June 1877.

[97]Charlotte Payne-Townshend, Commonplace Book, C. Shaw Papers, ADD MS 56504, vol. 15.

[98]C. Payne-Townshend, Commonplace Book, 29 March 1879, C. Shaw Papers, ADD MS 56521.

[99]Dunbar, Mrs. G.B.S., p. 48.

[100]Charlotte Shaw to T. E. Laurence, 17 May 1927, C. Shaw Papers, ADD MS 45922, British Library.

[101]Ibid.

[102]Ibid.

[103]Letter to C. Payne-Townshend, 1885, C. Shaw Papers, MS 56490.

[104]Charlotte Payne-Townshend diary, 1878, C. Shaw Papers, ADD MS 56500, vol. 11.

[105]C. Shaw to T. E. Laurence, 17 May 1927, C. Shaw Papers.

[106]Ibid.

[107]C. Payne-Townshend, translation from T. Gautier, Mademoiselle de Maupin, C. Shaw Papers, ADD MS 56522, 1871.

[108]C. Payne-Townshend, "Essay on Othello," C. Shaw Papers, ADD MS 56521, 13 August 1877.

[109]Ibid.

[110]Ibid.

[111]Ibid.

[112]Ibid.

[113]Ibid.

[114]C. Payne-Townshend, Untitled Short Story, C. Shaw Papers, ADD MS 56524, No. 28.

[115]Ibid.

[116]C. Payne-Townshend, Commonplace Book, 1884, C. Shaw Papers, ADD MS 56504, vol. 15.

[117]C. Payne-Townshend, 27 March 1885, C. Shaw Papers, MS 56490.

[118]C. Shaw to T. E. Laurence, 17 May 1927, C. Shaw Papers.

[119]Ibid.

[120]Ibid.

[121]General Clery to C. Payne-Townshend, 1892, C. Shaw Papers, ADD MS 56490.

[122]Ibid., 1893.

[123]A. Munthe to C. Payne-Townshend, 9 November 1894, C. Shaw Papers, ADD MS 56490.

[124]Augustine Henry to C. Payne-Townshend, 30 November 1895, C. Shaw Papers, ADD MS 56490.

[125]Major Hutton to C. Payne-Townshend, 18 July 1887, C. Shaw Papers, ADD MS 56490.

[126]C. Payne-Townshend, Commonplace Book, 6 June 1877, C. Shaw Papers, ADD MS 56521.

[127]Karen Horney, "The Problem of Feminine Masochism," in Psychoanalysis and Women, ed. Jean Baker Miller (Harmondsworth, Middlesex: Penguin Books, 1973).

[128]C. Payne-Townshend, Untitled Short Story.

[129]Ibid.

[130]C. Payne-Townshend to A. Henry (n.d.), reprinted in Dunbar, Mrs. G.B.S., pp. 130-31.

[131]C. Payne-Townshend to A. Henry, 1897, ibid., p. 128.

[132]Ibid., p. 129.

[133]Webb Diary, 16 September 1896.

[134]Ibid.

[135]Ibid.

[136]Ibid.

[137]B. Shaw to Ellen Terry, 5 December 1896, in Collected Letters, p. 709.

[138]B. Shaw to E. Terry, 24 December 1897, ibid., p. 831.

[139]B. Shaw to E. Terry, 8 March 1897, ibid., p. 733.

[140]Webb Diary, May 1897.

[141]Ibid.

[142]Ibid., 27 September 1897.

[143]B. Shaw to C. Payne-Townshend, 27 October 1896, Shaw Papers, MS 50550.

[144]Ibid., 7 November 1896.

[145]Ibid., 8 December 1897.

[146]Ibid., 16 March 1898.

[147]G.B.S. to B. Webb, 21 June 1898, Passfield Papers.

[148]Ibid.

[149]B. Shaw to C. Payne-Townshend, 26 October 1897, Shaw Papers, MS 50550.

[150]Ibid., 7 October 1897.

[151]Ibid., 15 October 1897.

[152] Dervin, _Bernard Shaw: A Psychological Study_, p. 332.

[153] B. Shaw to C. Payne-Townshend, 26 April 1898, Shaw Papers.

[154] Ibid., 29 March 1898.

[155] Ibid., 15 March 1897.

[156] Ibid., 29 November 1897.

[157] Ibid., 4 April 1898.

[158] Ibid.

[159] St. John Ervine, _Bernard Shaw: His Life, Work and Friends_ (New York: William Morrow, 1956), p. 315.

[160] B. Shaw to E. Terry, 1897, in _Collected Letters_, p. 831.

[161] B. Shaw to B. Webb, 7 May 1898, Passfield Papers.

[162] G.B.S. to Edward Pease, 5 June 1898, Shaw Papers, ADD MS 59784.

[163] St. John Ervine, _Bernard Shaw_, p. 304.

[164] Charlotte Shaw to the Webbs, 1898, Passfield Papers.

[165] Webb Diary, November 1906.

[166] C. Payne-Townshend, Commonplace Book, 1877, C. Shaw Papers, ADD MS 56521.

[167] Webb Diary, 7 March 1911.

[168] Sidney Webb to C. Shaw, 21 January 1899, C. Shaw Papers, ADD MS 56491.

[169] G.B.S. to E. Pease, 6 January 1899, Shaw Papers, ADD MS 59784.

[170] G.B.S. to Alfred Sutro, reprinted in Dunbar, _Mrs. G.B.S._, p. 176.

[171] C. Shaw to H. G. Wells, 4 September 1906, [rough draft], Shaw Papers, MS 50552.

[172]Ibid.

[173]Ibid.

[174]Ibid.

[175]Ibid.

[176]Ibid.

[177]H. G. Wells to C. Shaw, 5 September 1906, Shaw Papers.

[178]Fabian Society, "Executive Minutes," November 1906.

[179]Ibid., January 1907.

[180]See Sara Evans, Personal Politics: The Roots of Women's Liberation in the Civil Rights Movement and the New Left (New York: Alfred A. Knopf, 1979), chapters 7-9 passim.

[181]Daily Telegraph, 1 December 1913.

[182]C. Shaw, Letter to the Editor, 21 November 1911, London Times.

[183]Rowbotham, New World for Women, pp. 23-42.

[184]B. Shaw, "Biographers' Blunders Corrected," in his Self Sketches, pp. 132-33.

[185]Review of "Woman on Her Own," The Tatler, 17 December 1913.

[186]E. Brieux, Woman on Her Own, in Three Plays by Brieux, trans. C. Shaw (London: Fifield, 1911).

[187]Charlotte Shaw, "Forward" to E. Brieux, Damaged Goods (London: Fifield, 1914).

[188]B. Shaw to Granville Barker, 19 August 1908, in Bernard Shaw's Letters to Granville Barker, ed. C. B. Purdom (New York: Theatre Arts Books, 1957), p. 136.

[189]Dunbar, Mrs. G.B.S., pp. 203-04.

[190]G.B.S. to B. Webb, 1912, Passfield Papers.

[191]Pearson, Bernard Shaw, pp. 284-93.

[192] Webb Diary, 12 July 1913.

[193] Roger Fry to C. Shaw, June 1914, C. Shaw Papers, ADD MS 56491.

[194] Webb Diary, 26 March 1916.

[195] St. John Ervine, Bernard Shaw, p. 313.

[196] T. E. Lawrence to Lady Astor, 30 June 1929, Shaw Papers.

[197] Blanche Patch, Thirty Years with G.B.S. (London: Victor Gollancz, 1951), p. 116.

[198] Ibid., p. 62.

[199] Ibid., p. 10.

[200] C. Shaw to T. E. Laurence, 17 May 1927, C. Shaw Papers, ADD MS 45922.

[201] Patch, Thirty Years, p. 17.

[202] Simone De Beauvoir, The Second Sex, trans. H. M. Parshley (New York: Alfred A. Knopf, 1953), pp. 639-73.

[203] C. Shaw to T. E. Laurence, 17 May 1927.

[204] Ibid.

Chapter 3

THE HUBERT BLANDS

The most consistently reactionary views on the
"woman question" were held by the Hubert Blands. Founding
members of the Fabian Society, the couple played an important role in establishing the infant society. If G.B.S.
was a perceptive, if somewhat erratic, supporter of the
women's movement and Charlotte Shaw a late-blooming but
enthusiastic feminist, Hubert Bland was the quintessential
male chauvinist and his wife, Edith Nesbit Bland, an
unabashed anti-feminist.

The Blands' opinions on the "woman question" were
representative of a point of view at odds with feminist
demands but, in some respects, consistent from its own
perspective. Yet the Blands, like the two other Fabian
couples under consideration here, often expressed views
on the "woman question" which contradicted the sexual roles
they created for themselves. In their turn, and perhaps
in the most extreme form, the Blands provide another
peculiarly idiosyncratic compromise to the age-old question
of how the sexes are to relate to each other and how sexual
equality is to be defined.

I. Hubert Bland: The Fabian in the Frock Coat

In considering the Blands, it is clear that Hubert's personality was the dominant one. Certainly his role in the Fabian Society was of longer standing and far greater importance than his wife's. Unfortunately, Bland left little by way of personal documents or conversational encounters which might have supplied information about his early life. For a man who issued a steady stream of verbiage about all subjects great and small, in articles and essays over a thirty year period, he left surprisingly little information about himself.

Reputedly, Hubert's grandfather was a housepainter and plumber. His father, however, called himself a gentleman and maintained his family, three sons and a daughter, in a moderately comfortable middle-class home in Woolwich. The boys were given adequate schooling, but not a university education, and were imbued with patriotic and martial sentiments, the lasting effects of which will be seen. Hubert, in fact, had expressed the wish to be an army officer, but his father's death when he was still a youth prevented that possibility from occurring.[1]

All that is known of Hubert's first years is that he had "from the very earliest age, cherished and petted the conviction that [he] was a particularly and peculiarly masculine person."[2] This conviction seems to have rested upon the precocity of his love life and his willingness to do battle. He had his first love affair at eight, his first cigar at nine, at ten he indulged in a "prolonged battle with a drummer boy in the Royal Welsh Regiment" and left his "mark on the red-coated lad's honest face." For further proof of his masculinity he offered the fact of his formal engagement at age twelve, and that, at eighteen, he was "within a few hours of fighting a duel with one of the best swordsmen of Bonn University."[3] For the rest of his life Hubert Bland seems to have been offering proof--either to himself, his friends, or his readers--of his masculinity, and on just the same grounds: a prodigious number of love affairs and a pugnacious approach to the problems of life.

This is not to say that Hubert had little time for political and intellectual matters. As a young man he was a Disraeli Conservative; he experienced the fall of Disraeli's government as a "staggering blow."[4] His solace at first had been the artistic and literary coteries of the early 1880's, where he and his fellow aesthetes created "a little world within a world, a world of poetry, of pictures, of music, of old romance, of strangely designed wallpapers, and of sad coloured velveteen" (he wore it "only in the evening"). "Disgusted with the present, apprehensive of the future," they turned to the past.[5] With William Morris they celebrated the Middle Ages in rhyme and meter, with Burne-Jones they settled on their "Ideal Woman," with Swinburne they expressed the weariest pessimism about life, and, finally, with Schopenhauer they settled on the philosophical underpinning for their pessimism.

Hubert's revolt against Schopenhauer's malignant view of the universe, his growing belief that the world is rational, was his first step toward socialism. Within a short time the "red-hot rhetoric" of Henry George had alerted Bland, as it had Shaw, to the importance of economic problems. "The lectures and speeches of Mr. Hyndman . . . completed the conversion that Henry George had begun." Hyndman was the "predominant factor" in Bland's conversion, inducing him to read and accept at least part of Marx's teachings.[6] Bland belonged to the Social-Democratic Federation in the early 1880's and, as will be seen, continued to believe in many of the principles advocated by Hyndman and the Federation long after he had ceased to be a member. From an emphasis on military preparedness, to a preoccupation with political action, a disparagement of women, and the adoption of a businessman's dress in spite of sympathy with the workman's cause--the style and content of Bland's socialism often resembled that of H. M. Hyndman.[7]

But Bland was not a revolutionary. Much as he hoped for the development of a socialist party, the S.D.F. would not suffice. "Its schemes political have been persistently subordinated to its proposals revolutionary." Worse, "it was damned by its past," he claimed in 1887, referring to the "Tory gold" scandal. Above all, Bland was a middle-class intellectual, a party of the masses was no more appealing to him than it was to Webb or Shaw.

The middle-class intellectuals who gathered around the Scottish schoolmaster, Thomas Davidson, were more to Bland's liking. When this group split into the apolitical Society of the New Life and the more practical Fabian Society in 1884, Bland found the kind of socialism he could accept, and the organization to promote it, in the latter. According to Bland, Davidson taught him and his colleagues how to think for themselves and not to use catch words and slogans, socialist or otherwise, which might stand in the way of complete understanding of an issue.[9]

In the first years of his adulthood, Bland earned his living by working in a bank. The position soon proved unsuitable for a young man who had begun to wear velveteen "in the evenings." In 1880, aged twenty-five, Bland settled into a partnership for the manufacture of brushes, his first and last business venture. Within a year Hubert had contracted smallpox, encountered death at close hand, had been defrauded by his business partner, and had lost his brush factory.

After recovering from a double bout of smallpox, Hubert began contributing articles to several socialist and left-leaning periodicals--in the process discovering a far greater talent for journalism than he had thus far

evinced for business. From 1886 to 1888, he was editor of
the socialist weekly To-Day and author of its column
on "Books." In 1889 he became a regular columnist for
both the London Daily Chronicle and the Manchester Sunday
Chronicle. By the turn of the century, "Hubert of the
Chronicle" was the "star-turn of the Sunday Chronicle,
which at the time had a huge circulation," and he had a
reading public which "ranged from bishops to stableboys."[10]

Bland's major failure of this period was his
candidacy for the Finley District seat in the London School
Board election of November 1888. Along with fellow Fabians,
the Reverend Stewart Headlam and Annie Besant, he campaigned against "Digglism," the do-nothing philosophy of
the Chairman of the London School Board, the Reverend
J. R. Diggle. Headlam and Besant were elected to the
Board; Bland lost amidst accusations by his election
committee that Herbert Burrows, Mrs. Besant's election
agent, had invaded Finley District to obtain prospective
workers for Mrs. Besant's campaign in Tower Hamlets. The
victorious Besant-Burrows team denied the charges, and
Bland and company, though unconvinced, closed ranks with
their fellow socialists.[11]

Whatever the reasons for Bland's defeat, thereafter
he refrained from seeking public office. Contributing to
that defeat, no doubt more than inroads made by Mrs.
Besant's campaign, was the Blandian style. Despite his
ability to "debate with a barrister-like effectiveness,"[12]

and his unquestioned ability as a platform speaker, Bland's
aloofness, his "punctilious phrasing and cultured tones
. . . his dexterous and polished retorts to . . .
hecklers"[13] could, at times, be more irritating than
convincing to non-Fabian listeners. Moreover, Bland,
the "sartorial dandy," was an impressive but not always
an effective purveyor of the socialist message to his
working class audiences. The basic incongruity between
his public persona and the creed he trumpeted, as well as
the profession he followed, could be as disconcerting to
his audiences as it was puzzling, on occasion, to his
friends.

Mrs. Cecil Chesterton, a journalist and an admiring
younger friend of Bland's, described him at Fabian meetings
as "refulgent in eye glass, smartly cut clothes, stiff
shirt and exotic tie, he looked like a dashing company
promoter at a convocation of Rural Deans."[14] H. G. Wells,
one-time friend turned harsh critic, was less favorably
disposed to Bland's costume. In "top hat, tail coat,
greys and blacks, white slips, spatterdashes, and . . .
black-ribboned monocle," Bland presented himself, according
to Wells, as "a great Man of the World," when in fact "he
had no gleam of business ability."[15]

Certainly, Bland's one brush with the business
world had been an unfortunate one, and his costume belied
his profession and his politics. The paradoxes surrounding
Hubert Bland did not end, however, at his spatterdashes.

While his tenure in the Fabian Society was of longer
standing and of greater import than his business experience,
here too Bland's status was ambiguous and the positions he
championed often of a conflicting nature.

*   *   *

At first glance, Hubert Bland's input into the
Society seems more limited than it was. Given the fact
that he was not only a founding father of the Fabian, but
remained in the Society and on the Executive for the
next twenty-six years, and was treasurer for twenty of
those years, surprisingly few letters of his turn up in
the major repositories of Fabian files and correspondence.
Neither the Fabian Papers at Oxford nor the Passfield
Papers and Wallas Collection housed at the British Library
of Political and Economic Science contain much material
about or by Bland. This deficiency, however, reflects
other factors than the extent of Bland's involvement in
the Society. Graham Wallas, according to Shaw, aspired
continually and "fretfully towards a Blandless universe."[16]
The Webbs--whose collective Puritanical streak ran fully
as wide as Wallas's--could not abide the Blands and weeded
out Hubert's correspondence from their files, as, for the
most part, did Edward Pease from the Fabian files. According to Pease, Bland's work as treasurer did not amount to
much: "All he ever did for twenty years was to sign as
many banks cheques as I asked for. He never looked at
the accounts."[17] Nonetheless, his presence, at least until

1908 when his health began to fail, was constant, his influence pervasive. "He was always there," according to H. G. Wells: "The larger purposes of the Wallases, Webbs and Shaws had to defer continually to the dark riddle of 'what the Blands will do about it.' There was no reckoning without them for they turned up, excited and energetic, with satellites, dependents, confederates and new associates at every meeting."[18]

While Bland wrote only two tracts under his own name, "After Bread, Education" (1905) and "Socialism and Labour Policy" (1906), he played an important role in the editing of many a Fabian document. As S. G. Hobson, a member of the Executive for ten years, explained, draft copies of tracts were discussed and altered at the Executive meetings, but "Shaw and Bland naturally saw to the literary quality."[19] Moreover, Bland was an effective debater and a lively lecturer, with "a supreme gift of exposition,"[20] and he did his share in spreading the socialist word from platforms and press. Especially in the latter, Bland was a personality with whom to be reckoned. By 1903, if not well before, Hubert Bland was "established in the mind of Shaw . . . as a necessary evil," one whose views could never be ignored.[21] It is impossible to know to what extent Shaw's proposals to the Society were tempered by his anticipation of Bland's possible reactions and activities. But his correspondence with Bland, and about him, clearly reflects a strong concern over Bland's opinions and political machinations.

As a member of the "Old Gang," Bland was "a little difficult and a little of an outsider."[22] Indeed, Shaw was the only one of that gang who was on friendly terms with him. He alone shared with the Blands a streak of Bohemianism and, in the early years of their relationship, he often enjoyed their hospitality. Then too, Bland and Shaw were often useful to each other as fellow journalists and authors. As editor of To-day, Bland published one of Shaw's novels, The Unsocial Socialist, in 1886, and Shaw occasionally recommended Bland for journalistic work which he, himself, was too busy to accept. Both men, unlike Webb, Wallas, and Olivier, made their livelihoods entirely from their pens, and were, at first, quite slow to earn a sufficient living by doing so.

In a notably philistine environment, Bland and Shaw were among the few early Fabians concerned with the arts. Yet, both held their commitment to the arts as separate and apart from their socialism. Shaw rarely dealt with economic or socialist themes in his dramatic work. Bland as literary critic often warned against spoiling "a work of art by an attempt to preach a sermon," for "novels with objects are a weariness to the spirit. . . . By doing good work . . . outside the sphere of militant socialism, and at the same time quietly being a socialist," Bland felt that poets, novelists, and painters could be most effective as artists and as socialists.[23] Even as Bland became

increasingly involved with politics, he felt no need to
discard his apolitical, aesthetic tenets. Thus, he remained
an aesthete propounding l'art pour l'art in one breath and
social activism in the next. And he continued to celebrate
the experience of the moment a la Pater, while strongly
advocating the adoption of government schemes requiring
complicated and lengthy state planning.

The style adopted by the two authors was, at times,
similar. Shaw's continuous barbs at society and convention
were always done under cover of wit and humor. Bland,
while less successful than Shaw with the humorous touch,
prided himself on being concerned with "the things that
matter: love, religion, essential politics, and treating
the serious things lightly and the light things seriously."[24]
Indeed, some of his best essays on social and political
topics stimulate the same mix of moral indignation and
amused interest that Shaw's expositions so often do.

Both Bland and Shaw had read Marx and retained
portions they felt were useful, as they had read Darwin
and retained a belief in evolution, tempered in Shaw's
case by a Lamarckian interpretation and in Bland's by his
religiosity on matters of ultimate origins and ultimate
ends. When it came to practical politics, however, G.B.S.
and Bland often parted company. Bland was consistently
insistent on the importance of political action, as opposed
to permeation, whereas G.B.S. often waffled on the subject.
From the very beginning, Bland favored practical politics

over visionary concerns. In each instance, when the
issue of political participation was raised, he stood
solidly in favor of active partisanship rather than polite
propaganda or educational programs.

In 1886 Bland was closely involved in overcoming
the first group of political impossibilists within the
Fabian Society, the anarchists, led by Mrs. Charlotte
Wilson. Mrs. Wilson would "never split the Society";
she might at best "break off a small projection which
even now rather spoils its symmetry," he assured Shaw.
Furthermore, he, himself, could "make sure of 23 [Fabian
votes] on a question of political action," and Mrs. Besant
had a "formal following of at least 10."[25] Thus, Bland
seconded and helped carry Mrs. Besant's resolution of
September 1886: "That it is advisable that socialists
should organize themselves as a political party for the
purpose of transferring into the hands of the whole working
community full control over the soil and the means of production, as well as over the production and distribution of
wealth."[26] He also helped engineer the solution that was
to keep Mrs. Wilson and her faction within the Society,
at least temporarily, that is, the formation of a Parliamentary Committee which would handle political questions
without forcing practical politics down the collective
throat of the entire Society. Assuring Shaw he had "no
ambition to be a leader" on such matters, he offered his
services should the situation "merit a calvalry charge."[27]

The solution was short-lived, the victory Pyrrhic, as the Parliamentary Committee did little by way of direct political action and the Society, although quit of its anarchist wing, fell more and more under the sway of the "Big Four": Webb, Wallas, Olivier, and Shaw. The Webbian policy of permeation became the new and most lasting enemy for Bland. In his contribution to Fabian Essays in Socialism, Bland was the only contributor who argued for a split with the Liberals and the formation of a definitely socialist party. There was no longer any real difference between liberalism and conservatism, he argued; liberalism was aspiring to a "sham socialism," for it is not what the state does but its ultimate purpose that makes for socialism. That purpose, according to Bland, must be "the common holding of the means of production and exchange, and the holding of them for the equal benefit of all. . . . Democracy holds socialism in its womb," but, he cautioned, it may be "endlessly delayed."[28]

In the ensuing decade Bland kept up the pressure on his colleagues; he often led the attack against permeation or "Webbite opportunism," as he labeled it. In 1892 he insisted the Fabian make up its collective mind about the fledgling Independent Labour Party and whether or not to support their political candidates.[29] Occasionally, as G.B.S. complained to Graham Wallas, he managed to surprise Shaw and Webb with a "concerted attack" on their "flank" in favor of political action;[30] other times he managed to carry Shaw, along with many of the other members, with him in his enthusiasm. Shaw's "Fabian Election Manifesto" of 1892 came out firmly against support for the Liberal Party or its radical wing, but this proved to be a temporary aberration. Soon thereafter the Society went back to its permeating ways.

As a Hutchinson Trustee, Bland was ever in favor of using the funds for Fabian propaganda rather than as seed money for the London School of Economics, but Sidney Webb was far less susceptible to the blandishments of his colleague than Shaw. For the most part, Webb maneuvered the Trust to support his own purposes. It was not until 1909 that Bland's concept was actually funded and he became, along with Webb and Pease, a Trustee of the Fabian Parliamentary Fund. The purpose of this fund was to sponsor Fabian candidates for Parliament on the Labour ticket, but the arrangement was too little and too late to suit Bland or to effect any great changes in either the political representation of the Fabian Society or the number of socialists in the Commons.

In his last years on the Fabian Executive, Bland was increasingly disappointed with the progress of the Society. The London Program, the Minority Report, and the long list of reforms supported by the Fabian, he felt, had stood in the ways of a "direct march" to socialism.[31] Political inaction and an emphasis on palliative measures had sidetracked the Fabian from the socialism of the

"Basis," that is, from the transfer of industries to the state. "If all we are proposing were carried out we'd be no nearer to socialism than we are today," he complained to G.B.S. in 1910. "We know all about the paupers and invalids but nothing at all about the people who do the work." We have pledged ourselves to the care of the aged and the endowment of maternity but to "nothing that would put money in the workman's pocket. . . . If the Society cannot rejuvenate itself--and I don't think it can--then it had better die peacefully and die soon," he added pessimistically.[32]

If Bland was often on the losing side in matters of political activism, he was perfectly in accord with the majority position--a term almost synonymous with the opinions of Webb and Shaw in the period between 1890 and 1910--on questions of Imperialism, religious education, and tariff protection. Particularly with regard to the war in South Africa, Bland's views were in keeping with the position ultimately adopted by the Society, that is, limited support for the war and for colonialism based on a Fabianized version of the "white man's burden." A difference of degree, however, existed; Bland's support was far from "limited." As he wrote to Pease in the midst of the heated debate over the Fabian's position on the war,

> it looks as though you and I and the remnant of
> the Old Gang . . . will have to make one more big
> fight to secure the Society's usefulness in the

future. . . . We must now throw ourselves athwart
the Imperialist tendency or any other strong stream
. . . we would only be broken up by them. . . .
[We must try to] direct them and do for "sane
Imperialism" what we have done for "sane"
socialism.[33]

A year later, in an article commemorating the
soldiers who had fallen thus far in the South African War,
he assured his readers that a soldier was just as productive
as a miner, for he was "the guardian of wealth," the
guardian of Britain's Imperial possessions. Indeed, the
soldiers had given their lives in "a holier cause than
that of the defense of England's material property. They
fell fighting for English liberty and for England's civil
law. . . . Progress costs," he admonished, and the graves
of dead soldiers were "an altar of Empire."[34] In accord
with his appreciation of arms and Empire, Bland regarded
reservations about maintaining a large army as a "silly
socialist superstition."[35] On more than one occasion, he
informed his fellow Fabians that such an army did not
necessarily involve overt militarism, merely military
preparedness.

Bland had converted to Catholicism several years
after becoming a socialist, and he was also convinced that
no difficulties stood in the way of a reconciliation
between Catholicism and socialism: "Communism has ever
been the Church's ideal of life . . . in all ages it has
been practiced by some, at any rate, of her children. The
Church was the first organized body which upheld

internationalism and condemned and mitigated the evils of
racial prejudice."[36] Protestantism, on the other hand, was
"simply the religious expression of individualism."[37] By
1905, he felt that the radical wing of the Liberal Party
had "degenerated into a political committee of the Free
Church Councils."[38] Thus, he had willingly acquiesced
in Sidney Webb's, and subsequently the Fabian Society's,
support of the Conservative Education Bill of 1903.
Whereas Webb had found state support for religious schools
a necessary, though not necessarily desirable, concomitant
of achieving secular control and regulation of religious
schools, Bland had seen much that was desirable in the
preservation of religious traditions in private schools.[39]
On this he was worlds apart from the position taken by
most socialists who tended to be nonconformists or atheists.

On the issue of protective tariffs, Bland's idiosyncratic brand of socialism again separated him from the
Liberal left whence came many a Fabian socialist. According to Cecil Chesterton, a younger Fabian and close friend
of Bland's, a commitment to protective policies followed
almost inevitably from Bland's intense nationalism, which
in fact was at "the root of his socialism." Once nationalism, rather than an internationalist class consciousness,
was taken as the basis for his socialist creed--and for
middle-class socialists and intellectuals, Chesterton
argued, nationalism was the more logical source of identi-
fication--certain views followed quite naturally.[40] For

Bland, such was the case with his advocacy of protection
and conscription, two policies he deemed absolutely necessary to the existence of a democratic state. Support for
the latter may have been flogging a dead horse, but in the
Fabian Society, as in the minds of a growing number of
Chamberlain's Unionists, protection was very much a live
issue. In fact, G.B.S.'s pronouncement on the subject,
Tract 116, in which he tried to reach a Fabian consensus
but created confusion instead, did endorse protective
tariffs. Graham Wallas, whose links to liberalism were
as strong as Bland's were to conservatism, felt compelled
to resign from the Society over this tract; Hubert Bland
was enormously pleased with it.

Bland himself resigned from the Fabian Executive
in March 1911, primarily for reasons of poor health. To
the end of his tenure he had continued to press for a
more activist, propagandist policy, and continued to be
far ahead of most of his colleagues in terms of political
activism. Paradoxically, he remained far behind, and well
to the right, of his socialist brethren on matters of
religion, nationalism, militarism, and social convention.
With reference to these issues, Shaw's description of
Bland as a "Tory democrat"[41] seems fully justified.

It is interesting to note--and a commentary on the
ambiguous legacy of the early Fabian Society--that it is
precisely in the areas where Bland seems most conservative
that his positions were at one with those ultimately

proposed by the Society. Only when agitating for a more
activist socialist policy did Bland consistently find
himself in the minority within the Fabian.

II. Bland as Anti-feminist

On the "woman question" Bland's notions were as
conservative as were his views on Imperialism and tariff
reform, but they were somewhat less consistent. On this
issue in particular Bland's reaction tempered the efforts
of his more radical colleagues and gave the uninterested
or the uncertain an excuse for inaction.

Bland was firm in his opposition to the women's
rights movement and patronizing to most of its adherents.
Looking back on the "Emancipated Woman" of the 1880's,
he reminisced in 1910: "Let loose by Miss Olive Shreiner
from an African Farm, she had a lurid career in Europe.
She irritated, bewildered, fascinated, and finally bored
us."[42] In most of his articles and speeches, by innuendo
or, less often, by direct assault, Bland made it quite
clear that he did not find feminists "delightful," and
they were damned forever in his estimation on that account
alone. Worse, he felt they had added nothing to the world
of great art. Why was it, he pondered, when there was no
women's movement there were great women artists, and
"now when woman is clamorous and obtrusive, there are
none?"[43]

At the height of the battle over women's suffrage,

Bland's condescension reached its zenith. In <u>Olivia's</u>
<u>Latchkey</u>, his fictional alter ego, Stephen Yorke, purports
to have calculated the number of hours he had spent waiting
for women while they were "patting their hair before a
looking glass." He multiplied the sum by the number
of men in the civilized world to discover the number
of hours wasted, then admonished his young woman friend:
"Think what we might have done instead. . . . And yet they
want to give women votes."[44]

Bland had strong views on the connection between
women's economic emancipation and the coming of socialism.
However, he belonged neither to the group of socialists
who felt that the fight for socialism involved a continual
attempt to secure equality of rights and opportunities for
all, regardless of gender or class, nor to the great
majority of socialists who believed that indulging in
feminist activism was superfluous; one need only work
for socialism--women would automatically be emancipated
"after the revolution." "No!" Bland insisted in 1886,
socialism would not necessarily bring about the economic
independence of women. Under socialism, most men would
probably earn enough to keep their wives at home as a
luxury or toy and wives would be, therefore, less likely
to need or want to assert their economic independence.[45]

On this point Bland was far more consistent than
G.B.S. As stated previously, Shaw oscillated between
linking socialism and the emancipation of women and

disavowing any such connection. Bland's opposition to
such a linkage remained constant, and he was unmoved by
the pressures exerted by the growing women's movement.
He reiterated the same position he had taken in 1886 in a
lecture to the Fabian Society in 1907:

> The increasing economic independence of women
> . . . is due to the very causes that the economic
> revolution seeks to remove. The stimulus to the
> economic independence of women to-day is not a
> moral but an economic stimulus. The northern factory
> girl who spends her ten hours a day amid the whirl
> of machinery, the London "general" the whole of
> whose waking hours are passed in slavery to another
> of her own sex . . . do so, not from any newly-
> developed desire to escape the chains of matrimony,
> but to avoid the pangs of starvation. . . . For
> women of the middle class the economic pressure
> is neither so great nor so obvious . . . it is
> a question of maintaining a certain not very lofty
> standard of comfort. . . . The increasing compe-
> tition has rendered it impossible for the heads
> of families to maintain by their own earnings adult
> sons and daughters at the standard of comfort to
> which they themselves have been accustomed. Then
> either the standard must be lowered or the income
> supplemented by the children's earnings. . . .
> One of the effects of . . . public ownership
> proposed in the Fabian Basis will be to increase
> the earnings, the real wages, of the wage and
> salary-earning classes, that is, to make it easier
> for husbands and fathers to support wives and
> daughters. This being so, it seems to me a great
> and unwarrantable assumption . . . that the daughters
> and wives will, in greater numbers and more vehe-
> mently than they do now, insist on supporting them-
> selves . . . better economic conditions . . . will
> tend rather to reintegration than to further dis-
> integration of family life.[46]

Within the Fabian Society, Bland stood foursquare
in defense of marriage, the family, and traditional morality. In 1894 he lectured to the Society on the implica-
tions of collectivism. He assured his fellow Fabians that
even in the collectivist associated home being advocated

by the most vocal Fabian feminist of the time, Harriot
Blatch, monogamy and parental love would continue to
survive, just as it had survived individualism. "Sex
relations and parentage seem to defy all consideration,"
he intoned.[47] Thirteen years later, Bland responded in a
similar fashion, endorsing the family and sexual restraint
in the midst of the controversy created by the actions and
proposals of H. G. Wells.

Many new members of the Fabian had been particularly enthusiastic about Wells's notions favoring greater
sexual freedom for men and women and fewer restrictions
on, and more public support for, maternity outside the
traditional family. Bland felt strongly that the "sex
and child question," as he labeled it in a letter to
Edward Pease, should be forced to a vote in the Fabian.
A majority of the members did not support Wells's views,
he suggested, but the more vocal minority was apt to
carry the day unless the matter were settled by a ballot.
"We had to do it with the anarchists," he reminded Pease,
"and we may have to with the Free lovers."[48] The resigna-
tions attendant upon a definitive vote were not troublesome
to Bland. As he noted in another letter to Pease, it would
be "excellent to shed those that have joined for every
reason but socialism this year."[49]

The vote which was taken in the excitement created
by Wells did not clarify the controversy as Bland wished,
for it turned more on questions of loyalty and internal

Fabian politics than on specific moral issues. What was clear, however, was Bland's commitment to the preservation of the family, monogamous marriage, and traditional morality as a means of preserving both the quality of the racial stock and the stability of society. One might also assume he was anxious to uphold the purity of the Fabian Society; on more than one occasion, Bland blackballed a prospective member of the Fabian on moral grounds, to the dismay of the other Executive members.[50]

Bland worked not only within the Society as a whole for support of conventional values, but in one of the several special interest groups, the Biology Group, that evolved during the "second blooming" of the Fabian as well. Dedicated to such questions as how "biological explanations can run parallel to and explain change,"[51] especially such manifestations of change as the contemporary women's movement, this particular group was a refuge for Fabian social conservatives in the Edwardian era. The participants in this relatively short-lived body favored monogamous marriage, women in the home, and the breast feeding of infants. In open meetings, its members were generally most vociferous in their opposition to resolutions suggested by the Fabian Women's Group, a case in point being their objection, in June 1909, to the strongly worded denunciation of the dismissal of married teachers by the L.C.C.[52] issued by the Women's Group. Hubert Bland often chaired the Biology Group and inspired it. As his health declined and his participation waned, the organization became less provocative on the "woman question." In December of 1910, the Group embarked on the "serious study of biology," using a textbook by Galton,[53] and soon was heard from no more.

Outside the Fabian Society, Bland's concern with social convention did not extend to a condemnation of the harmless diversions of the working classes. Quite the contrary: in the prewar years he was a co-founder of the Anti-Puritan League, constituted generally to limit "the interference of wealthy Puritans with the pleasures of the populace,"[54] and specifically to halt the flow of local and national government emissaries and regulations to the music halls and pubs. Bland had nothing but contempt for "the practical, the prudent, and the Philistine,"[55] especially when they interfered with the pleasures of men--of any class.

* * *

Unlike many a polemicist opposed to female emancipa-tion--but willing to grant women a separate but equal value based on their superiority in the sphere of domesti-city, nurturance, or morality--Bland was unwilling to concede anything to women other than their inspirational and reproductive functions. "Men could do most of the things that are done in the world without woman's help. Men could reap and sow, and bake bread, and cook dinners; they could build battleships and bathe babies--supposing of course, they could achieve them without feminine co-operation."[56] In Olivia's Latchkey, Bland indulged in one of his favorite devices, placing the anti-feminist or derrogatory remarks against women in the mouth of a female character. Bland's views were expressed by Olivia Brent:

> I really believe that it is all the good we
> women are--to provoke men to do things, to write
> things, poems and music, to create, to fight.
> I said so last night at Tooting. I was goaded
> to it by an advanced woman who was there, and
> she hated me for it. She said, with pride . . .
> she had never provoked a man to do anything
> except to lose his temper.[57]

But, in his nonfictional essays, he expressed the same idea: "Woman's métier in the world . . . is to inspire romantic passion. . . . Men . . . could construct and maintain the world of material things pretty much as it is, without women."[58]

Even in the rearing of children, Bland was not willing to grant women their due. The bringing up of children, he complained in 1904, was not scientific at all, and was utterly unsatisfactory, because "it has always been left to women."[59] A few years later, he lavishly praised Kipling for, inter alia, his portrayal of his feelings for children, that is, "of the man's feelings as distinguished from the woman's." "He has recognized," wrote Bland, "that the maternal instinct is not the sole monopoly of one sex."[60] Such sentiments are laudatory and, to this author's mind, absolutely correct.

The difficulty lies only in Bland's inability to extend this insight on the mutability of characteristics commonly thought of as masculine or feminine, and to run the argument the other way. Nowhere in the writings and ruminations of Hubert Bland does one find the suggestion, for example, that women, like men, might possess intelligence, loyalty, bravery, or scientific acumen.

Unwilling to grant women pre-eminence in the realm of domesticity or nurturance, Bland was equally uncharitable in the moral sphere. If "the eternal feminine" beckoned Goethe "ever upwards," this was not so for Hubert Bland. Women's business, he opined, was not to moralize the world and raise men to higher things: "Their business is, and has been, to make the world a comfortable place for themselves to dwell in, and to make the best and the most of men as they are down here on these lower levels."[61] Women are not more moral than men, according to Bland, they are less so:

> Of course women are not honest, and what an extraordinarily distasteful place the world would be if they were! . . . Considering that three-fourths of an ordinary man's comfort in life depends upon what his women folk think of him, or, more correctly, on what he fondly thinks they think of him, have we not sound cause to thank our lucky stars that we were born into a world in which women are not honest?[62]

For Bland, reproduction, not morality or ability, was woman's primary concern. In the light of his fervent nationalism and his belief in evolutionary theory, his eugenic view of woman's role is not surprising. Like many

a late nineteenth-century Imperialist who feared his
nation might lose in battle or in the colonial scramble
if its population fell or showed signs of weakness, Bland
believed that "from the point of view of the evolution of
the race . . . a woman's function is to bear and rear
healthy children."[63] The means of optimizing this function
is open to varying interpretations; for Bland the institution of marriage took on a new significance as the study
of eugenics became "a real science": "Marriage is the
central fact of life, because [it] must precede good
breeding, and upon good breeding the future of the race
depends."[64] Defining a "good marriage" as "the deliberate
selection of man by woman and of woman by man for parenthood,"[65] Bland extended his concern with the race to a
condemnation of divorce. "Any measure," he wrote, "which
tends to facilitate divorce, tends inevitably to . . .
inhibit well planned thoughtful marriage."[66]

Similarly, Bland's preoccupation with nation
and Empire, and his consequent acceptance of bellicose
behavior, carried in its wake an admiration for characteristics and attributes usually associated with men, and
a penchant for emphasizing the differences between the
sexes rather than the similarities. That "men and women
are very different," he was certain, though "strong women
and weak men deny it."[67] He was equally certain that no
change in the environment could make men and women
physically equal: "By her sex and her child-bearing,

she is for all time handicapped."[68] Given the differences
between the sexes, Bland reasoned, to treat them "in
precisely the same way and then imagine that equality of
treatment has been secured" was a grave error.[69] Thus,
arguments for sexual equality of any sort were anathema
to Bland.

However much one may disagree with Bland's delight
in the Empire or his endorsement of those values he thought
necessary to protect it, one sees a certain consistency in
his argument, and in his concern for maintaining the sexes
in their separate functions by means of divergent treatment. Granted, an equal but opposite argument could
easily be made beginning with the same premises. G.B.S.,
for one, supported the Empire, as a means of spreading
civilization and its expertise to the uneducated, but
generally found war and military values distasteful. He
argued for the encouragement of maternity outside the
confines of marriage as a means of increasing the population, and he argued vehemently for easing the laws governing divorce as a means of saving the institution of
marriage. And on most occasions, he stressed the similarities rather than the differences between the sexes.
Nonetheless, Bland's line of reasoning seems not only
internally consistent but representative of a larger
portion of the population in late Victorian and Edwardian
England, socialist or not, than was Shaw's.

At closer look, however, the consistency of Bland's

argument breaks down. The institution of marriage he
supported so enthusiastically as a socialist, an Imperialist, and a Catholic, he castigated soundly when speaking
ex cathedra as a member of the fraternity of middle-class
males. First of all, according to Bland, men do not
even like women. In his book Letters to a Daughter,
he interrogated his favorite child: "Do men, men as
a whole, men as a sex, love women, women in the lump,
women as a sex? As I live, I don't believe they do!"[70]
This is to be clearly seen, he claimed, in the proverbs,
aphorisms, and epigrams from all languages, written by
men, scarcely one of which has a word to say in praise of
women. More conclusive still is the evidence presented by
the habits of men after a dinner party:

> Do they . . . hurry up to the drawing-room
> after dinner, or do they linger down there over
> their wine and their talk till the hostess loses
> her patience and every feminine eye keeps turning
> to the door. . . . And oh! if you were to see
> us the moment after the dining-room door has
> closed behind you, you dears! If you were to see
> how we draw our chairs up, to note the change in
> our voices, the air of comfort with which we finger
> our glasses, the heavy reluctance with which we
> rise when the host gives the word![71]

Not only do men not like women, most men fear
marriage "with a craven, shrinking, shivering terror."
Men marry "just as they die, because they can't help themselves." If any bridegroom were to confess why he married,
it would be obvious that he wanted his woman but he did
not "actually want to take upon himself the life long
responsibilities, the life long expenses, the life long

risks, the life long limitation of liberty" which marriage involves.[72] Thus, wrote Hubert Bland, the fact that the Registrar-General's returns show men marrying less freely than they had before is evidence of "the growth and development of intelligence among his sex," and the fact that at last women are "being found out."[73]

Specifically, men were "finding out" that women benefited more from marriage than did men. Worse, the poor male marries for love, but women marry only for "social precedence" or "a feeling of dignity or importance."[74] Marriage is their profession; one need not love one's profession. In addition, wrote Bland, "women find it easier to settle down in a loveless marriage than do men. For women, who knows why, find it easier to submit."[75] That submission might be a necessary fact of life for women who possessed few alternatives, rather than an ability inherent in the female nature, seems to have escaped Bland. As a socialist, supposedly sensitive to the importance of economic determinants, Bland evinced a surprising lack of perspicacity on the possible ramifications of women's economic subordination.

In full fraternal garb, then, Bland showed himself to be highly inconsistent. How justify marriage, castigate divorce, or deify the propagation of the race if marriage is such hell for mankind? One wonders why marriage has ever occurred between consenting adults and, to what purpose beyond perpetuating the race and decorating the

landscape, women have been placed upon this earth. The
truth, as conceived by Hubert Bland, is close at hand, but
at this point the edifice of his intellectual argument on
the role of women breaks down completely. To understand
fully his view of women one must leave such subjects as
race and family and discuss instead his notions of what
constitutes life's pleasures.

Flirtation, he wrote in 1906, is, like virtue, its
own reward:

> Like art, it must exist only for its own sake;
> and it is remarkably like art. Indeed, it is no
> inconsiderable part of the art of life. The
> object of art, as Pater says somewhere, is to
> render radiant, to intensify our moments. That
> and nothing else is the object, so far as it has
> an object, of flirtation.
> Of course it gratifies our vanity, and of all
> gratifications, or nearly all, the gratification
> of vanity is the sweetest. . . . There are few
> things in this world which give a man, who is a
> man and not a pudding, such a tingling thrill of
> pleasure as the consciousness that a woman, an
> ordinarily discreet woman, has run the ever-so-
> slightest risk of compromising herself for his
> sake.[76]

If flirtation was the great gratifier of vanity, it was
also "a sort of preliminary to the duel of sex."[77] "Duel
of sex" and "battle of the sexes" are terms which appear
often in Bland's lexicon, and they help to complete his
definition of woman's role in society.

Thus, in addition to their existence as objet
d'art, women, according to Bland, are to function as
gratifiers of male vanity and male sexuality; objects
they remain, but of a different sort. For the most part,

the overtly sexual overtones of Bland's expectations were
sedately clothed in euphemisms. Woman's major responsibility was "to be delightful": "Middle-aged ladies who
are not delightful are not anything; they simply don't
count."[78] Nonetheless, the sexually exploitive underpinning of his theories on women can be inferred from much
that he wrote. How he reconciled such an attitude with
his concerns for the purity of marriage and the family
resists explanation.

Considering Hubert Bland's negative attitude toward
women and his contradictory notions on the subject of
marriage, one wonders what kind of woman he would have
deigned to marry and what sort of marriage they would
establish. The nature of the woman he did marry and the
facts of the marriage they maintained seem to have been
fully as complicated and as contradictory as one might
have expected.

III. From Daisy Nesbit to Edith Bland

Edith Nesbit was born on August 15, 1858 at Lower
Kennington Lane. She was the youngest child of John Collis
and Sarah Nesbit. Her half-sister Saretta, child of Mrs.
Nesbit's first marriage, was fourteen at the time of
Edith's birth; Mary was six or seven, Alfred was four,
and youngest brother Harry was three. John Collis Nesbit,
grandson of a Northumberland farmer, son of a schoolmaster,
had by then converted his father's Classical, Comercial,

and Scientific Academy, in which he himself was teaching, into the first Chemical and Agricultural College in the country. A bright and able educator, much interested in chemistry, he was the first to introduce natural science into his curriculum. John Nesbit died when Edith was not quite four years old. Her few memories of him present a portrait of a loving, playful father, all the more to be missed in the years after his death.

Mrs. Nesbit, widowed twice, never married again. She kept the school going for several years, but as time went on she devoted more and more of her energy to her daughter Mary's precarious health. This necessitated a rather peripatetic existence for the Nesbit family, with continual forays to better climates in hopes of curing or alleviating Mary's consumptive condition.

Thus, from the age of seven, Daisy--as Edith was called throughout her childhood--found herself placed in a series of schools. Her first experience, in a boarding school at Brighton, was an horrendous one. "Stuart plaid," a fiendish tormentor disguised in a plaid frock, destroyed Daisy's pewter tea set, her paint box, and any joy she might previously have taken in being alive. The extent of the blight may be judged by the extreme joy Daisy felt when she contacted a severe case of measles and was sent home, carefully wrapped in blankets.[79] Subsequent experiences were little better; only the cause of her torments changed. At a "select boarding establishment" at Stanford,

the reason for her grief was a particularly meticulous and
unsympathetic teacher and her own inability to make her
unruly hair tidy, her rough and grubby hands clean, and
her answers to long division problems correct.[80] After a
year of unalloyed trauma and tears, Daisy convinced her
mother to let her go with the family on its journey to the
south of France.

Daisy's relationships within her family were
both more rewarding and more uncertain than those she
experienced at school. Her mother was loving and affectionate when she was present, but this was never often
enough for Daisy. Her extended absences on Mary's behalf
must have made her seem unreliable to her youngest daughter.
Daisy's eldest sister Saretta, whom E. Nesbit later
described as a second mother, had a "genius for telling
fairy stories"[81] and could be counted upon, when they were
all together, to regale her younger sister and brothers
with tales on a rainy day. Mary, Daisy's "favorite sister,"
read stories and graciously accepted "confidences" from the
younger ones,[82] proximity and her health permitting. Most
important of all to Daisy were her brothers, Alfred and
Harry. Closest to her in age and temperament, they provided the companionship of her younger years, that is, when
they were not away at school.

Summers, when her brothers were at home, were
Daisy's happiest times. The summer her family rented a
country home at Dinan was an especially idyllic one for

Daisy and the boys. While their elder sisters and mother engaged in parties and picnics, they were allowed to "run wild." The adventurous threesome built a fort with hay and straw, sailed a homemade raft on their pond, traced a local stream to its source through tunnels, swamps, and muddy fields, and dug pirates' caves in the nearby cliffs.[83] If Daisy felt a "sneaking appreciation" for a pretty dress donned on one of the rare occasions they were groomed to meet guests, she was never so foolish as to let it be known to her brothers.[84]

Daisy spent the next school year in an Urseline Convent near Dinan; she was a troublesome, but not quite so unhappy, student. A letter sent to her mother reveals that she wished to become a Catholic, but was not able to convince her mother of the wisdom of such a conversion.[85] (The conversion was long in coming, but did occur several years after her marriage to the like-minded Hubert. Their conversion seems to have been a mutual idea.)

The Franco-Prussian War brought the Nesbit family back to England. By this time Mary was engaged to the young, blind poet Philip Bourke Marston. Staying with Mary, Daisy met Swinburne, the Rossettis, and other artists connected with the pre-Raphaelite movement. In this stimulating environment, Daisy began her first serious attempts at writing poetry. Unfortunately, this situation did not last long. Her attractive sister began to weaken, was taken to Brittany in 1871, in hopes of improving her health, and died there at the end of the year.

Grief-stricken, Mrs. Nesbit settled her family at last in a long, red brick house at Halstead, Kent. "The Hall," as it was called, was Daisy's favorite house. It had a lush garden, "nooks where one could hide with one's favorite books," trap doors that led to dark passages and on to the roof itself, and her own little room, complete with writing table.[86] Here, in her early teens, Daisy wrote poetry in earnest: "I used to sit and write--verse, verse, always verse--and dream of the days when I should be a great poet, like Shakespeare or Christina Rossetti!"[87] She was careful to keep her more sentimental poems from her brothers, lest they tease her. She did show some of her work, "a non-committal set of verses about dawn, with a moral tag,"[88] to her mother, who in turn sent them to the editor of the Sunday Magazine. Thus, at fifteen, Daisy became a published poet and the enormously proud recipient of "a whole guinea."[89] Within a few years she was also contributing verse to other publications such as Argosy and Good Words.

Mrs. Nesbit was forced to give up the much loved home in Halstead sometime in the late 70's. Her finances greatly reduced (possibly due to the prodigality of her sons), she moved her family to a much lesser abode at Barnsbury in London.[90] Shortly thereafter Daisy met Hubert Bland and succumbed to his charms. She promptly threw over a young man to whom she was engaged and began a three year romance with Bland. The culmination of this affair occurred in a Registrar's office on April 22, 1880 when the not quite twenty-two year old--and very pregnant-- Daisy became Mrs. Hubert Bland.

Paul Bland was born in 1880, shortly after the young couple had settled in a small house in Lewisham; Iris was born in 1882. In the space of these same two years Hubert was twice stricken with small pox. Thus, in addition to her maternal responsibilities, Edith found herself the sole support of her family. She put to good use all of her considerable talents. With the proceeds from the sale of her poetry, short stories, newspaper articles, hand-painted greeting cards, complete with her own verse, and with the profits from recitations, which she wrote and performed, she kept the wolf from their door.

* * *

As Hubert recovered and began to engage in polit- ical activities, his enthusiasm for socialism completely won over his young wife. In 1884, Edith, like her husband, was a member of both the newly established Fabian Society and the Social Democratic Federation; she too found the middle-class Fabians more to her taste. She thought the Fabians "quite the nicest set of people I ever knew."[92] In the first few years of the Society's existence she spent a good deal of time attending meetings and reading books which might help her understand the issues being discussed. This in spite of the fact that she was also churning out short stories to keep her family solvent and raising small children.

Edith's commitment to socialism was strong, although not all of her Fabian efforts were constructive. She was not above making scenes or pretending to faint if the proceedings became monotonous.[93] Too, she would on occasion raise a fuss about inconsequential issues, as she did when she loudly protested and almost prevented the hiring of Edward Pease as the Society's first paid secretary in 1890. Yet, as Pease himself admitted, she was "the most attractive and vivacious woman of our circle,"[94] and she added wit and charm to the meetings, if not always high seriousness. She was on several committees, including the original Pamphlet Committee which revised the first Fabian tract, "Why Are the Many Poor?" At one point, Shaw suggested that she also be on the Fabian Executive,[95] but this never came to pass. Basically her vote was indistinguishable from her husband's, and she was content to acquire Executive information secondhand.

Her attitude toward women's issues had a similarly secondhand quality to it. She read Mill's On the Subjection of Women, and she conducted herself like an "advanced woman": smoking in public, cutting her hair short, and wearing all-wool clothing. But, like her husband, she was not impressed with the woman's movement of the 1880's. At one of the few women's rights meetings she attended in this period, she was "infinitely bored,"[96] and thought the

speaker was "hideously like a hippopotamus."[97]   Aside from
Hubert's influence, however, her own circumstances provided
a negative inducement. She was a married woman with a
good deal of work to keep her occupied, in one of the few
professions traditionally open to women. She had little
to impede her but the hourly limits of the day. The group
of mainly single women, agitating for the vote or for
entrance into the professions, and their cause were of
no particular interest to her. Thus, Edith turned her
back on the suffragist movement and, at first, devoted
much of her prodigious energy to socialism.

As the Fabian Society evolved from its drawing room
stage to the larger, less intimate meetings at Clifford's
Hall in the 1890's, Edith's participation began to lessen.
Whether she attended meetings or not, Edith's contribution
to the cause of socialism was mainly literary, from an
occasional lecture on a literary figure to a collection
of poems devoted to socialism (<u>Ballads and Lyrics of
Socialism</u>, 1908). Literature, not economics or main
drains, was her field. Unmarried women or men might
devote themselves to both--the Fabian novelist, Emma
Brooke, made a valiant attempt to do so, Bernard Shaw was
quite successful at the dual program--but for Edith Bland
neither time nor inclination allowed for such diversity.
As she herself admitted, her reading was "mixed and
miscellaneous" for "it is the fate of most women only
to be able to get a smattering" of all the doctrines and

ideas floating about.[98]

Not surprisingly, much of Edith's poetry echoed her husband's ideas, particularly his bellicose nationalism and his dedication to socialist activism. What seemed to be distinctly Edith's own was her anarchistic distaste for the fruits of urbanization and industrialism. For her the "great vile cities" represented all that was ugly, evil, and grasping:

> I want to think no more of all the pain
> That in the city thrives, a poison-flower--
> The eternal loss, the never coming gain.[99]

The antithesis of urban degradation, of "blank unhappy towns,"[100] existed in the beauties of nature and in the loveliness of the country where "sweet are the lanes and hedges,"[101] "and white sheep crop the grass, and seagulls sail / Between the lovely earth and lovely sky."[102] She repeatedly suggested, however, that socialists, if they are to be true martyrs to the cause--a pose which her husband rarely struck in his urbane and witty essays--were duty-bound to leave the joys of the countryside. Only among the toiling multitudes can one "do battle till this strife shall cease!"[103] "Here," in the city, "We fight for freedom and the souls of men-- / Here, and not there, is fought and won our fight!"[104] And only in the battle for liberty or freedom is there any real glory. To labor for fame or gold insures unhappiness; "to work for the world" assures one a name in "the book of eternal life."[105]

The socialism expressed in Edith Bland's poetry
is basically a plea for a more equitable division of
wealth based on the belief: "Brothers in nature, pulse,
passion, and pains. . . . Basest or best, we are all of
us men!"[106] Equality was not a theme which concerned her,
however, when it came to subject races. Like her husband,
to whom she gave credit for her views, she firmly defended
British Imperialism. She dedicated Songs of Love and
Empire (1898) to Hubert: "You taught me first what love
and Empire mean, / And to your hands I bring my harvest
home." A few of the poems strike the same combative
note Hubert often played, but, for the most part, she
filled the Imperialist frame she borrowed from him with
shapes and colors of her own design.

The effect thus achieved is of a gentler, more
maternal Imperialism than that of her husband, even if
the underlying concepts are similar. In "After Sixty
Years," for example, she celebrated the Queen's greatness,
not only as monarch, but as mother and wife:

> She has seen joy unveiled even as we,
> Has laid upon cold clay the heart-warm kiss,
> She has known sorrow for the King he is;
> She has held little children on her knee.
>
> Mother, dear Mother, these your children rise
> And call you blessed, and shall we not, too,
> Who are your children in the greater wise,
> And love you for our land and her for you?[107]

This emphasis on parental and filial roles is similar to
that in several of her religious poems. In "Evening
Prayer," for example, she speaks:

To no vast Presence too immense to love,
    To no enthroned King too great to care
To no strange Spirit human needs above,
    We bring our little, intimate, heart-warm prayer;

But to the God who is a Father too,
    The Father who loved and gave His only Son
We pray across the cradle, I and you,
    For ours, our little one![108]

In her love poetry, Edith borrowed little conceptually from her husband, but she simulated his gender entirely. In her romantic lyrics, the narrative voice she invariably chose was that of a male, a fact which added not a little to the insincerity of the verse. In part she paid homage to the traditions of her times, and she chose her nom de plume, E. Nesbit, to aid her in the ruse.

Only on a few occasions did E. Nesbit write poetry with a woman's voice, and then it is primarily as a mother delighting in the joys of motherhood. Not only Victorian restrictions, but her own inhibitions prohibited her from assuming a feminine voice when discussing nonmaternal love. "In Trouble" recounts the sorrows of an illegitimate mother-to-be, and would seem to be an exception, but it is spoken in the tones of a lower class woman punished for her love.[109] The portrait is entirely sympathetic, the faithless lover is soundly castigated, but the message conveyed is of the cost of careless love for women and has nothing to do with a feminine assertion of sexual love or the right to love. As she admitted, a few years before her death, when discussing why most of her published poems were in the form of dramatic lyrics: "Right or wrong I could never bring myself to lay my soul naked before the public."[110]

For all the hiding, disguising, and borrowing involved in E. Nesbit's poetry, it is remarkable how many of her real concerns and attitudes do manage to slip through. Her anarchic disdain for economic "progress," her aesthetic distress over the ugliness of modernization, her fascination with martyrdom in the name of the cause, all distinguish her brand of socialism from that of her husband. In some of Edith's poetry, her husband's militant Imperialism and his tradition-bound religiosity are so transformed as to be almost unrecognizable. Edith's maternal Empress ruling "great nurseries" of her children,"[111] and her gentle God "who is a father too" are concepts of her own conjecture issuing from the depths of her own understanding and experience.

IV. E. Nesbit: Children's Author

Given the kind of internal and social constraints Edith experienced when writing adult poetry and fiction, it is, perhaps, not surprising that she found her most effective narrative voice as a writer of children's books. In children's literature she was less constrained by Victorian notions of sexually appropriate behaviors and assertions. Peopled with pre-pubescent youngsters, her juvenile fiction did not deal with sexual love at all and

spared her the confusions and ambivalence, to say nothing
of the maudlin sentimentality, with which she masked them
in her adult prose and poetry.

Thus, more than half a century after her death,
those of us who have come in contact with E. Nesbit's
work did so as avid, young readers of her children's books.
In her fast-paced, often fantastic, stories in which
children with skinned knees, impertinent tongues, and
endless curiosity abound, Nesbit found her most original
mode. Here she broke fresh ground. She wrote with a
child's enthusiasm, at times with a mother's sentiment,
and occasionally with a true artist's competency, but not
as the wife of Hubert Bland or in the guise of a love-
struck man. It is, therefore, in her children's books
that one must look for E. Nesbit's attitudes on social
issues, especially on sexual roles, to find those attitudes
that are uniquely her own.

E. Nesbit adopted the narrative voice of a young
boy for her first three full-length children's books.
Given her preference for male narrators, this is surprising
only in the fact that it proved to be such a felicitous
disguise. The trilogy, based on the adventures of the
Bastable family, is narrated by Oswald Bastable, the
oldest son and heir-apparent of the House of Bastable.
Through most of the series Oswald covers himself in anonymity, leaving his readers to guess which of the Bastable
children--Dora, aged thirteen or fourteen; Oswald, twelve;

Dicky, eleven; the ten year old twins, Noel and Alice;
or H.O., aged eight--is narrating the story. His slips
in substituting "I" for Oswald, and his "objective" descriptions of Oswald's actions and motivation, add enormously
to the warmth and humor of the tale. In the midst of an
avalanche of falling crockery and a screaming housekeeper,
caused by a marauding goat dressed as a circus performer,
for example, "Oswald, though stricken with horror and
polite regret, preserved the most dauntless coolness."[112]
Similarly, the narrator says of Oswald, he "is a very
modest boy, I believe, but even he would not deny that
he has an active brain . . . and . . . is tenacious of
purpose."[113]

The impetus for the Bastable books, as well as
much of the material within them, came from "My School-
days," a series of twelve autobiographical reminiscences
which E. Nesbit wrote for The Girl's Own Paper from
October 1896 to September 1897. The writing of this
series seems to have brought to the surface a wellspring
of information and vivid memories of her past. The fact
that her dearly loved eldest brother, Albert, had died
two years earlier, at the age of forty, contributed, no
doubt, to the power of these memories. In any event,
Edith was not long in putting them to good use, not
suspecting in the least that she might by so doing create
some of her best, most original work. The similarities
between the recollections of "My Schooldays" and the

events and characters of the Bastable trilogy is striking.
How a middle-aged woman could create a narrator as con-
vincing as Oswald becomes understandable in the light of
Daisy's experiences with her older brothers. Daisy herself
comes through cast as the androgynous and creative twins,
Noel and Alice.

Edith wrote the first chapter of what was to be
The Treasure Seekers in October 1897; it and each successive chapter were issued at first in serialized form.
Published as a book in 1899, The Treasure Seekers received
wide acclaim. It traced the exploits of the Bastable
brood as they tried to restore the fallen fortunes of
their family through a number of ingenious schemes. They
had little supervision as they did so, since their mother
had died the year before and their father was in the midst
of some very difficult business transactions which kept
him away much of the time. The occasional tradesman who
appeared, red-faced and angry and waving bills, had given
them a clue as to their family's financial straits. So
had the scarcity of pocket-money and of servants (only
one "general" remained) and the length of their "vacation"
from school.

This being the case, the children took turns at
devising money-making schemes. A few netted them a limited
profit, insufficient to restore a fallen house but helpful
by way of providing an occasional sweet or a modest toy.
Digging for gold under the house, for example, turned up

a half crown. Its appearance coincided with that of
"Albert-Next-Door's Uncle," who had come to retrieve his
nephew buried in the collapsing hole in which it had been
his turn to dig. Albert's uncle was one of the few adults
to whom the Bastables could turn if all went wrong; coinci-
dentally he was often on the scene when events began to
take a turn for the better.

Of E. Nesbit's notions of the relationships between
parent and child little can be said, for the adults are
most notable for their absence in the Bastable tales.
There is clearly a good deal of respect and admiration,
mingled with fear, and a great reserve on the part of the
children. As one would expect in a tale of late Victorian
England, the worlds of the parents and their children are
distinctly separate from each other. In the Bastable
family, however, the gap is not mediated by servants
attendant upon the nursery and the kitchen. This is
especially true in the first book, The Treasure Seekers,
when the family "lived in humble hard-upness in the
Lewisham Road."[114]

The lack of servants, governesses, or teachers,
like the lack of parents in the story, gave the children
freedom from the restraints of adulthood and offered them
a golden opportunity to indulge in every sort of mis-
adventure. By arranging her material this way, E. Nesbit
secured for herself full license to describe those adventures and to examine and delineate the relationships among

the children. Consequently, the Bastable stories, like most of Nesbit's best children's books, are fascinating studies of sibling interaction in a Victorian setting; they are, in addition, excellent models of sexual role stereotyping.

Sibling society à la Bastable is a microcosm of English bourgeois society; it is extremely hierarchical, with pride of place going to males and to older children. Oswald, being the oldest male, is well aware of the impor- tance of his position as "representative of the House of Bastable, which, of course, he is whenever father is not there."[115] To his credit, as he would be the first to note, only occasionally did he take advantage of or flaunt his authority. As the youngest, H.O. was considered the responsibility of the entire family. Oswald, in particular, was anxious to teach him to respect his elders and not to blame others, especially Oswald, for his own errors: "He is our little brother, and we are not going to stand that kind of cheek from him."[116] Far more than age, however, gender seems to account for the hierarchical differences among the children.

The girls, Dora and Alice and their friend Daisy, are never allowed to smoke the peace pipe: "It's not right to let girls smoke. They get to think too much of them- selves if you let them do everything the same as men."[117] Oswald is forever commenting on the peculiar and vastly different nature of girls: "They seem not to mind saying

things that we don't say." They confided to Albert's
uncle, for example, why they had not thought of Albert-next-
door's mother while they were holding Albert prisoner
(because they tried "very hard not to think of other
people's mothers").[118] They also cry a good deal: "It
is their nature, and we ought to be sorry for their
affliction."[119] And they faint, and they giggle, and
they "will kiss everybody" at the slightest provocation.
They are, in short, "strange, mysterious, silly things."[120]

Dora, the oldest sister, seems to suffer from most
of the afflictions of her sex. When Dennis and Daisy
Foulkes visited the Bastables in the country, thereby
bringing the number of children up to eight, Daisy's
presence exacerbated Dora's faults and flaws. They read
"too many books about being good,"[121] according to Oswald,
and "they seem really to like sitting still."[122] Dora and
Daisy originated the "Society for Being Good in" which was
christened the "Wouldbegoods." They were responsible in
some measure, therefore, for the dreadful misadventures
that befell the group in their attempts to commit good
deeds. Yet, having decided on the Society, Daisy and
Dora were often "entirely out of it"[123] when it came
to carrying out its plans, and they didn't even mind
being so. In Dora's defense, she has promised her mother,
as she lay dying, that she would take care of her brothers
and sisters. When Oswald learned of this he was sorry
about having been hard on Dora for her overprotectiveness

and her priggishness. He tried to be more understanding
after that; he was not always successful.

"Brothers ought not to have favorites,"[124] he well
knew, but Alice was a different matter entirely. She
almost seemed to be the exception to Oswald's definitive
descriptions of girls and boys. Granted, she did not like
fishing because of the worm work; nor could she tolerate
watching the cats catch rats and dismember them. And she
had a warm and sensitive way with others which Oswald
uncomprehendingly and begrudgingly admired. For example,
when poor, old Widow Simpson received the news of her
son's death in the South African War, just after she
discovered that the "Wouldbegoods" had "weeded" all of
the turnips and cabbages from her garden, it was Alice
who made amends. The children tried to comfort her in
her sorrow by inscribing a tombstone in her son's honor
in the garden near the churchyard. But only Alice ever
could have convinced Mrs. Simpson that they were not
"making fun of people's troubles" and could have gotten
her to come and see the tombstone with the wreaths of
flowers they had laid upon it. Alice had hugged Mrs.
Simpson and cried with her over the wreaths that afternoon,
and Mrs. Simpson had forgiven them all for the turnips and
cabbages. They were friends after that, "but she always
liked Alice the best." Oswald had to admit that "a great
many people do somehow."[125]

If Alice was softer than her brothers, she was just

as likely to come up with brilliant ideas; it was her idea
to follow their local stream, alias the Nile, to its
source, a plan that proved to be rich in adventure. And
it was her idea to bury the broken crockery in the area of
the Roman ruins to fool the "antiquities" who were coming
to dig there. And Alice was "plucky." She stood up to
the Magistrate who wrongly accused Noel of killing a fox,
and stopped him from taking her twin brother off to jail.
Oswald had to admit, probably not for the first time: "She
is almost worthy to be a boy for some things."[126] On
another occasion, the Bastable clan was scouring England
for their lost dog, Pincher, and found themselves in a
rough area of gas works, tanneries, and a good many
ruffians. When they came across five of the latter beating
up on a wrinkled "blue Chinaman," Alice slapped the largest
boy in the face as hard as she could, and was shaking the
second largest before Dicky and Oswald could get their
hands "into the position required by the noble art of
self-defense."[127]

But even Alice was not able to escape her feminine
nature entirely, for after the battle was over and their
attackers had fled, Alice burst into tears: "That is the
worst of girls--they never can keep anything up. Any brave
act they may suddenly do, when for a moment they forget
that they have not the honour to be boys, is almost
instantly made into contemptibility by a sudden attack of
cry-babyishness."[128] Simiarly, when Alice made as much

fuss as did Dora over Albert's uncle's wedding, Oswald could only conclude in despair: "It's no good. You may treat girls as well as you like, and give them every comfort and luxury, and play fair just as if they were boys, but there's something unmanly about the best of girls. They go silly, like milk goes sour, without any warning."[129]

Alice's twin brother, Noel, could be as perplexing as his sister. Edith seems to have chosen ten year old twins to demonstrate some of the flaws in Oswald's clearly defined sexual universe. In the Bastable books, Dora was always a "girlish" girl, Oswald and his younger brother Dicky were ever brave and manly, or as close an approximation to it as they could manage, but the twins were utterly inconsistent. Alice kissed, and cried, and went "soft," yet she could be as brave as the boys sometimes. Noel, on the other hand, was frail and asthmatic, required more protection than most ten year old boys should require, and was "disgustingly like a girl in some ways."[130] While Noel was not a coward, he joined in on every lark as manfully as the rest; "he's not strong, and he easily gets upset."[131]

To make matters worse, Noel was a poet; he spent most of his time chewing on a pencil stub and thinking up poems for every occasion. Neither Oswald nor Dicky thought very highly of poetry, unless it was of a manly, Kipling sort. They thought Dennis, their visiting friend who did appreciate Noel's poetry, must have gone to a girls' school to have learned the quantity of poetry which he regularly quoted. After Oswald and Noel had ventured to London and sold three of Noel's poems to the editor of The Recorder for a "whole guinea," however, even Dicky and Oswald were impressed with the family's poet laureate.

If poetry was a feminine pastime, which gained only partial acceptance from the older Bastable boys, this was not the case when it came to prose. A love of literature and of language seems to have been one of the few values uncomplicated by gender or age distinctions. All of the Bastables were inveterate readers; they enjoyed nothing more than enacting scenes from their favorite books. In fact, it was their rendition of Kipling which caused so much trouble that they had been sent to the country "to learn to be good." They also loved to use the language of the books they read.

The use of literary allusions and "talking like a book" not only added to the fun of acting out an adventure, they were ways of recognizing their own kind of people, especially among grownups. Albert's uncle was a writer himself and frequently broke into literary speech with the children. According to Oswald, "he always talks like a book, and yet you can always understand what he means. I think he is more like us, inside of his mind, than most grown-up people are. He can pretend beautifully."[132] The friendly lady poet Oswald and Noel met on the train to London was immediately accepted when she recognized the literary source of H.O.'s send-off ("Good Hunting!") at

the train. Once they had compared favorite authors and
found several similarities, the friendship between Mrs.
Leslie and the two boys was ensured. Oswald offered the
final seal of approval by thinking her "too jolly for
a poet" and more "like a jolly sort of grown-up boy in a
dress and hat" than a "real lady."[133]

Patriotism ranked even higher than love of language
and literature on the Bastable scale of values, particularly in The Wouldbegoods written in the midst of the South
African War. Not a trace of irony mars the children's
delight in a parade of marching soldiers or in the fate
that awaited them. "If they have to die, it is a glorious
death; and I hope mine will be that," noted the patriotic
narrator. "And three cheers for the Queen, and for the
mothers who let their boys go, and the mothers' sons who
fight and die for old England. Hip hip hurrah!"[134] In
the light of E. Nesbit's Imperialist poetry, one can
infer that the Oswald factor, that is, the role of the
adolescent narrator in shaping the material, is not solely
responsible for such blatant flag-waving.

On matters of family loyalty, love of literature,
and especially on the issue of sexual stereotyping, it is
necessary to compare the other works of E. Nesbit to rule
out the "Oswald factor" as the source of the values
expressed. The New Treasure Seekers, the last of the
three Bastable books, was published in 1904 and signed
at the end by Oswald Bastable, surprising no one with this

revelation of his identity. This last, however, shows the strain of the continued format. With chapters occasionally ranging backward in time and using material from their days as poor treasure seekers living in the semi-detached house on Lewisham Road, it is the least consistent, least satisfying of the Bastable books. E. Nesbit published three more children's books based on stories of everyday life: The Railway Children (1906), The Wonderful Garden (1911), and Five of Us and Madeline published posthumously in 1925. In each of these a different family is employed, with an omniscient narrator rather than an Oswald equivalent.

The Railway Children involves a family of three children: Roberta, twelve; the oldest, Peter, ten, "who wished to be an engineer"; and Phyllis, eight, "who meant entirely well."[135] They, like the Bastables, found their circumstances altered and their parents removed from their lives. They--no surname is given for the family--had been ordinary suburban children living in a large house, Edgecombe Villa, with "perfect" parents and many servants, including a parlor maid, housemaid, between maid, and a cook, when their father was whisked off to prison. He was charged with having sold state secrets to the Russians.

Off they went to a small white house, Three Chimneys, in the middle of nowhere "to play at being poor for a bit." With father gone and mother shut up in her room writing stories to support them, and no money

left to send them to school, the children were very much on
their own. They were less mischievous than the Bastables,
however; their adventures often involved helping or being
helped by people in their new neighborhood. Their chief
source of amusement was the railroad which ran near their
home. Many of their friends were connected with the
railway. Perks, the porter, was their dearest friend,
and the "old gentleman" to whom they waved daily turned
out to be a high official for the railway. He awarded
them gold watches for flagging down the train when the
track was broken, and generally played the deus ex machina
in their trials and tribulations. It was he who secured
medicine for mother, who found the poor Russian immigrant's
family, and who finally turned up the evidence to free
father.

In many ways the "old gentleman" resembles the
grand uncle from India who rescued the Bastable family
from poverty at the end of The Treasure Seekers, provided
them with suitable surroundings and wealth in The Wouldbegoods and The New Treasure Seekers, and eventually helped
their father to restore his good name and his fortune.
But for all the similarities between the Bastable series
and The Railway Children, there is a major difference
between the books. Unlike the former, the tone of the
latter is clearly feminine, despite the occasional adventure, and despite the family's involvement with the railroad. In The Railway Children the central characters,

unlike those in the Bastable books, are female. The
narrator never reveals him or herself, but one has the
feeling the narrator is someone's mother or, at the very
least, someone's daughter. Instead of constantly reminding
the reader of what is or is not manly and brave, the
narrator of The Railway Children takes the reader aside
to share personal observations of an entirely different
sort:

> I hope you don't mind my telling you a good deal
> about Roberta. The fact is I am growing very fond
> of her. The more I observe her the more I love
> her. And I notice all sorts of things about her
> that I like.
> For instance, she was quite oddly anxious to
> make other people happy. And she could keep a
> secret, a tolerably rare accomplishment. Also
> she had the power of silent sympathy. That sounds
> rather dull, I know, but it's not so dull as it
> sounds. It must means that a person is able to
> know that you are unhappy, and to love you extra
> on that account, without bothering you by telling
> you all the time how sorry she is for you. That
> was what Bobbie was like. She knew that Mother
> was unhappy, and that Mother had not told her the
> reason. So she just loved Mother more and never
> said a single word that could let Mother know how
> earnestly her little girl wondered what Mother
> was unhappy about. This needs. practice. It is
> not so easy as you might think.[136]

What Oswald Bastable would have said about such a rapturous
discussion of "silent sympathy" one can only imagine,
although, if he really thought about it, he might have
realized that it was akin to his sister Alice's way with
people and that there might be something said in its
favor.

The sexes are regarded as distinctly different here
as they are in the Bastable books. But, as the above

quotation plainly demonstrates, the differences are not
used to point up the inferiority of females; rather the
reverse is true. A few attempts are made to show similarities between the sexes, that is, to show that girls are
on a par with boys in areas usually thought of as masculine.
"Girls are just as clever as boys, and don't you forget
it,"[137] Father tells Peter with reference to the possibility of girls helping mend toy engines. And Jim says
Bobbie is "just as brave as a boy"[138] when she stays in
the dark railway tunnel with him while the others get help
for the injured boy. But, for the most part, the emphasis
of the narrative is on valuing qualities that girls, at
least some girls, possess in greater quantity than do boys
and on the differences between the sexes in terms of
interests and tastes.

     In most situations Peter was braver and more
adventurous than his sisters, and certainly more blood-
thirsty. After the threesome saved a baby from a burning
barge, and were allowed access thereafter to the barge
and to the baby, it was clear that Peter preferred playing
on the barge while Bobbie loved playing with the baby. On
one occasion, when Peter was harassing his sisters with
gory tales of make-believe medical procedures, their
friend, Dr. Forrest, had to restrain him:

     "You'll excuse my shoving my oar in, won't you?
     But I should like to say something to you. . . .
     Something scientific. . . . You know men have
     to do the work of the world and not be afraid of
     anything--so they have to be hardy and brave.

But women have to take care of their babies and
cuddle them and nurse them and be very patient
and gentle. . . .
   "Well then, you see, boys and girls are only
little men and women. And we are much harder and
hardier than they are . . . and much stronger,
and things that hurt them don't hurt us. You know
you mustn't hit a girl. . . . Not even if she's
your own sister. That's because girls are so much
softer and weaker than we are; they have to be
. . . because if they weren't, it wouldn't be nice
for the babies. And that's why all the animals
are so good to the mother animals. They never
fight them, you know.
   . . . "And their hearts are soft, too . . .
and things that we shouldn't think anything of
hurt them dreadfully. So that a man has to be
very careful, not only of his fists, but of his
words. They're awfully brave, you know. . . .
Think of Bobbie waiting alone in the tunnel with
that poor chap. It's an odd thing--the softer
and more easily hurt a woman is the better she
can screw herself up to what has to be done. I've
seen some brave women--your mother's one," he ended
abruptly.[139]

Clearly, the message is that girls are meant to

have babies, and men "to do the work of the world." A

woman can be brave if she must be, and can support her

family if need be, but that is not the way the sexes were

intended. The difference here is that woman's work--

mothering--is considered more thoroughly than in any

of E. Nesbit's other children's novels. It did help,

of course, that Bobbie's mother was neither killed off nor

placed on holiday for her health. Instead the relationship

between mother and daughter is examined, albeit in a

highly idealized, sentimental light. And mothering itself,

and the qualities it requires, are depicted as extremely

important.

The narrator makes definite distinctions, however,

between admirable mothers and not so admirable ones:

> Mother did not spend all her time in paying
> dull calls to dull ladies, and sitting dully at
> home waiting for dull ladies to pay calls to her.
> She was almost always there, ready to play with
> the children, and read to them, and help them to
> do their home-lessons. Besides this she used to
> write stories for them while they were at school,
> and read them aloud after tea, and she always made
> up funny pieces of poetry for their birthdays and
> for other great occasions, such as the christening
> of the new kittens, or the refurnishing of the
> doll's house or the time when they were getting
> over the mumps.[140]

When Mother had to write to support her family, she did

so, uncomplainingly. But when the "old gentleman" paid

her to nurse Jim until his broken leg mended, and hired a

cook and a housemaid to relieve her of some of her chores,

she was delighted to stop writing and have time for her

children.

Considered in the light of Hubert Bland's remarks

about the ineffectiveness of most mothers, and their

unscientific treatment of children, The Railway Children

is a virtual panegyric to mothers and motherhood, to

females and "feminine" qualities. Mothers, like their

little girls, remain in a different realm from their male

counterparts, but it is an enlarged and enlightened realm

with room for responsibility and accomplishment. Alice

Bastable's occasional flights of bravery and intelligence

are herein magnified; her warmth and ability to communicate

with others are expanded and given a name: "silent

sympathy."

In the process of delineating the very positive

relationship between Mother and Roberta, E. Nesbit sacri-
fices the finely drawn interaction among the siblings
which exists in her other books. Not only Mother's
presence, but her preference gets in the way: "Of course,
mothers never have favorites, but if their mother had had
a favorite, it might have been Roberta."[141] Thus, the
relationships of the children to each other are not as
important or as convincing as those portrayed in the
Bastable series. This is clearly meant to be a girl's
book, written from a woman's perspective, an unusual event
in E. Nesbit's juvenile fiction.

* * *

In her books of magic and fantasy, of which there
are six, E. Nesbit developed many of the same themes she
had dealt with in her books of everyday life. The most
noteworthy of the lot are three which involve a family of
children, again without a surname, and an assortment of
fantasy facilitators. In Five Children and It (1902),
Cyril, Robert, Anthea, Jane, and their baby brother Lamb
(named after the primary word in his vocabulary, "baaa")
find a Psammead or Sand-Fairy while digging their way to
Australia in a local gravel pit. It grants them a wish a
day. In The Phoenix and the Carpet (1904), this same lucky
fivesome is delivered a carpet for their nursery which
holds the egg of a Phoenix and has, itself, the power to
fly. The winter holidays are thus relieved of all possible
boredom and filled with daily adventures. The Story of

the Amulet (1906) recounts the children's rescue of the
Psammead from a pet shop and their travel through time to
places and periods in ancient history.

In this trilogy the children's parents are usually
absent. Father is either working very hard or traveling
on business, and Mother is ill and resting in Madiera or
staying with Granny who is not well. The "Lamb" is rarely
with them in their adventures, being with Mother most of
the time, so the stories involve Cyril, the oldest, Robert,
Anthea, and Jane, the baby of the group, and their fast-
talking, often pedantic, usually ill-tempered, magic
friends.

In each of the three books, the action is so
lively, and the wish-granting friends so interesting that
the omniscient narrator spends less time than did Oswald,
or the sentimental narrator of The Railway Children,
describing the feelings and thoughts of the children or
the exact circumstances of their lives. Nonetheless, there
is sufficient information to indicate that the children
come from a middle-class family with less money than they
need for vacations and a decent nursery. It is also clear
that, even without the "Oswald factor" at work, there is
a good deal of sexually stereotypical behavior occurring.

Anthea, the eldest daughter, is the representative
of her sex, Jane being too young to be anything but a
scaredy-cat and a nuisance. Anthea resembles Alice
Bastable and Roberta of The Railway Children. If there

was a duty to be done, hugging to be given, or feelings to be felt or expressed, Anthea was the one to do it. In The Phoenix and the Carpet, Anthea, alone, wished that the carpet might take them somewhere where they could do some good deeds.

"All of them, but more particularly Anthea, hated to keep the secret of the Phoenix and the carpet from Mother . . . [for Anthea's] inside mind was made so that she was able to be much more uncomfortable than the others."[142] Especially in The Phoenix and the Carpet where Mother is away less often, Anthea seems to have the special relationship to her that Roberta maintained with her mother:

> Anthea knew exactly what to do for mothers with headaches who had breakfast in bed. She fetched warm water and put just enough eau de cologne in it and bathed mother's face and hands with the sweet scented water. . . .
> "Is your head better, Mammy dear?" she asked, in the soft little voice she kept expressly for Mother's headaches. "I've brought you brekki."[143]

(It is enough to make the reader yearn for the vain and self-serving Phoenix and his obscure historical references and multi-syllabic pedantry.)

Mother is something of an enigma. The reader learns that she occasionally has headaches, and that she turned pale when cook threatened to quit because of the antics of the children. She was "really a great dear," pretty, loving, kind, and "almost always just."[144] The children knew she wanted to do what was best, but she was not always "clever enough to know exactly what was the best."[145] Father suffered from no such deficiency, but he worked very hard and was rarely at home. On Saturday evenings, however, when the family lived in Camden Town, he always brought flowers home for the breakfast table the next morning. On Sunday he read aloud to his assembled brood while Mother listened "quite nicely with her eyes shut."[146]

The clear division of labor which existed between Mother and Father (she worried about the cook and the children and her mother's health, and he went to work) also existed among the children. Except for the "Lamb," who was just a baby, gender was far more important than age in determining function. The girls had to darn the carpet while the boys went for a walk. They took most of the responsibility for the baby, and on cook's and maid's day off they had to help make the beds and wash the dishes while the boys waited impatiently to be off on another adventure.

When it came to leading the way in a dark French castle, however, and telling frightening stories about dungeons and such, the boys took over. When the children's request to the carpet for "the most beautiful and delightful productions of . . . your dear native home" netted them 199 mewing Persian cats, the boys had to go off into the dark night to get rid of them; the girls were too sleepy.[147] "That's all women are fit for--to keep safe and warm, while

the men do the work and run dangers and risks and things,"
Cyril charged as he trudged out.[148] He was gone before
Anthea could deliver a rebuttal from under her warm blanket.
Of course, Anthea and Jane cried under trying circumstances,
but "boys never cry."[149] In dreadful situations, Cyril and
Robert "made faces in their efforts to behave in a really
manly way,"[150] or "tried to pretend that no boy would be
such a muff as to cry."[151]

Yet, as in each of E. Nesbit's books, there are a
few mitigating incidents which alter the monotony of the
stereotypical behavior she presents. For instance, the
boys' "inward monitor" told them that it was "sneakish to
begin without the girls" on the day's adventure.[152] Thus,
if they were anxious to begin they ought to help the
girls with the dishes and dusting. Consequently, they
spent at least one morning engaged in housewifely chores.
Anthea, on the other hand, emotional and squeamish as she
was, would occasionally surprise everyone, including
herself, with her bravery.

The most intriguing example of non-stereotypical
behavior takes place in The Story of the Amulet, while the
children are wandering through London of the future, a
social utopia of green parks, calm, happy citizens, and
clean streets. Sitting on one of the numerous benches
bordering a lovely park near the British Museum, the
children noted the many fresh-faced, colorfully dressed
people seated around the park watching the babies playing

in the grass: "Men as well as women, seemed to be in charge of the babies and were playing with them."[153] This would seem to indicate that even if E. Nesbit's characters usually acted according to sexually determined roles, in the future, the far distant future, there was some hope for a less convention-bound society.

Such behavior, however, was not central to her point in describing this British Utopia. Two notions were far more important to her: the attention paid to the care and well-being of the children, and the elimination of poverty and its attendant dirt and ugliness. The house the children visited had a large room in the middle with padded walls, a soft, thick carpet, and padded chairs and tables. Unlike the children's nursery at home, which was all "cornery and hard," there was not a single thing in it which might hurt a child. "Why the children are more than half of the people, it's not much to have one room where they can have a good time and not hurt them-selves,"[154] explained the woman of the house.

The streets in the utopia were so free of smoke and dirt and lined with so many lovely trees and shrubs, the children could not believe they were really in London:

> "Usedn't people to have no homes and beg because they were hungry? and wasn't London very black and dirty once upon a time? and the Thames all muddy and filthy? and narrow streets, and. . . ."
> "You must have been reading very old-fashioned books," said the lady. "Why, all that was in the dark ages!" . . .
> "I haven't seen any working people," said Anthea.

"Why, we're all working people," said the lady;
"at least my husband's a carpenter."
"Good gracious!" said Anthea, "but you're a
lady!"
"Ah, . . . that quaint old word!"[155]

E. Nesbit's jibes at the state of the lower classes
in Britain were not limited to comparisons with a utopian
future. In another instance, the Queen of Babylon returned
their visit to her ancient land with one of her own to
London. She commented on the dreadful state of their
"slaves" and "how wretched and poor and neglected they
seem." Told they were not "slaves" but "working people,"
she scoffed: "Of course they're working people. That's
what slaves are. . . . Why don't their masters see that
they're better fed?"[156] Although Cyril insisted they had
the vote which made all the difference, he had to admit
that "they don't do anything particular with it." The
Queen understood immediately that a vote was "a sort of
plaything."[157] Thus, The Story of the Amulet published
in 1906 was the first children's story in which E. Nesbit
evinced a concern for the inequities of her time. The
dismay expressed by anachronistic visitors to London
over the "poor, tired, miserable, wicked faces"[158] is
a far cry from the disdain with which her earlier middle
class characters regarded most members of the lower classes,
especially servants and tradesmen.[159]

Yet, even in The Story of the Amulet, Nesbit's
message is not a distinctly Fabian critique. The outrage
she expresses is directed more tellingly at the ugliness

and squalor of contemporary times than at the inequities of
the economic system. As in her poetry, urbanization
seems as much at fault as capitalism for the destruction
of nature and the absence of beauty. The utopian dream
Edith depicts is suggestive of notions advanced by William
Morris, not by Sidney Webb. One vaguely perceives in her
utopia an economy of skilled artisans producing beautifully
hand-crafted products, rather than a system of efficient
factories bringing forth utilitarian wares.

In her concern for children's welfare, and especially in her occasional references to technological
inventions which would aid in setting up a utopian society,
Nesbit clearly reflects the influence of a more forward-
looking reformer than Morris. The effect of fellow Fabian
and, at that time at least, friend H. G. Wells and his
A Modern Utopia is clearly evident. One of her utopian
characters acknowledges, when explaining why she named
her boy "Wells" after the "great reformer of the dark
ages," that Wells "saw that what you ought to do is to
find out what you want and then try to get it. . . .
We've got a great many of the things he thought of."[160]
Most of the "great many things," however, she leaves to
the pages of Wells's fiction, for she is far more concerned
with magic and magicians than with technology, and more
interested in historical civilizations than in utopian
ones.

In two related historical fantasies, The House of Arden (1908) and Harding's Luck (1909), E. Nesbit makes this preference quite clear. Instead of ancient times, however, it is the England of King James which provides the contrasting setting to the ugliness of contemporary Britain. The magic is provided by a trinity of mouldi-warps--mouldiwarp, mouldierwarp, and mouldiestwarp--who conduct the characters back and forth in time.

In The House of Arden, Edred and his sister, Elfrida Arden, search for their family's lost treasure in the past, fail to locate it, but are able to bring back their missing father. Harding's Luck, the more interesting of the novels, details the adventures of Dickie Harding, a lame, slum child. Dickie is an orphan living with his mean-tempered "aunt"; his only possession is a cherished rattle, Rattler, given him by his father before he died. Befriended by a gentle tramp, Beale, Dickie leaves New Cross with "its dirty streets, its sordid shifts, its crowds of anxious, unhappy people, who never had quite enough of anything" for a life of tramping, begging, and sleeping in the beautiful out-doors.[161] Gradually Beale assumes the role of "Father" to the lame boy, and Dickie loves him as if he truly were.

The plot is complicated by Dickie's journey through time which is expedited by "Rattler." He discovers that in the seventeenth century he was an Arden of noble birth

and great wealth, a cousin to Edred and Elfrida, and
was not lame. The noble lad leaves this comfortable past
to be with Beale again and to help his beloved "father"
learn a trade. In the end, however, Dickie goes back to
the time of King James for good, so as not to deprive his
cousins and their father of the Arden inheritance. Before
leaving the present, Dickie sees to it that Beale is
properly settled with a wife and a job and a comfortable
home. He also manages a joyful reunion between Beale and
his old father whom Beale had not seen in twenty years.
Thus Beale loses a "son" but gains a father.

Dickie Harding is nothing if not self-sacrificing
and loving, but in spite of this feminine aberration in his
character, Dickie is very much in the masculine mold.
E. Nesbit had not given up on separating the sexes according to their interests and abilities:

> Girls like dolls and tea-parties and picture-books,
> but boys like to see things made and done; else
> how is it that any boy worth his salt will leave
> the newest and brightest toys to follow a carpenter
> or a plumber round the house, fiddle with his tools,
> ask him a thousand questions, and watch him ply
> his trade? Dickie at New Cross had spent many
> an hour watching those interesting men who open
> square trapdoors in the pavement and drag out from
> them yards and yards of wire. I do not know why
> the men do this, but every London boy who reads
> this will know.[162]

Dickie's cousins Elfrida (aged twelve) and Edred
(aged ten), who enter the story at midpoint and confuse
matters and readers no end, are cardboard children of
little interest, except that Elfrida is not only kinder

and more enthusiastic than her brother, she is also braver
and more clever. Yet, after Edred, under the direction
of a mouldiwarp, commits the heroic act of rescuing cousin
Dickie from his kidnappers, this imbalance is set straight.
It is not clear if Edred became more clever than he had
been, but Elfrida "now looked up to him in all things
and consulted him about everything."[163]

Thus, Harding's Luck fits the pattern set by the
Bastable books: male supremacy reigns almost supreme.
The boys are heroic, and fathers, or father figures, are
very important. Unlike mothers, they are not done away
with entirely; if absent they may be brought back. Edred
and Elfrida find their lost father and bring him back to
life. Dickie finds a substitute father in Beale, then
helps Beale to reunite with his own father after a twenty
year hiatus, discovering in the process his dead father's
identity and his own noble lineage. Indeed, the two
historical fantasies might be called "The Return of the
Fathers."

Clearly, in her later fiction, as in the Bastable
trilogy, E. Nesbit had continued to mine the banks of her
childhood for material, although never as precisely as in
the Bastable stories. The "Five Children" series with
Mother always gone tending to someone's health, but loving
when she was at home, is reminiscent of Mrs. Nesbit's many
absences on behalf of Mary's health. The search for
fathers in the Arden books seems all the more significant

in the face of Daisy's loss of her father at such an
early age. And the fact that all of E. Nesbit's fiction
depicts children on holiday from school, or withdrawn
indefinitely as a result of their family's altered economic
circumstances, is easily understandable given the horrendous
accounts she offered of her own schooling. Second perhaps
only to Bernard Shaw in her distaste for formal education,
E. Nesbit described school as an institution than which she
would "have preferred a penal settlement."[164]

All of which is not to say that experiences of
her later years were not occasionally grist for the
authorial mill. Mother in The Railway Children resembles
Edith Bland in the early years of her marriage, just as
Mrs. Leslie, the jolly poet of The Treasure Seekers,
resembles the accomplished middle-aged Mrs. Bland. That
Edith Bland happened to be the mother of a growing family
no doubt helped her work, but it was far more important
for her juvenile fiction that she had been the irrepressi-
ble Daisy and remained so at heart.

* * *

In summarizing E. Nesbit's views, one finds a
favorable but somewhat ambiguous attitude toward parents
expressed in her juvenile fiction. Fathers are very
important, but never more so than in their absence.
Indeed the only paternal relationships she depicts are
of surrogate fathers like Albert-next-door's uncle and
Beale. Mothers, on the other hand, when present, have

very specific relationships to their children, especially
to their daughters. They take care of them but, as often
as not, are taken care of by them. Daughters seem to
spend much time worrying about their mothers' feelings,
or their headaches, or their health in general. Mothers
may be brave and talented, but they are neither healthy
nor strong.

Creating parental characters or establishing
parent-child relationships, however, was not E. Nesbit's
forte. What she did best and most often was to describe
the interaction of children, especially siblings. The
codes of honor they constituted among themselves, the ways
in which they cared for each other or were ornery with each
other are what take center stage. The message that emerges
is: parents are important for reasons of love and security,
but siblings are important for the paramount aspect of
life--play. An important link between a child's play
and a writer's fiction is the imaginative process which
inspires both. Clearly recognizing this kinship, E. Nesbit
found the fullest scope for her imaginative powers in the
domain of children's adventures. Further, by creating
middle-class characters, more likely to be literate than
their poorer counterparts, she allowed herself to indulge
fully a love of fine and fancy language and of literary
allusions.

E. Nesbit's views on the matter of sexual differences and gender stereotyping seem, at first glance, to

be similar to her husband's. She accepted differences
between the sexes as a given, and she accepted society's
assignment of disparate roles and behaviors based on
gender. At the same time, she redesigned the limitations
placed on some members of her sex and expanded the possibilities of their existence. She did so by claiming,
indirectly, that allowances must be made for a particular
young girl's adventurous spirit or a specific woman's
talent. One must not forget, she reminded her readers,
the talents of the special few, life's "favorites," like
Alice Bastable, Mrs. Leslie or Roberta. More important,
while agreeing that most women were very different from
men, she insisted that they were valuable nonetheless, a
point which her husband badly neglected. Thus, she called
attention to, and lauded, those qualities which, by common
consent, were considered feminine attributes: the capacity
to nurture, to provide "silent sympathy," and to take
emotional risks, that is, to communicate with others.
And she added several traits to the list, such as bravery,
intelligence, humor, and creativity. By the time one
finishes with such a list, the differences between the
sexes are quite small indeed.

Yet, with regard to the woman's movement, there are
no feminist surprises in E. Nesbit's juvenile fiction, no
closet suffragist peeking out from behind her husband's
views. She treated the suffragettes only once in her
children's books, and then fleetingly and unflatteringly.

In The Magic City, one of her lesser works, the protagonist
is a young boy who builds a city of blocks and whatever is
handy, only to find it come to life. In this magical
kingdom, he is stalked by a woman whose avariciousness
and unprincipled pursuit of power has earned her the
title, the "Pretenderette." Hers is as unattractive a
portrait of a would-be claimant to political power as has
ever been penned. She comes to grief in the end and does
a proper penance, having to be loving and docile to an
ogre. Written in 1910, the book's message is clear:
magic is laudable; suffragettes are deplorable. No sympathy
here for the woman's movement then in full swing.

When E. Nesbit confronted the issue of women's
rights at all, she seemed to demand recognition for the
exceptional female rather than for the multitude. One
suspects she demanded recognition for the kind of girl
she must have been and the woman she certainly was.

V. The Blands: An Odd Compatibility

The Blands were married for thirty-four years,
that is, until Hubert's death in 1914. The relationship
they established was an interesting and unusual one. It
was more central to each of their lives, more influential
on their individual careers, than that of the Shaws, yet
hardly the "partnership" the Webbs were to establish.

E. Nesbit was responsible in large measure for
the fact of her husband's journalistic career. It was

she who first persuaded him to help her write the articles
and stories with which she supported the family in the
first two or three years of their marriage. As his health
improved, his participation in their literary output
increased. By 1884 they were collaborating fully in
their literary efforts. Edith regularly contributed
her own poems to the Weekly Dispatch, but on all of the
short stories submitted she and Hubert went "shares,"
using the pseudonym "Fabian Bland."[165]

     In 1889 the Blands completed a novel, The Prophet's
Mantle, which met with little notice and less acclaim. It
did much to disprove a theory of Hubert's expounded in
1886, that to round "the full circle of social experience,"
and thereby produce the best works whether sociological,
scientific, or imaginative, it was necessary to employ
the joint talents of a man and a woman.[166] The Prophet's
Mantle demonstrated instead: two imaginations may do
better than one in dreaming up adventures for a half dozen
characters and moving them through endless twists of plot
and circumstance, but two authors are prone to alternative
styles and differing interpretations of characters, and
might deprive their joint effort of a central theme or a
convincing, consistent development of characters. The
Prophet's Mantle was the high point--an unkind biographer
might declare it the nadir--of the Blands' collaboration;
thereafter their cooperative efforts were infrequent.

     Despite the addition of two more children in the

family, Fabian, born in 1885, and Rosamund, born in 1886,
Edith's literary efforts never slackened. She continued
to produce a stream of articles, short stories, and poems
which contributed a great deal to the family income. She
had, as one friend commented, the ability to "write uncon-
cernedly in the midst of a crowd, smoking like a chimney
all the while."[169] Her first book of poetry, Lays and
Legends, had been published in 1886, a fact which brought
her much satisfaction since she entertained to her last
days the notion that her most important talent was as a
poet. Other volumes followed, with little import for
posterity but much personal significance for the author.

Hubert found his own voice as a writer, a very
masculine one at that. And he slowly began to make his
way as a journalist. By way of encouragement, during
this period, G.B.S. once wrote to Hubert commending him
on his choice of professions and assuring him that the two
of them were doing their respective women a favor by
following their own inclinations:

> If . . . a man is to attain consciousness of him-
> self as a vessel of the Zeitgeist or will or what-
> ever it may be, he must pay the price of turning
> his back on the loaves and fishes, the duties,
> the readymade logic, the systems and the creeds.
> He must do what he likes instead of doing what,
> on secondhand principles, he ought. . . . You
> and I, according to the most sacred secondhand
> principles, should be prosperous men of business,
> I for the sake of my poor dear mother, who in her
> old age, has to . . . eke out the domestic purse
> by teaching schoolgirls to sing, you for the sake
> of your clever and interesting wife and pretty
> children. . . . My mother, the victim of my

selfishness, is a hearty, independent, and jolly
person, instead of a miserable old woman dragged
at the chariot wheels of her miserable son, who
had dutifully sacrificed himself for her comfort.
Imagine Mrs. Bland as the wife of a horrible city
snob with a huge villa, a carriage, and several
thousand a year, which is exactly what, on moral
principles, it was your duty to have made her.
You and I have followed our original impulse, and
our reward is that we have been conscious of its
existence and can rejoice therein.[170]

One would like to have seen Bland's response to
such a portrayal of his family situation; unfortunately,
there is no such letter in existence. It is a measure of
the differences between the two men that Shaw was always
quick to point out, indeed to exaggerate, his culpability
in neglecting his economic responsibilities, whereas
Bland covered up such details with a smokescreen of urbani-
ties on male superiority and female inadequacy. Further,
he dressed the part of a "horrible city snob" even if he
could not supply the "huge villa."

Shaw was certainly right, however, that Edith Bland
would not have done nearly so well as the wife of a "city
snob." From the beginning of their marriage, the Blands
lived the life of avant-garde Bohemians at odds with
almost every aspect of bourgeois culture. They enjoyed
the literary life of London, belonged to the Browning
Society and the Shelley Society, and went "out a good bit"
to public meetings, debates, and readings.[171] They were
much involved, of course, with the Fabian Society and its
activities.

Their homes, as they gradually increased in size

over the years, were open to an increasingly large number of "enthusiastic youth, artists, writers, flaming socialists, and decorous Fabians."[172] Edith was a gracious and innovative hostess, well versed in the domestic arts, and capable of making very little money go a long way. The scale of their parties grew in proportion to their income, with dinners for thirty or forty not unusual in later years. The Blands treated their guests to informal dances or games of badminton. Edith entertained at the piano; Hubert led, and usually dominated, the animated conversations which took place. He also performed handsomely in their Saturday evening debates; she provided costumes and enthusiasm for complicated games of charades.

Clearly, Edith's literary exertions and her family responsibilities were never allowed to stand in the way, at least not for long, of her love of play. Her playfulness and _joie de vivre_ enlivened and shaped her life, as it did her juvenile fiction. Whether the activity involved dressing up for charades, riding a tricycle, rowing a boat, or climbing a tree, if it was good fun, it would hold her undivided attention. Richard le Gallienne described the impression she made upon him when she was in her early thirties:

> [With her] tall, lithe boyish-girl figure, admirably set off by her socialist gown, her short hair, and her large vivid eyes, curiously bird like, and so full of intelligence and a certain half-mocking, yet friendly humour . . . she suggested adventure, playing truant, robbing orchards, or even running away to sea.[173]

Not one to settle for a sedentary middle age, two
decades later Edith was entertaining guests at her home
by building huge "magic cities" of the sort she described
in her book, built of odds and ends and kitchen utensils.
About this time, she was also given to the making of
cardboard houses and factories and burning them in effigy
on her lawn. She thereby showed her increasing anger and
intense distaste for the ugliness of industrialization and
urbanization, while indulging her need for creative and
fanciful play.

The thought of the frock coated Hubert Bland
sharing in such frivolity evokes incongruous images. Yet,
his pretensions in dress and bearing rarely kept him from
participating in, or at least tolerating the amusements
she enjoyed--even if his chief concerns lay elsewhere.
More than this, his domineering and conventionally conservative presence gave some ballast to her childish antics and
her Bohemian tastes. He alone was capable of calming her
when her volatile temper got out of hand. Storming away
from the dinner table in a fit of pique, Edith could be
lured from her room to offer penance to all only by the
soothing ministrations of her husband. Kisses and pet
names--"Cat" in particular was a favorite of theirs--
usually worked the necessary magic.[174]

The relationship between the Blands was as complex
as it was long-standing. Adding to the complexity, far
more than a disparity between her childlike behavior and

his conservative demeanor, was Hubert's own particular
notions of what constitutes pleasure and what passes
as morality. With reference to the latter, his personal
position is clear, even if it conflicted egregiously
with his public pronouncements on the subject: "Break
the rules as you wish, but respect the power of people's
prejudice, and use your superior intelligence to cover
your tracks."[175]

In her biography of E. Nesbit Bland, published in
1933, Doris Langley Moore was the first to bring to light
how numerous were the "tracks" Hubert Bland had to cover.
The Blands had been married less than a year when the young
bride discovered that her husband had not broken off
his relationship with another woman upon his engagement
to her; in fact he had fathered a child by this woman,
Maggie.[176] The shock was seismic but of a lesser magnitude
than that created by similar incidents in the years that
followed.

Alice Hoatson was an editorial reader for Sylvia's
Home Journal when Edith Bland submitted her first story to
the magazine in the early 1880's. The two women became
friends, and Miss Hoatson gave up her job to work for the
Blands a year or two later. She became housekeeper,
nurse, governness, typist, collaborator, and close friend
to the Blands. She was for Edith what many a contemporary
working woman has claimed to need: a wife sans sexual
responsibilities. For Hubert, however, her role had no

such restrictions. When Miss Hoatson became pregnant in
1886, Edith generously offered to raise the baby as her
own, even when the errant Miss Hoatson would not reveal
the paternity of the child. Edith did not discover her
husband's role in the affair until the baby was six months
old. One can imagine the tumultuous rising of the roof
at the Bland home when Edith received the news. In spite
of her rage, however, she accepted the situation and
continued to claim the child, Rosamund, as her own.
Her motivation for such generosity is open to speculation;
her response to Miss Hoatson's second pregnancy, thirteen
years later, is far easier to surmise. But once again
Edith adopted a child her husband had fathered, and Miss
Hoatson continued to live with the Blands and their assorted
children.[177]

Bland's public persona spoke, especially at Fabian
meetings, in tones of moral purity, and it was further
defined by the pen of "Hubert of the Chronicle" who stood
for conventional morality, traditional roles for women,
and the importance of the family. Obviously, the gap
between personal myth and actual fact was enormous. If
in his writings "Hubert of the Chronicle" occasionally
see-sawed between promoting conventional morality and
extolling the joys of flirtation, in the Fabian Society
Bland never wavered in his support for traditional attitudes toward social and sexual behavior. In his private
life, however, he never faltered in his flaunting of the

same sexual codes he preached.

A visitor to Well Hall, the Blands' huge old "rambling and romantic" home at Eltham, to which they had moved in 1899, described how Hubert held court at their Saturday evening soirees amidst "a springtide of femininity fluttering around him, waiting for a sultanesque sign to approach. There was always an inner group of devotees, mostly of the Victorian type. He had a great attraction for the ingenuous."[178] Bland, himself, sweetened and sanitized his version of his relationship to young women in a statement by his fictional alter ego, Stephen Yorke: "I am convinced the one role I am fitted for is that of guide, censor, confessor, and friend of young womanhood."[179] In truth, he considered himself, according to one private confidant, "a student in illicit love." He was not a Don Juan, but "Professor Juan,"[180] and he indulged in a prodigious number of affairs throughout his not very long, by Fabian "Old Gang" standards, life. (One suspects Bland of having tried to burn the candle in the middle, as well as at both ends; his heart began to falter in his mid-fifties and gave out entirely after fifty-nine years of trying to keep the pace.)

Edith's response to her husband's infidelities was best expressed in a poem she wrote in 1885:

"The Husband of To-Day"

. . .
After each fancy has sprung, grown and died,
Back I come ever, dear, to your side

The strongest of passions--in joy--seeks the new
But in grief I turn ever, sweetheart, to you.

"The Wife of All Ages"

I do not catch these subtle shades of feeling,
Your fine distinctions are too fine for me.
. . .
Why should one rule be fit for me to follow
While there exists a different law for you?
. . .
What do I care to be the first--or fiftieth,
It is the only one I care to be.
. . .
And so good bye! . . .
. . .
The world no doubt has fairer fruits and blossoms
To give to you; but what, ah what for me?
Nay, after all I am your slave and bondmaid,
And all my world is in my slavery.
So, as before, I welcome any part
Which you may choose to give me of your heart.[181]

As time went on Edith placed more emphasis on the question "Why should one rule be fit for me?" and less on her "slavery." She enjoyed a few relationships with admirers which went beyond the realm of friendship. George Bernard Shaw was one of the first men she developed a passion for, in 1885-86, but, as his diary plainly shows, that relationship remained within the pale--due to his insistence rather than hers. Two decades later, a frequentor of the Blands' Saturday evening parties at Well Hall found Mrs. Bland

> always surrounded by adoring young men, dazzled
> by her vitality, amazing talent, and the sheer
> magnificence of her appearance. She was a very
> tall woman, built on the grand scale, and on
> festive occasions wore a trailing gown of peacock
> blue satin with strings of beads and Indian
> bangles from wrist to elbow.[182]

One suspects that her acceptance of her husband's

behavior was eased not only by an occasional indiscretion of her own but by her delight in play and make-believe. Hubert Bland was not alone in enjoying the pretense and the drama of illicit situations. As H. G. Wells suggested with reference to the "fantastic concealments and conventions" that masked Bland's philandering, Mrs. Bland "detested and mitigated and tolerated but presided over and, I think, found [it] exceedingly interesting."[183]

How the children fared in the midst of these "concealments" is another matter. They were, at least, spared the details for a long while. Rosamund and John did not know who their real mother was until their respective teen years. Rosamund discovered the ruse in October 1900, a year after John's birth and just days after the death of fifteen year old Fabian, Edith's own, much favored son. The boy died unexpectedly of complications from a simple tonsillectomy; Edith was not able to contain her grief or her bitterness. Overhearing her distraught "mother's" lamentations and her protestations against life's injustices, Rosamund deduced the truth about her own maternal lineage. John, on the other hand, was told directly that Miss Hoatson was his real mother to stop the youth from treating her so unkindly.[184]

Rosamund, the most strikingly attractive and talented of the Bland children, maintained a close relationship with her father and felt a strong sense of loyalty to him. In later years she seems to have forgiven him his part in the deception, and blamed much of her peculiar parental situation on her adoptive mother,[185] a sleight of hand possible only in the dealings of a doting daughter with her glamorous father. It was Rosamund, at age nineteen, to whom Hubert dedicated his book of essays, <u>Letters to a Daughter</u>. He must have derived a perverse kind of pleasure from the "letter" entitled "The Limits of Flirtation" in which he mentioned, in passing, "I am told that the 'menage a trois' is one of the commonest of social phenomena."[186] One wonders if it was this kind of arrangement that he was safeguarding in his continuing defense of the British family?

That Rosamund felt Edith favored her own children did not improve relations between the two. Aside from the complications which affected this relationship, however, one might expect E. Nesbit, writer of children's books par excellence, to have been a consummate mother. Yet according to reports from both her daughters, she was hot-tempered, overly emotional, and given to storming off to her room if anything upset her.[187] And she was not the most interested, understanding, or consistent of mothers. But then, playful, highly imaginative children, who lead very busy lives, do not usually make the best mothers.

* * *

Given the many peculiarities in the Blands' marital arrangements, perhaps what is most surprising is that the

marriage worked as well and as long as it did. Hardly one
to indulge in self-revelatory expositions, Bland suggested
that good tempered men philander, but make pleasant husbands, whereas "good" men use up all their energy in
being good and are, therefore, mean-spirited husbands.[188]
Such a generalization may have been soothing to the rough
edges of his constantly tried conscience, but it offers
little by way of explaining the Bland marriage or the
Blands themselves.

Hubert Bland was indeed a man of provocative
poses and puzzling inconsistencies. In the context of
his conservative notions on women and the family, Bland's
marital and extramarital relationships seem as out of
place as his socialist activism in the face of his conservative views on race and nation. Beyond the paradoxical
nature of his attitudes and activities, however, one
wonders about the driven quality of his sexual exploits.
Why did he need to indulge in them so often and discuss
them so endlessly? According to H. G. Wells,

> the fundamental interest insisted upon coming to
> the surface. . . . He would talk about it. He
> would give hints of his exceptional prowess. He
> would boast. He would discuss the social laxities
> of Woolwich and Blackheath, breaking into anec-
> dotes, "simply for the purpose of illustration."
> Or he would produce a pocket-worn letter and read
> choice bits of it--"purely because of its psycho-
> logical interest."[189]

Wells, no fan of Bland's in later years, offered as partial
explanation of Bland's compulsion that it was a way of
getting "even" with his wife's "wit and freaks and

fantasies and with a certain essential coldness in her."
Further, that "the clash of their personalities" confirmed
him in this tendency.[190]

However much one might question Wells's impar-
tiality,[191] Bland's insistence that his wife accept both
his mistress and her children under their roof and practice
a lifelong deception as to the children's maternity does
smack of cruel and retaliatory behavior, especially the
second time around. Similarly, his continual references
to the inferiority of women in the light of his wife's
many talents also suggests an element of reprisal in his
conduct. One can assume, however, given the fact of
Bland's conduct with Maggie, even before his marriage
to Edith, that the pattern had already been drawn before
their relationship began, and their marriage only served
to fashion the design more intricately.

Considering Bland's response to women on purely
socioeconomic grounds, his contempt for women's abilities
and his limited perspective on their activities could be
connected to the fact that, as a writer, he made his
living in a field that was being increasingly permeated
by women. As a sympathetic newsman describing the identity
of interests between the middle-class intellectuals of the
Fabian Society and the working-class poor, noted in 1890,
"it is the unprecedentedly severe competition produced by
the spread of education and the admission of women to the
professions that is driving the 'brain workers' into the

camp of the 'hand workers.' The Fabian Society is a sign
of the times."[192] Bland's response to women working
might be seen, then, as similar to that of most industrial
workers whose jobs were being threatened by the infiltra-
tion of female workers.

For middle class "brain workers," a lack of unions
and of the conditions conducive to unionization, that is,
large numbers of workers congregated in small areas, made
the problem of sexual competition for a limited number of
jobs appear less blatant. The competition and the difficulties and resentments it inspired were discernible
nonetheless. One suspects that Bland's need to denigrate
the talents and abilities of women was fueled, in part,
with concerns provoked by the specter of feminine competition in his own areas of competence. But in his case,
the issue was not only a general social trend to be
encountered at the workplace, it was a fact to be endured
in his home.

The more determinedly Bland painted the role of
women as secondary to man, the more money his own wife
seemed to contribute to their family income. (Perhaps
one should say, the more his own wife contributed to their
family income, the more determinedly he painted the role
of woman as secondary to man.)

Aside from his daily and weekly newspaper articles,
which were popular but transient by nature, the sum total
of his literary output was four volumes of journalistic

essays, one of which, _Essays by Hubert_, was published posthumously by his wife in 1914, and a slim volume of fiction, _Olivia's Latchkey_ (1913). A catalogue of E. Nesbit Bland's novels, collected stories, and poetry would fill a good many pages. There is no doubt that her creativity far outdistanced his. Bland's narrow-minded opinion of female abilities seemed to fly in the face of his wife's artistic and financial success. Such notions may have been comforting, but they were out of touch with reality as he lived it.

Why the compulsion to trifle with women, or why Bland chose that particular way to "get even" with his wife, if that were the case, remain unanswerable questions. One is tempted to speculate along the lines of Melanie Klein's psychoanalytic explanation for such behavior. Compulsive infidelity, according to Klein, represents the repeated turning away from a loved person, which springs in part from a fear of dependence. The unfaithful individual proves to himself that his own greatly loved object, originally his mother, is not indispensable, since he can always find another to replace it. By rejecting and deserting some woman, or a series of women, he is, unconsciously, turning away from his mother and saving himself from his dependence.[193]

In Hubert's case, the death of his father while he was a youth threw him back on his mother and intensified his ambivalent feelings about her. The more he felt dependent upon her, the more frightened he was of losing her, and the angrier he became at his helplessness. As Hubert matured, his feelings of dependency kept alive the angry little boy within him who could neither separate completely from his mother nor forgive her his dependence. This angry little boy, artfully disguised in a powerful frame and a pugilistic manner, found solace in numerous love affairs and, one suspects, in notions of male supremacy. What better way to "get even" than to damn the whole sex and laugh at its infirmities and incompetence?

In this regard, Bland's sexual compulsions were related to his male chauvinism and his conservative attitudes toward the role of women in society. Both sprang from his need to overcome feelings of dependence, that is, to prove himself the master of his feelings by proving himself master in the battle of the sexes. Thus, the same fears and anxieties helped generate inconsistencies in his persona and in his views of women. In addition, a negative opinion of women made it easier to misuse them. Yet, one cannot generalize about the causal relationship between conservative attitudes toward the role of women and sexual acting out. Many a conservative gentleman, given to placing women on pedestals of powerlessness, does in fact maintain a consistency between his views and his sexual activities, just as many an ardent male feminist, H. G. Wells chief among them, proposes every sort of feminist reform while exposing his own wife and children

to numerous social indignities due to his sexual esca-
pades.[194]

      For even the most superior of males, the strut and
swagger of superiority is difficult to maintain, and the
little boy who hides beneath it all will out. At times
Bland played the part of the poor injured male and sounded
almost Shavian in his admission of male weakness before
the feminine colossus. Now and then he displayed the
wistfulness of an overwhelmed or under-appreciated young
boy. "Most women behave as though their mere existence
were a blessing to men,"[195] he complained; "this world is
the best of all worlds for women--and cats."[196] Such
lapses in his pose of male superiority, however, were
infrequent. For the most part he remained as insistently
supercilious toward women as he was inconsistent in his
views of women.

      Hubert Bland was a misogynist who alternated
between belittling women and finding them "delightful,"
and a misogamist who attacked marriage as more beneficial
to women than men, and as utterly destructive of the
joys of romance, while loyally supporting marriage and
the family in most of his public pronouncements. He
was a moralist intent upon maintaining conventional morality in order to flaunt it. The continual collision of
Bland's aesthetic notions, misogynous views, patriotic
aspirations, and his lecherous designs wreaked havoc
with the consistency of his thought and the purity of

his purpose. Bland the quintessential poseur remains in one's memory long after expositions by "Hubert of the Chronicle" have faded away.

Perhaps more curious than all of Hubert Bland's inconsistencies was the fact that his wife, Edith Nesbit Bland, put up with them and stayed with him through thirty-four years of marriage. Granted the insurmountable difficulties divorce presented to a young married woman with several children, one wonders, still, how and why she bore it. One wonders too if, after years of living with Hubert Bland, she ever revolted against his chauvinistic opinions of women in the light of her own obvious talents, energy, and income. Did she continue to acquiesce in his negative negative estimation of the women's movement once the discrepancies within his thought, and between his ideas and his actions, had become undeniably apparent?

Edith had almost as many reasons for staying with her unfaithful husband as she had grounds for leaving him. Aside from the compatibility of their interests, habits born of years spent together, and the strictures against divorce of her new faith, Edith's inability to leave him was influenced by certain aspects of her past.

The peripatetic nature of her childhood with its stark contrasts between the settled interludes of happiness and the gloomy periods at school, the very unpredictability of her situation, must have made separations as well as certain aspects of growing up very difficult for her.

That she was not able to give up some of her childlike
behaviors and needs emanated from this difficulty--one
cannot give up being a child if one has not had the
security a child requires to take the slow, painful steps
toward maturity. After she was married, the insecurity
generated by Hubert's unfaithfulness duplicated the situation she had experienced as a young child. The comradeship
and love which they clearly shared would disappear when new
evidence arose of his extramarital activities. That, in
the course of their married life, she never rid herself of
her tantrums or erratic behavior owed as much to this
continuing cause of insecurity as it did to the original
source. That she was equally unable to rid herself of her
husband followed, paradoxically, from the very insecurity
he generated and the consequent feelings of dependency she
experienced. She had a "cat-like fondness for things
[she was] accustomed to,"[197] born of her years of imperma-
nence, and she seems to have had similar needs in terms of
her relationships.

Even the tranquillity of Edith's earliest years had
been marred by the death of her father. The ramifications
of such a loss were numerous, including a greater dependency
on her mother, the same mother who habitually left Edith in
order to seek more healthful climates for the consumptive
Mary. Possibly the oddest ramification of that loss was
Edith's obsession with the Shakespeare as Bacon question.
Between 1908 and 1918 she spent enormous amounts of time

and money, which she could ill afford in the later years,
pursuing the matter, looking for proof mathematical and
semantic that Bacon had written all of Shakespeare's
works. Edith began her investigation of this question
about the time she was creating the Arden stories in which
everyone is either in the process of looking for, or
finding, their fathers. It was also the period when
Hubert's health began to fail; his first heart attack
occurred in 1908. Possibly, Edith's concern for her
husband's health brought back feelings of loss she had
experienced after her father's death. Thus, one suspects
a connection between Edith's obsessive search and her
fictional pursuit of fathers, both influenced by a longing
for her dead father, a longing exacerbated by her fears of
losing Hubert.

In this context, it is interesting to note how
differently Hubert and Edith handled their dependency
needs. He feared such feelings and did all in his power
to hide from them, in the process disguising himself in a
confusing mix of conservatism, male bravado, and promiscuity. She, on the other hand, was less frightened of
feeling dependent, and far more willing to give into such
feelings and to acknowledge their power. Rather than
clothing herself in superiority, she dwelt upon her needs
and weakness and, at times, generalized them to her gender.
Perhaps, the disparity in their methods of handling the
problem of dependency says as much about the nature of the

options each perceived as open to him or her as it does about the relative natures of the Blands themselves. The existence of the problem itself, in each of their personalities, however, bespeaks an odd kind of compatibility.

The Blands were compatible in a number of other ways, as has been noted. For one, he was the complete older brother and playmate for her. It was, perhaps, this brilliant older brother quality in Hubert which caused her to look up to him as she had to Alfred and Harry. That his mind had a better store of facts, figures, and social theory than hers made this all the more likely. Caught up in the demands of family and the exigencies of writing to earn a living and to satisfy her need to write poetry, she had no time to notice when some of the theories espoused by her husband and endorsed by herself did not match their lives as they lived them or her role as she had created it.

Thus, a quarter of a century after her initial unfavorable impression of the feminist movement, despite her own achievements in the interim, she remained steadfast in her opposition to the woman's movement. Notwithstanding her own economic independence, incredible energy, and talent, she gave a speech to the Fabian Women's Group on the disabilities of women as workers which set her well apart from the feminist position of most members of the Group. And, her quarrel with the political system and her less than overwhelming faith in the talents of the working class notwithstanding, she refused to sign an authors'

memorial in favor of the Conciliation Bill for women's
suffrage, stating: "I cannot sign the enclosed Memorial as
it does not embody my views. I am for adult suffrage, but
primarily my political interest is all for socialism, and
I do not wish socialism to be endangered by an extension
of the franchise to a class of women mainly conservative."[198]

It is hard to imagine that if Edith Bland had felt
an emotional affinity with the women of the movement or the
issues being raised, she would have allowed herself to be
deterred by the possible incongruence of socialism and
feminism on matters of class and timing, as she suggested.
Intellectual coherence was not a primary concern of hers.
It is equally difficult to think that she followed her
husband blindly on this issue. Her own values certainly
played a role in her decisions and opinions.

For Edith, work, and higher education, or entrance
into the professions or the political world would not be
liberating achievements for women. Instead, play and the
beauties of nature ought to be the universal liberators
for both sexes. Work was not a blessing to be sought
but a necessity to be endured: "Work is what you hate
doing and have to do for your living."[199] One suspects
that if the solemn soldiers of the movement had demanded
for women more freedom to indulge in play, more room for
adventure, they might have had a convert in Edith Bland--
whether or not her husband agreed.

It is relevant in this regard that E. Nesbit
earned her fame and fortune in a profession which, with
certain restrictions, had always been open to women of
talent. Like Beatrice Webb, she felt few of the hindrances
experienced by women seeking recognition in other fields.
She herself seemed unaware of the price she paid for some
of the restrictions, that is, in the quality and sincerity
of her verse and adult fiction in which she assumed the
male voice. She seemed rather to revel in the fact that
"all the reviewers took [her] for a man, and [she] was
Mr. Nesbit . . . til [she] was fool enough to dedicate
a book to [her] husband, and thus gave away the secret."[200]

After Hubert's death in April 1914, Edith was
beset by myriad problems created by her own ill health,
her financial insolvency (complicated by her involvement
in the Shakespeare controversy), and the difficulties of
living in a nation at war, a war which, true to her past
principles, she supported. Her fondest wish was for a
government pension. She felt "quite unable to do any
work" after the "crushing blow" of Hubert's death. Having
"worked hard for thirty-seven years and . . . written
forty books" and having been told that her "books for
children are the best there are," she hoped she might
be entitled to some sort of government help.[201] A small
civil pension of £60 a year was awarded her in recognition
of her service to literature in 1915, and as her health
improved she regained some of her old spirit.

The last years of her life were gladdened considerably by her marriage in 1917 to the gentle Thomas
Terry Tucker, a retired ship's engineer and a friend of
long standing. "Skipper" ran the Woolwich Ferry for the
County Council and was a general handyman. "Everyone is
very much surprised at my marrying Mr. Tucker," she wrote
to a friend,

> but no one is more surprised than I am. . . .
> It is extraordinarily rum that I should have
> found someone who suits me like this. It is
> like a consolation prize for all sorts of failures.
> And the knowledge that I have a friend and com-
> rade to sit on the other side of the hearth while
> life's dying embers fade, is incredibly comfort-
> ing.[202]

To her brother she wrote telling him that her husband was
the best man she had ever known and that she felt as though
she had "opened another volume of the book of life [the
last volume] and it [was] full of beautiful stories and
poetry."[203]

The Tuckers' financial situation was not overly
comfortable, nor her health entirely good, yet her old joy
in life and writing and her many interests returned. The
couple even collaborated on several sketches of nautical
life for the Westminster Gazette. The comfort of having
a husband whose love never wearied or wandered was indeed
"a consolation prize for all sorts of failures." The
serenity of her last years attested to the depth of that
"consolation"; the last "volume," she often reported, was
the best. Sadly, it was also the briefest. E. Nesbit

Bland-Tucker died in the Tuckers' nautical bungalow at
Jesson, St. Mary's, Kent on 24 May 1924.

Footnotes

[1] Norman and Jeanne MacKenzie, The Fabians (New York: Simon and Schuster, 1977), pp. 67-68.

[2] Hubert Bland, "If I Were a Woman," in his Essays by Hubert Bland (London: Max Goschen, 1914), p. 203.

[3] Ibid.

[4] H. Bland, "The Faith I Hold," in his Essays, p. 214.

[5] Ibid.

[6] Ibid., pp. 221-25.

[7] See Chushichi Tsuzuki, H. M. Hyndman and British Socialism (London: Oxford University Press, 1961).

[8] H. Bland, "The Need for a New Departure" [Lecture to the Fabian Society], reprinted in To-Day, October 1887.

[9] Bland, "The Faith I Hold," pp. 221-25.

[10] Mrs. Cecil Chesterton, The Chestertons (London: Chapman and Hall, 1941), p. 57.

[11] Arthur H. Nethercot, The First Five Lives of Annie Besant (Chicago: University of Chicago Press, 1960), p. 268.

[12] H. G. Wells, Experiment in Autobiography (New York: Macmillan, 1934), p. 516.

[13] "The Fabians," Glasgow Herald, June 1916.

[14] Mrs. Chesterton, The Chestertons, p. 14.

[15] Wells, Experiment, p. 514.

[16] George Bernard Shaw to Graham Wallas, 16 December 1890, Wallas Collection, British Library of Political and Economic Science.

[17] Edward Pease, "Webb and the Fabian Society," in The Webbs and Their Work, ed. Margaret Cole (London: Frederick Muller, 1949), pp. 18-19.

[18] Wells, Experiment, pp. 518-19.

[19]S. G. Hobson, Pilgrim to the Left (London: Edward Arnold, 1938), pp. 81-82.

[20]Mrs. Chesterton, The Chestertons, p. 57.

[21]Wells, Experiment, p. 519.

[22]Pease, "Webb and the Fabian Society," pp. 18-19.

[23]Hubert Bland, "Books," To-Day, April 1886.

[24]Hubert Bland, Olivia's Latchkey (London: T. Werner Laurie, 1913), p. 55.

[25]Hubert Bland to George Bernard Shaw, 25 September 1886, Shaw Papers, MS 50557, British Library.

[26]George Bernard Shaw, "Early History of the Fabian Society," Fabian Tract No. 41, reprinted in Edward R. Pease, The History of the Fabian Society (New York: Barnes and Noble, 1963), p. 67.

[27]H. Bland to G. B. Shaw, 25 September 1886, Shaw Papers, MS 50557.

[28]Hubert Bland, "The Outlook," in Fabian Essays in Socialism, ed. G. B. Shaw (London: Walter Scott, 1908), pp. 202-14.

[29]See G. B. Shaw to G. Wallas, 20 September 1892, Wallas Collection, 9a, British Library of Political and Economic Science.

[30]G. B. Shaw to G. Wallas, 28 October 1892, Wallas Collection, 9a.

[31]Hubert Bland to Edward Pease, 5 December 1911, Fabian Papers, A/6/2, Nuffield College, Oxford.

[32]Hubert Bland to G. B. Shaw, 13 October 1910, Shaw Papers, MS 50557.

[33]H. Bland to E. Pease, 17 October 1899, Fabian Papers, A/6/2.

[34]Hubert Bland, "An Altar of Empire," in his With the Eyes of a Man (London: T. Werner Laurie, 1905), pp. 35-36.

[35]Hubert Bland to Kensington Group, reported in Fabian News 17, no. 4 (1907).

[36] H. Bland, "Books," To-Day, May 1888.

[37] Ibid.

[38] Hubert Bland, Lecture to Fabian Society, reported in Fabian News 15, no. 4 (1905).

[39] See H. Bland, "Religion and the Child," The Happy Moralist (London: T. Werner Laurie, 1907), pp. 178-90.

[40] Cecil Chesterton, "Introduction," in Essays by Hubert Bland, p. xi.

[41] G. B. Shaw, "Early Days," in The Webbs and Their Work, p. 7.

[42] H. Bland, "The Decadence of Kipling," in his Essays, p. 35.

[43] H. Bland, "Men's Love," in his Letters to a Daughter (London: T. Werner Laurie, 1906), p. 108.

[44] Bland, Olivia's Latchkey, p. 68.

[45] H. Bland, "Books," To-Day, July 1886.

[46] H. Bland, "The Faith I Hold," in his Essays, pp. 229-31.

[47] H. Bland, in Fabian News 4, no. 1 (1894).

[48] H. Bland to E. Pease, 14 October 1906, Fabian Papers, A6/2.

[49] Ibid., 23 September 1908.

[50] Anne Fremantle, This Little Band of Prophets (New York: New American Library, 1959), p. 51.

[51] Fabian News 19, no. 8 (1909).

[52] Ibid. 19, no. 5 (1909).

[53] Ibid. 20, no. 10 (1910).

[54] Cecil Chesterton, "Introduction," p. xi.

[55] Bland, Olivia's Latchkey, p. 50.

[56] H. Bland, "The Honest Woman," in his Essays, p. 257.

[57] Bland, <u>Olivia's Latchkey</u>, p. 87.

[58] Bland, "The Honest Woman," p. 257.

[59] H. Bland, "On Spanking," in his <u>With the Eyes of a Man</u>, p. 38.

[60] Bland, "The Decadence of Kipling," p. 44.

[61] Bland, "The Honest Woman," p. 259.

[62] Ibid., p. 254.

[63] H. Bland, "Concerning Heredity," in his <u>With the Eyes of a Man</u>, p. 190.

[64] H. Bland, "About Divorce," in his <u>Essays</u>, pp. 155-56.

[65] Ibid.

[66] Ibid.

[67] H. Bland, "The Man's Point of View," in his <u>Letters to a Daughter</u>, pp. 123-24.

[68] H. Bland, "Books," <u>To-Day</u>, July 1886.

[69] Ibid.

[70] Bland, "Men's Love," p. 115.

[71] Ibid., pp. 116-17.

[72] Bland, "The Man's Point of View," pp. 130-31.

[73] H. Bland, "The Rudeness of Women," in his <u>Letters</u>, pp. 161-62.

[74] H. Bland, "Modern Romance," in his <u>Letters</u>, p. 182.

[75] H. Bland, "To a Lady," in his <u>Essays</u>, p. 83.

[76] H. Bland, "The Limits of Flirtation," in his <u>Letters</u>, pp. 98-99.

[77] Ibid., p. 100.

[78] Bland, "The Rudeness of Women," p. 52.

[79]E. Nesbit, "My School-Days," in The Girl's Own Paper, October 1896, p. 28.

[80]Ibid., November 1896, p. 106.

[81]Ibid., April 1897, p. 436.

[82]Ibid., July 1897, p. 635.

[83]Ibid., pp. 635-36.

[84]Ibid.

[85]Daisy Nesbit to Mrs. Nesbit (n.d.), cited in Doris Langley Moore, E. Nesbit: A Biography (Philadelphia: Chilton Books, 1966), p. 45.

[86]E. Nesbit, "My School-Days," September 1897, pp. 788-89.

[87]Ibid.

[88]E. Nesbit, John O'London's Weekly, November 1919, quoted in Moore, E. Nesbit, p. 57.

[89]Nesbit, "My School-Days," p. 788.

[90]Moore, E. Nesbit, pp. 58-59.

[91]Ibid., p. 185.

[92]Edith Bland to Ada Breakell, 1884, in Moore, E. Nesbit, p. 76.

[93]George Bernard Shaw, "Early Days," in The Webbs and Their Work, pp. 7-28.

[94]Edward Pease, quoted in Moore, E. Nesbit, p. 75.

[95]G. B. Shaw to E. Pease, 1898, Shaw Papers, MS 50557, British Library.

[96]E. Bland to Ada Breakell, 1884, in Moore, E. Nesbit, p. 82.

[97]Said speaker, Miss Lydia Becker, tireless leader of the women's constitutional movement, was editor of the Women's Suffrage Journal and parliamentary agent for the National Societies for Women's Suffrage. She was, in addition, "plump, bespectacled, and homely." Constance Rover, Women's Suffrage and Party Politics in Britain

(London: Routledge and Kegan Paul, 1967), p. 57. No
other sources, however, have suggested she possessed
a hippopotamian appearance.

[98]E. Bland to A. Breakell, 1885, in Moore,
E. Nesbit, p. 77.

[99]E. Nesbit, "August," in her Ballads and Lyrics
of Socialism, 1883-1908 (London: A. C. Fifield, 1908),
p. 60.

[100]E. Nesbit, "The Garden Refused," ibid., p. 37.

[101]E. Nesbit," Two Voices," ibid., p. 28.

[102]E. Nesbit, "Here and There," ibid., p. 43.

[103]E. Nesbit, "London's Voices," ibid., p. 39.

[104]Nesbit, "Here and There," p. 43.

[105]E. Nesbit, "Two Lives," in her Ballads, pp.
12-17.

[106]E. Nesbit, "Brothers," ibid.

[107]E. Nesbit, "After Sixty Years," in her Songs
of Love and Empire (Westminster: Archibald Constable,
1898), p. 15.

[108]E. Nesbit, "Evening Prayer," ibid., pp. 162-63.

[109]E. Nesbit, "In Trouble," in her Ballads, p. 76.

[110]Nesbit, John O'London's Weekly.

[111]E. Nesbit, "After Sixty Years," in her Songs,
p. 15.

[112]E. Nesbit, The WouldbeGoods, in her The Bastable
Children (New York: Coward-McCann, 1929), p. 125.

[113]E. Nesbit, The New Treasure Seekers, ibid.,
p. 72.

[114]Ibid., p. 74.

[115]Ibid., p. 121.

[116]Ibid., p. 25.

[117]E. Nesbit, The Treasure Seekers, ibid., p. 138.

[118]Ibid., p. 76.

[119]Ibid., p. 132.

[120]Nesbit, The WouldbeGoods, p. 53.

[121]Ibid., p. 65.

[122]Ibid.

[123]Ibid., p. 276.

[124]Nesbit, The Treasure Seekers, p. 208.

[125]Nesbit, The WouldbeGoods, p. 62.

[126]Ibid., p. 192.

[127]Nesbit, The New Treasure Seekers, p. 89.

[128]Ibid., p. 86.

[129]Nesbit, The WouldbeGoods, p. 263.

[130]Nesbit, The Treasure Seekers, p. 49.

[131]Ibid., p. 114.

[132]Ibid., p. 180.

[133]Ibid., p. 45.

[134]Nesbit, The WouldbeGoods, p. 64.

[135]E. Nesbit, The Railway Children (1906; reprint ed., Middlesex: Puffin Books, 1960), p. 9.

[136]Ibid., p. 114.

[137]Ibid., p. 13.

[138]Ibid., p. 199.

[139]Ibid., pp. 216-17.

[140]Ibid., pp. 9-10.

[141]Ibid.

[142]E. Nesbit, The Phoenix and the Carpet, in her The Five Children (New York: Coward-McCann, 1930), p. 80.

[143]Ibid., p. 233.

[144]Ibid., p. 80.

[145]Ibid.

[146]Ibid., p. 57.

[147]Ibid., p. 152.

[148]Ibid., p. 169.

[149]Ibid., p. 239.

[150]Ibid.

[151]E. Nesbit, The Story of the Amulet, in her The Five Children, p. 7.

[152]Nesbit, The Phoenix and the Carpet, pp. 35-36.

[153]Nesbit, The Story of the Amulet, p. 247.

[154]Ibid., pp. 252-53.

[155]Ibid., p. 253.

[156]Ibid., pp. 167-68.

[157]Ibid.

[158]Ibid., p. 256.

[159]In The Wonderful Garden, written in 1911, E. Nesbit delivered her harshest indictment of servants. They represented both unwanted authority and an uneducated lower class--the worst of all possible combinations in the eyes of the young protagonists. And whether cruel or merely "common" none of the servants in the novel managed to do anything at all to redeem themselves or overcome such a handicap.

[160]Ibid., p. 255.

[161]E. Nesbit, Harding's Luck (London: Ernest Benn, 1961), p. 207.

[162]Ibid., p. 87.

[163]Ibid., p. 251.

[164]E. Nesbit, "My School-Days," The Girl's Own Paper, November 1896, p. 106.

[165]E. Bland to Ada Breakell, 1884, in Moore, E. Nesbit, p. 79.

[166]H. Bland, "Books," To-Day, July 1886.

[167]"Fabian Bland" [pseudonym for Hubert and Edith Bland], The Prophet's Mantle (London: Henry J. Drane, 1889), p. 241.

[168]Ibid., p. 142.

[169]Mrs. Chesterton, The Chestertons, p. 58.

[170]G. B. Shaw to H. Bland, 18 November 1889, in Bernard Shaw: Collected Letters 1874-1897, ed. Dan H. Laurence (London: Max Reinhardt, 1965), pp. 228-29.

[171]E. Bland to Ada Breakell, 1884, in Moore, E. Nesbit, p. 79.

[172]Mrs. Chesterton, The Chestertons, p. 58.

[173]Richard le Gallienne to D. L. Moore (n.d.), in E. Nesbit, by Moore, pp. 116-17.

[174]Moore, E. Nesbit, p. 122.

[175]H. Bland, "Life at Large," in his Letters to a Daughter, pp. 10-23.

[176]Moore, E. Nesbit, pp. 71-72.

[177]Ibid., pp. 102-04.

[178]Mrs. Chesterton, The Chestertons, p. 59.

[179]Bland, Olivia's Latchkey, p. 27.

[180]Wells, Experiment, p. 517.

[181]E. Nesbit, "The Husband of To-Day," To-Day, September 1885.

[182]Mrs. Chesterton, The Chestertons, p. 58.

[183]Wells, Experiment, p. 516.

[184]Moore, E. Nesbit, pp. xx and 161-62.

[185]Ibid.

[186]Bland, _Letters_, p. 100.

[187]Moore, _E. Nesbit_, pp. 120-21 and 196.

[188]H. Bland, "Confidences," in his _The Happy Moralist_, pp. 165-77.

[189]Wells, _Experiment_, pp. 516-17.

[190]Ibid.

[191]According to G.B.S., the big fuss in the Fabian Society had begun as a result of H. G. Wells's attempted affair with Rosamund Bland in 1906. Wells's plans had been foiled by the intervention of an irrate Bland--the more so when he discovered that Wells had told his daughter of his own indiscretions--and a few of his Fabian friends. The episode had not served to endear Bland to Wells or vice versa. Three years later, Wells was more successful, at least temporarily, with Amber Reeves, the daughter of another Fabian couple.

[192]"The Fabian Society," _Scottish Leader_, 4 September 1890.

[193]Melanie Klein, "Love, Guilt, and Reparation," in her _Love, Guilt and Reparation, and Other Works 1921-1945_ (London: Hogarth Press, 1975), pp. 323-24.

[194]According to Wells, both he and Bland were "disposed to great freedoms by the accepted standard." The difference between them was that Wells proposed to make all love-making "licit," whereas Bland's view was "the more barriers the better." Wells, _Experiment_, p. 517. (One wonders how impressed the long-suffering Jane Wells was with these subtle distinctions.)

[195]Bland, "The Rudeness of Women," p. 52.

[196]H. Bland, "If I Were a Woman," in his _Essays_, p. 205.

[197]E. Nesbit, "My School-Days," June 1897.

[198]E. Bland to Miss Sharp, 13 June 1910, quoted in Moore, _E. Nesbit_, p. 244.

[199]E. Nesbit, _The Red House_ (New York: Harper and Row, 1902), pp. 66-67.

[200] E. Bland to Berta Ruck, 1924, cited in Moore, E. Nesbit, p. 298.

[201] E. Nesbit Bland to Mr. Thring, 3 June 1914, Society of Authors Collection, MS 56762, British Library.

[202] E. Nesbit Bland-Tucker to Professor Andrade, 1917, cited in Moore, E. Nesbit, p. 275.

[203] E. Nesbit Bland-Tucker to Harry Nesbit, 1917, ibid.

Chapter 4

THE SIDNEY WEBBS

Sidney Webb, primary architect of Fabianism, served on the Executive Committee for fifty years. He wrote 37 of the 175 tracts published before the First World War, and edited or supplied the information and initiative for a great many more of the Fabian publications and projects. His wife, Beatrice Potter Webb, did not begin to serve on the Executive until 1912, but well before that time she had established herself as a powerful force within the Society, and certainly was so thereafter.

Webb was neither a feminist nor an anti-feminist; he was merely indifferent to such matters. In fact, he was not even sure there was such a thing as a "woman question." Beatrice was a staunch anti-feminist for most of her long life, given to descriptions of the "essential inferiority" of women and their lack of intellectual power. Neither did much to promote the women's cause within or without the Fabian Society; both agreed on the existence of differences between the sexes and advocated measures to maintain those differences.

Yet these two earnest, public-spirited, and extremely industrious souls created a marital partnership which was and remains a model of affection, productivity,

and comradeship. Moreover, if their talents lay in different spheres--they were "second-rate minds," Beatrice
insisted,[1] "but . . . curiously combined"--their roles, at
times, were almost interchangeable. Sidney usually was the
"man of affairs," except when Beatrice took over, and
Beatrice usually was the primary social investigator
except when Sidney predominated. Why it was they maintained one set of views with regard to women's role in
society, and lived their lives according to another, has
more to do with their personal idiosyncrasies, especially
Beatrice's, than with feminist or socialist ideologies.
The relationship one advocates between the sexes, and the
relationships one devises, are often miles apart; the
Webbs, like their Fabian colleagues the Blands and the
Shaws, were particularly adept at maintaining a great
distance between the two.

I. Sidney Webb: The Development of
a Committeeman

Sidney James Webb was born on 13 July 1859, the
second of three children. His beginnings were less than
auspicious. He was brought up in a family firmly ensconced
in the lower middle classes of inner London's shopkeepers
and tradesmen, a class background which was to remain
clearly stamped on his speech and manner. His physical
appearance did little to improve his position: he was
short, like the rest of his family, and ill-favored in

looks. Sidney's intellectual gifts, however, were out of all proportion to his physical stature. Scholastic achievement, which he easily attained, opened a great many doors for him, a fact which he never forgot. Indeed, he spent much of his adult life improving London's educational system and extending its range to those on the lower rungs of the social ladder. He became, in effect, a spokesman for the kind of person he had been, advocating the extension of opportunities from which he had already benefited.

His mother, Elizabeth Mary Stacey, was the stronger and more practical of his parents. One of four children orphaned by the death of their ne'er-do-well father, she had borrowed money from a relative and opened a millinery and hairdressing shop near Leicester Square. A "matter-of-fact woman, somewhat cold,"[2] Elizabeth showed the same determination in running her shop she was to show in launching her children on their educational and professional paths. She informed Sidney, when he was a very small boy watching the Lord Mayor's Show from the steps of St. Martin's Church, that he himself might one day be Lord Mayor of London.[3] No doubt such faith did much to inspire Sidney's own "absurd self-confidence"[4] in his abilities and in his future. In later years, Sidney considered her to have been "a good mother--much better than she is in the least aware of" and felt he owed her "a great deal."[5]

Sidney's father, the son of a Kentish innkeeper,

came to Elizabeth's shop as an assistant and married his
somewhat older employer in 1854. His health was poor and,
in general, he "was managed by his far abler and more
energetic wife."[6] Accounts vary as to his occupation;
he has been described as a hairdresser, tax collector and
public accountant.[7] In time, his main duty seems to have
been keeping the books for the family shop and for various
other businesses in the neighborhood. This allowed him
ample time for his public-spirited interests. He served
on the local Board of Guardians and the Vestry, and he
filled the Webb household with political pamphlets and
radical politics. In 1865 he was a staunch supporter of
John Stuart Mill as candidate for Westminster. It was,
no doubt, the senior Webb's ardent political beliefs and
activities which created the pervasive atmosphere of
Sidney's childhood, that is, of always having been "in
the thick of the fight," of having lived in a "happy
family" but by no means a peaceful one.[8]

Despite a family income of something like £300 a
year, Mrs. Webb managed to educate her children quite well.
She sent Sidney and his brother Charles, eighteen months
his senior, to a decent middle-class school near their
home and to the Continent to learn language skills appropriate to careers in international business. The boys
spent two years in Neuveville learning French, followed
by almost two years living in the home of a Lutheran pastor
in Wismar, mastering German. At this time, sister Ada, six

years Sidney's junior, was sent to a boarding school in
England.[9] She had sufficient intelligence and education
to sit for and pass the Newnham College entrance examinations in 1885. She chose, however, to stay at home and
care for her aging parents. She was "a most capable,
unselfish, and devoted woman."[10]

Upon the brothers' return to London in 1875,
Charles went into clerical work, eventually progressing
to a partnership in a prosperous rubber stamp business.
Sidney's talent and energy were not so easily satisfied.
He took a job in a colonial broker's office but, almost
immediately, began taking classes, first at the City of
London College, then at the Burbeck Literary and Scientific
Institute. Quickly distinguishing himself as exceedingly
bright and able, he won several first-class prizes in a
variety of subjects. Finding himself intellectually
limited by his commercial occupations, he sat the Lower
Division civil service examination in 1881, and became a
clerk in Inland Review. A year later he sat for the
more difficult Upper Division examination, placing second
to Sidney Olivier, a tall, distinguished looking Oxford
graduate. Both were appointed to the Colonial Office and
soon became close friends. Continuing his studies, Webb
read law and was called to the Bar in 1886, having won
£450 in prizes along the way, a sum which more than offset
the £130 which his studies had cost him.

Webb's education and training did not end with

evening classes and external examinations. He also made
considerable use of the debating clubs, study groups, and
political societies which abounded in London in the late
1870's and 1880's and catered to aspiring working-class
reformers and self-improvers. Among others, Sidney belonged
to the Holborn Literary and Debating Society, the Dia-
lectical Society, and the Reform Union. Having absorbed
John Stuart Mill's politics while still a boy, he grappled
with the issues raised in Mill's works with fellow members
of the Zetetical Society. This was a discussion group,
strongly influenced by the ideas of Mill, which met on
alternate Wednesdays to discuss "all matters affecting the
interests of the human race."[11] Mill's stepdaughter,
Helen Taylor, was a member of this group; George Bernard
Shaw joined in 1880, a year after Webb, and first met him
there. Shaw so admired Webb's brilliance and his debating
skills that he thought Webb "quite the ablest man in
England."[12]

Hyperbole aside, Sidney Webb was indeed an extremely
intelligent man, and he had already begun to develop the
style and methods which suited him. With his massive
head, adorned by protruberant features and thick spectacles,
perched atop his short stubby body--itself attended by tiny
hands and feet--he was not in the least prepossessing. He
spoke with a slight lisp in a rapid monotonous manner,
interrupting himself with a steady flow of "ers" and
"ums." His somewhat unkempt appearance, his "bourgeois

black coat shiny with wear"[13] and the absence of "h's"
in his speech clearly identified the class whence he
had come--a political disadvantage in class-conscious
Britain. In short, his public demeanor could never be
characterized as charismatic. He was not the man to move
the masses, but his ability and willingness to digest
voluminous facts and figures and to know more about a
given subject than anyone else, allowed him to shape most
discussions to his way of thinking.

This gift of persuasion, coupled with his public-
spirited concern, made Sidney Webb the quintessential
committeeman. In fact, he lived his life as if "he was
acting as a member of a committee," and he aspired "never
to act alone" or for his own benefit.[14] The role of
committeeman was a comfortable one for Webb in several
ways. It not only made use of his talents and satisfied
his sense of obligation to the community, it provided him
with a situation in which his shyness could be hidden
behind a calculating exterior and disguised by a brash
and brainy arrogance. That he was more comfortable with
numbers than with people is clear. Why his well deserved
intellectual self-confidence did not extend to everyday
social intercourse is less obvious. Perhaps, the lack of
warmth in his family ill-prepared him for convivial society.
The fact that his family "kept itself to itself" and had
"practically no friends"[15] did not help matters. In
addition, his class status and physical appearance were

not such as to inspire confidence in social situations.
Where there was an agenda to be followed, however, or
information to be mastered and dispensed, these considerations mattered little, and Sidney J. Webb was at his best.

In considering Webb's willingness to "submerge"
himself in committees and to forego individual recognition
for much of his work, one ought not to forget the real
enjoyment he derived from his powers of persuasion. "To
play on . . . millions of minds, to watch them slowly
respond to an unseen stimulus, to guide their aspirations
often without their knowledge--all this, whether in high
capacities or in humble, [he found to be of] extravagant
excitement." It was this "big and endless game of chess,"[16]
and not the capacity in which he played it, that fascinated
Sidney. Although he felt that "altruism and emotion"
sanctified the process, his reputation in later years as
a "wire-puller" testifies to the fact that, at times, the
game itself became more important to him than the principles behind it.

* * *

Webb's committeeman mentality was untroubled by
vestiges of religious faith. As a child, he had been taken
to many different churches by his mother, "in search of an
eloquent preacher free from sacerdotalism."[17] And he
claimed to have known then the terrors of Hell. But, by
the time he was twenty he considered himself an atheist;
he accepted Darwin's theories and Huxley's science and,

in doing so, suffered none of the raging conflicts experienced by many of his generation. On the rare occasion he attended church, as an adult, he found himself bored by the sermon and disgusted with the institution. Sidney was equally unimpressed with "the Jesus type"; he had a "vague feeling" that Jesus ought to have "taken it fighting," at least to the extent "of making a reasonable defence."[18] Introduced by his friend Olivier to the teachings of Auguste Comte in 1883, Webb tempered his "irreligious condition"[19] with elements of Comte's religion of humanity. He was never tempted, however, to return to the religion of God.

As Webb began to construct his own version of socialism, he again found Comte's philosophy helpful, particularly Comte's belief in the importance of a governing elite. Given Webb's abilities to manipulate and direct the actions of others, he must have felt little doubt as to where his own place might be under such a scheme. With regard to socialism, however, Sidney was most influenced by the works of John Stuart Mill. He recognized early that the continuous changes in Mill's Political Economy were bringing Mill to the doorstep, if not through the very portals of socialism. Like Mill, Webb based his economic beliefs on Ricardo's theory of rent, but he went beyond Mill's concern with land reform. He extended the theory of unearned income to include returns on capital from manufacturing or commerce. More socialist than Mill, and more democratic, Webb disagreed with Mill's notions of plural voting, open ballots, and a property basis for the local franchise.[20] Yet Webb's endorsement of experts in administrative roles, and of the intelligentsia as mentors for the working classes, bears a close resemblance to Mill's views, with echoes of Comte in the background.

The major difference between Webb's political thought and Mill's evolved out of Webb's concern for the collective whole--the committee rather than the individual. Mill felt government ought to stay out of the affairs of its citizens in all "self-regarding" matters, interfering only when a person's actions impinged upon the lives of others. But for Webb "there [was] no such thing as a self-regarding act"; all of one's actions affect others in the community.[21] Consequently, government ought to regulate or intervene in the lives of its citizens. The unit of measure for Mill remained the individual. For Webb the freedom of individuals was illusory; his concern was for the "higher freedom of collective life."[22]

If Mill's theories were not sufficient grounding for Webb's outlook, neither were those of Marx. In 1884 Sidney had begun to attend meetings of the Hampstead Historic, the socialist study group attended by many of his future Fabian colleagues. There, he read and discussed Das Kapital; in fact he attempted to teach Shaw German using that awesome tome as a primer. But Webb was not impressed with Marx's revolutionary brand of socialism.

Indeed, he spent at least one evening at Hampstead, as he
put it, "gaily dancing on the unfortunate Karl Marx,
trampling him remorselessly underfoot, amid occasional
feeble protest."[23]

Neither class conflict at the barricades nor
political propaganda at the polling booth appealed to
Sidney Webb. He much preferred manipulation in the committee room or the ward meeting. Thus, when he officially
became a socialist, joining the Fabian Society in May of
1885, he joined a group and forged a policy which would
allow him to indulge this preference. His policy was
"permeation," the inseminating of other groups, parties,
or caucuses with one's own ideas. Webb had "permeated"
the fledgling Fabian Society with this policy by 1886, and
set it on its permeating course--a course it was to follow
with only brief interludes of political activism until
after the First World War.

Webb himself assiduously attended Liberal caucuses,
council meetings, and political gatherings of all sorts,
using his considerable talents to get lesser minds than his
to pass resolutions and adopt policies favorable to the
common good--as he construed it. "Evidently," he wrote
to Edward Pease, during the first Fabian dispute over
whether or not to support a separate socialist party,
"I am not a man of action."[24] At that time he regarded
collectivist socialism as "a mere academic ideal like
Plato's republic." He worked toward its adoption, "knowing

that no such change can come for many centuries," and
feeling uncertain as to how it would work when it did
come. Even then, he expected, he would "be a reformer,
wanting a better ideal education."[25]

In later years Webb's committee man's brand of
socialism was at times indistinguishable from Radical
politics or even Conservative policies, but his commitment
to an "ideal" system of education never faltered. Having
made his way from petit-bourgeois beginnings to the level
of Upper Division bureaucrat, via night classes and external
examinations, and on the basis of effort and intellectual
merit, Webb was a convert to the process. At first he
taught extension classes for the Working Men's College
in Bermondsey, and involved himself in promoting the
program. When he became involved in local politics, his
most intense efforts, and his clearest accomplishments,
lay in the development of a rational and comprehensive
educational system.

Webb had resigned his civil service post to run
for the London County Council in 1892, which having been
established by the Local Government Act of 1888 had only
begun to bring a semblance of public order and administration to London. Elected on the Progressive ticket, Webb
served for six years as the chair of the L.C.C.'s Technical
Education Board, a committee which he himself set up. In
that capacity he was responsible for the allocation of
funds being channeled to education from the new duties

on liquor. Webb constructed an elaborate system of scholarships to secure technical and university educations for an
increasing number of students. Still more, this funding
gave him the authority to require the inspection and
regulation of technical institutions throughout the greater
London area, and to introduce new schools into the system.

The most successful school engineered by Webb was,
at first, a private enterprise. He founded the London
School of Economics and Political Science (L.S.E.) in
1895, using some of the funds bequeathed to the Fabian
Society by H. H. Hutchinson for purposes of spreading
socialism. As one of five trustees named by Hutchinson
to administer the money, Webb made the decision to use it
for a school. He then secured the independence of the
Hutchinson trustees from the Fabian Society, amid some
protest, and found additional funds to support the School--
including a grant of £500 yearly from his own Technical
Education Board. Ultimately, he assured the School's
financial stability by maneuvering its inclusion, as the
economic faculty, in the restructured University of London.
In keeping with his pragmatic approach to ideology, Webb
did not restrict the School or its professors to the
teaching of socialist interpretations of history or economics; in fact, the first Director of the L.S.E., William
Hewins, was a conservative economist. This, no doubt,
eased Webb's job in establishing the School; it did not
endear him to a good many of his socialist colleagues.

In like manner, Webb's pragmatic approach to
the "woman question" did not enhance his standing with
feminists. His notions of the collective good precluded
acceptance of arguments for sexual equality, like those of
John Stuart Mill, based on individual liberties. Webb had
even less sympathy with the issues being raised in and by
the plays of Henrik Ibsen: "Perhaps women have got, just
now, to go through the stage of 'self-realization' as the
Ibsenites call it. It does not seem to me a very worthy
ideal. I evidently fail to understand it, for it seems to
me as selfish to try to "realize oneself" as to try to save
one's own soul."[26] Similarly, in response to Shaw's book
on Ibsen in which he advocated greater opportunities for
women,[27] Webb commented, "I can see no alternative to
treating women as human beings, coûte que coûte,"[28] but
he seemed far from enthusiastic about the prospect of
doing so.

Sidney was never blatantly anti-feminist in his
public pronouncements--certainly not in the way that Hubert
Bland was. In Webb's first major tract for the Society,
"Facts for Londoners" (1889), he had declared the Society
in favor of "adult suffrage," that faintly equivocal
term considered insufficient by feminists and revolutionary
by traditionalists. For the most part, Webb was merely
insensitive to the needs of women and oblivious to many
of the problems they faced.

In a lecture to the Fabian in 1891, Sidney

attributed women's general difficulties to the fact that
they were unskilled labor, unprotected by combination, in
a redundant market. If they were paid less, it was usually
for different kinds of work from that of their male counterparts. Their position, he claimed, could be likened to
agricultural laborers; for both groups the solution to low
wages and poor work conditions lay in more education and
increased organization of their members.[29] More than
that, Webb went on to speculate on ways in which women
deserved or, at least, contributed to their lower wages
and lesser status. He pointed to the "general but not
invariable inferiority of productive power, usually in
quantity, sometimes in quality" of women's work, and
suggested that women's low pay in some occupations was
due, in part, to "their lower standard of life and their
incidental inefficiency, especially as to coping with
emergencies."[30] Despite the "imperfect statistics" available, he was also willing to propose that women seemed to
interrupt work for reasons of illness more often than did
men.[31]

Having reduced the "woman question" to an economic
problem, Webb felt no obligation to comment on the subjuga-
tion of women within the family situation. It was clear
to him that women were very different from men, certainly
not "men in petticoats" as Shaw would have it. If different, they were not necessarily inferior to men in all areas
as Hubert Bland was prone to claim; Webb accepted, for

example, Comte's description of women as "inspirers and guardians of morality."[32] But he seemed to have little understanding of the relationship between the sexes or of the difficulties women encountered in that relationship. Further, he seemed little impressed with the talents and abilities of women as a group. As a friendly observer noted in a fictionalized description of Webb, "women moved a little outside his plane, and he was troubled by a feeling of the strange and unaccustomed in dealing with them."[33]

* * *

It was not that Sidney Webb was adverse to romance. According to Shaw, it was easy to tell when Sidney was in love: he always broke out in spots, usually to no avail. When he was twenty-seven, a young woman with whom he was much in love dropped him somewhat unexpectedly and married another. Describing the experience to his close friend, Graham Wallas, he reported that he had remained in the "deepest depth" of Hell for seventeen or eighteen days, then was relieved to discover he "had been moved into a milder compartment, with less flame."[34] Afterwards he felt that the experience had given him "an additional cynicism and hardness." More important, it convinced him that "man is still 9/10th an irrational animal," and demonstrated "how little influence the intellect has, compared with that exercised by the emotions."[35]

In January 1890, Webb was still living at home with

his mother and sister, presumably still feeling, as he put it, "left out" in certain departments of life.[36] He was debating with himself whether or not his civil service position and his political activities were in conflict, and if he ought to become a candidate for Parliament. It was in this state that he met the illustrious Beatrice Potter.

As a result of knowing Beatrice, Sidney claimed, he "was revising his estimate of the feminine mind!" for, he felt, he "must get to understand such an important factor in the world." (In typically Webbian fashion, he hoped that women "won't always resent being considered factors.")[37] If ever a bright young woman could cause an intelligent young man to "revise his estimate of the feminine mind," one suspects Beatrice Potter could have done so. If anyone might have helped Sidney Webb to appreciate the abilities and needs of women who did not want to be reduced to subjection or legislated into the home, that is, of women who did not fit the stereotypical pattern drawn for them, it should have been the independent-minded Miss Potter.

II. Beatrice Potter: The Apprenticeship of a Social Investigator

Beatrice Potter was born in January 1858, at Standish House, in the Cottswolds of Glouscestershire. This was one of four homes among which her large family--

Beatrice was the eighth of nine daughters--and its attendant servants, nurses, and governesses divided its time. Unlike Sidney, whose early life remains enveloped in mystery and petit-bourgeois obscurity, Beatrice's childhood and family life have been amply documented.[38] The picture which emerges is that of a "poor, little, rich girl," badly neglected, emotionally starved, and permanently scarred. Her relationship with her mother was unsatisfactory, although her feelings about her softened after her mother's death. Her sisters were rivals for parental attention, rather than companions in adversity--they brought no solace. Only her father seemed a suitable candidate for her affections, but she was one of many contenders for his.

Not surprisingly, Beatrice suffered from most of the physical complaints unhappy children are prone to manufacture. In time she discovered that "brain work" offered some compensation for poor health and emotional deprivation. Professional ambition, on the other hand, which she gradually began to acknowledge, was a mixed blessing. It was perpetually at war with her emotional needs and her notions of womanhood. In her own case, ambition was the victor. She became, nonetheless, an ardent supporter of the type of mothering she had never had, on behalf of the kind of woman she would never become.

Her father, Richard Potter, was a financial specu-lator of considerable wealth; he was president of British and Canadian railway corporations, and involved in various

timber and construction companies. He was, his mildly
disapproving daughter noted in later years, committed to
profit-making, and utterly unguided by notions of the
public good. Notwithstanding frequent absences, Mr. Potter
"was the central figure of the family life--the light and
warmth of the home. . . . He worshipped his wife, he
admired and loved his daughters; he . . . genuinely believed
that women were superior to men, and acted as if he did."[39]
He discussed with his daughters, "as equals," not only
business affairs, but religion, politics, "and the problems
of sex, with frankness and freedom."[40] Moreover, despite
his business preoccupations, he enjoyed poetry, drama,
history, and philosophy. Obviously, his virtues were
legion, but, according to Beatrice, "his peculiar charm,
lay in his appreciation--his over-appreciation of the
intellect and character of those with whom he lived."[41]
His daughters thought him "far too long-suffering of
Mother's arbitrary moods; [his wife] thought him far
too acquiescent in his daughters' unconventional habits."[42]
When his daughters were adults themselves, his "assumed
clappings or sympathetic groans" continued to be heard,
"through miles of space."[43]

Beatrice's mother, Laurencina Heyworth Potter, had
been raised by an adoring, wealthy father and doting
brothers as "a scholar and a gentlewoman."[44] As a young
woman she wrote political essays and lectures and became
a zealous supporter of anti-corn law legislation. She had

expected a life of "close intellectual comradeship" with her husband, and "intellectual achievement" of her own.[45] But within a year of her marriage in 1844, her first child was born, followed quickly by a second, and a breakdown in her health. The loss of her husband's inherited income in the financial crisis of 1847-48 dashed her hopes for a life of learned leisure. Frequent separations from her husband as he began to make his own way as "a capitalist at large"[46] added to her unhappiness and further thwarted her expectations. Her greatest disillusionment, however, was in her children: "She had been reared by and with men and she disliked women. She was destined to have nine daughters. . . . Moreover, her daughters were not the sort of women she admired or approved. . . . [They] refused to be educated and defied caste conventions."[47]

Laurencina Potter was almost forty, and in frail health, when Beatrice was born. The birth of an only son when Beatrice was four, and his death when she was seven, was "the crowning joy and devastating sorrow" of her life.[48] It separated Beatrice from "her care and attention," and the coming of a youngest daughter, a few months after the death of her son, "completed [their] separation."[49] Mrs. Potter confided to her diary, when Beatrice was still a child, that she was "the only one of my children who is below the average in intelligence."[50] Years later, Beatrice thought this may have explained her mother's "attitude of indifference" toward her; it said little, however, for her mother's prescience.

Throughout Beatrice's childhood, her mother seemed to her

> a remote personage discussing business with my
> father or pouring over books in her boudoir; a
> source of arbitrary authority whose rare inter-
> ventions in my life I silently resented.   I
> regarded her as an obstacle to be turned, as a
> person from whom one withheld facts and whose
> temper one watched and humoured so that she could
> not interfere with one's own little plans.[51]

When she was sixteen, Beatrice mused: "What is this feeling between mother and me? It is a kind of feeling of
dislike and distrust which I believe is mutual. . . . She
is such a curious character, at times . . . wise judgment
and affectionate advice . . . and at other times the spoilt
child comes out so strong in her."[52] It was not until the
last years of her mother's life, when Beatrice was the only
grown-up daughter remaining in the home, that the two began
to understand each other. They discovered that they had
"the same tastes," were "puzzling over the same problems,"
and harbored the same secret ambition to write books.[53]
In fact, Mrs. Potter had written a novel, Laura Gay,
published in 1856, which had not been well received.[54]
Thereafter she had resigned herself to a life of domesticity, punctuated by learning esoterica for its own sake.
Her last project had been to master twelve languages, using
the grammar book of one in the language of another to do
so. After Mrs. Potter's death, Beatrice found that her
mother exercised a far greater influence on her than she

had while she was living. Her mother's "intellectual
strivings," which they had all been "too ready to call
useless," would serve as a stimulus to her own ambition;
her "best habits" she discovered had come from her mother.[55]

It seems unlikely, judging from Beatrice's reminiscences, that she derived much pleasure from her sisters
in her earliest years. In the course of a three month tour
of America with her sister Kate and her father, whose habit
it was to take one or two of his daughters with him on his
extended business trips, Beatrice began to regret the
estrangement. "Hitherto," wrote the fifteen year old
traveler, "I have lived a great deal too much apart from my
sisters, partly from indolence, and partly from my own
unfrank disposition." She had grown "quite fond" of "dear
Kitty," who was eleven years her senior, and wondered why
Kate did not "get on better at home."[56] Possibly, Kate's
independent course of later years--exceeded only by
Beatrice's own--had begun to cause the difficulty.[57]

The sister closest in age and interests to Beatrice
was Maggie; she was also the sister Beatrice most admired.
Four years older than Beatrice, but miles beyond her
in amicability, Maggie was her mother's favorite daughter--
the one who was called for at her deathbed. Beatrice
resolved, upon her return from America, "to make more
a friend of Maggie,"[58] and so she did. The two of them
enjoyed the "Season" together, went on walking and sketching trips, studied Greek and Roman history, and avidly

read and discussed the works of Ruskin, Balzac, Goethe, and Comte. Only on the last named did the two sisters disagree consistently; Beatrice was far more impressed with the "religion of humanity" than was Maggie.

The relationship with Maggie was new to Beatrice; clearly she had experienced nothing like it before. "I do believe I have started on a brighter path of existence . . . with a spirit of love instead of with a spirit of jealous ambition,"[59] she remarked in her diary after a particularly pleasant week spent sketching with Maggie. From 1878, when Beatrice was eighteen, until 1880, Maggie was a "complete companion" to her. The "necessary break" in their "absolute intimacy," brought about by Maggie's marriage to Henry Hobhouse in 1880, was very painful to Beatrice. She felt that Maggie was "not to be replaced."[60]

As Beatrice became more involved with her studies and with thoughts of a career, she occasionally grew concerned that as a result she was "losing ground in the affections of [her] sisters, but she decided it was "no use being over-sensitive"[61] and was not deterred. In later years, Beatrice got on quite well with her sisters, and was closer to most of them than she had ever been as a child. Yet, her unfailing "objectivity" with regard to them shows up repeatedly in her diaries, and testifies to the residual bitterness she felt toward them.[62]

Looking back, Beatrice described her childhood as an unhappy one. It was marred by "ill health and starved

affection and the mental disorders which sprang from
these: ill temper and resentment."[63] She remembered
"long dreary times of brooding and resentfulness" and very
little of "intimacy or tenderness" in her early life: "Its
loneliness was absolute."[64] "Creeping up in the shadow of
my baby brother's birth and death . . . I was neither
ill-treated nor oppressed: I was merely ignored. For
good or for evil, I was left free to live my own little
life within the large and loose framework of family circumstance."[65]

* * *

Beatrice's formal education was limited--chronic
illness, mostly of a psychosomatic nature, kept her out of
the schoolroom. Her "main occupation" from an early age
was reading, continuous and self-selected, from the masses
of books, periodicals, and newspapers available in her
family's houses. She engaged in a "continual struggle to
learn and to think,"[66] an often painful process which did
little to improve her poor health, but satisfied her
intense intellectual curiosity and assuaged, to a limited
degree, the loneliness and boredom of her childhood.

By the time Beatrice was thirteen all pretense at
formal education ended, and the last governess was dismissed. But, by then, she had invented her own method of
acquiring an education: reading books as she chose, then
"extracting, abstracting, and criticising" what she had
read in her private manuscript books. To this she added,

at first only occasionally, "confessions of personal
shortcomings" or reflections on the affairs of others.[67]
Her first entry, written at the age of ten, shows signs
of precocity, as well as a priggishness she never shed.
The education of young girls was, she wrote, sadly lacking:
"The object in reading is to gain knowledge. A novel now
and then is a wise recreation to be offered to a crowing
[sic] mind, it cultivates the imagination, but taken as the
continual nourishment, it destroys many a young mind."[68]

Fortunately, the Potters entertained a number of
interesting guests over the years. Of all the politicians,
literateurs, and businessmen who passed through their
doors, the most important to Beatrice was Herbert Spencer,
a close family friend whom she later christened "the
philosopher on the hearth." Spencer showed concern for
her ill-health, encouraged her in her studies, patiently
corrected her "untutored scribblings" on Greek and Roman
philosophers, and introduced her to the scientific method.
It was from Spencer's First Principles that she began to
fashion an intellectual creed for herself, a task which
proved onerous and unending.

At the age of sixteen, having lost her religious
faith in the thickets of scientific materialism, Beatrice
gave up conventional Christianity. For years afterwards,
however, she was subject to interludes when "the old
religious feeling" returned. The battle between religious
faith and rationalist philosophy continued most of her

life, and was not unlike the one that had been waged by her mother. Beatrice remained an agnostic, but she felt that "one has a faith within one which persists in the absence of direct contradiction."[69] Eventually, she settled on "an intuitive use of prayer as, for one of my temperament, essential to the right conduct of life."[70] She accepted prayer as the medium through which "the soul of man discovers the purpose or goal of human endeavor."[71]

The sudden and unexpected death of her mother in the spring of 1882 "revolutionized" Beatrice's life. It elevated her position in the Potter household, freed her from many of the neurotic symptoms from which she had suffered, and allowed her to begin her search for a career. In the ten "crucial years" which followed, Beatrice intensified her studies and slowly acquired the craft of a social investigator. Neither task was made easier by the concomitant emotional strain of a prolonged and painful love affair.

The changes in Beatrice's life after her mother's death were profound. Instead of being "a subordinate carrying out directions," she became "a principal, a person in authority," her "father's counsellor" and her youngest sister's "virtual guardian."[72] This newfound responsibility was extremely pleasing to Beatrice; running other people's lives seemed to be a particular talent of hers. But, the most revolutionary change, and the most telling, was the one which occurred in her health:

"From being an anaemic girl, always paying for spells of
dissipation or study by periods of nervous exhaustion,
often of positive illness, [she] became an exceptionally
energetic woman, carrying on persistently and methodically
several separate, and, in some ways, conflicting phases
of life."[73]

By this time, Beatrice fully acknowledged her
"restless ambition" for "a life with some result," and
she arranged her schedule accordingly. She set aside the
morning hours for the study of such diverse topics as
English history, algebra, and psychology, then dedicated
the rest of the day to domestic cares and social duties.
But she worried endlessly over the "presumption" of her
ambition:

> All my duties lie in the practical direction, why
> should I, wretched little frog, try and puff myself
> into a professional? If I could rid myself of
> that mischievous desire to achieve, I could defend
> the few hours I devote to study, by the truly
> satisfactory effect it has on my physical nature.
> It does keep me in health.[74]

She felt a continual pull to give herself over completely
to society, to go "with the stream" and please her family:
"It is risking less, . . . walking on a well beaten track
in pleasant company . . . and . . . there is less presumption in the choice."[75]

In the course of 1883, armed with a thorough
knowledge of Spencer's scientific methods, tempered by
Comte's religion of humanity, she determined at last, in
spite of all her reservations, to become a social

investigator. Like many of her contemporaries, her intellectual inquiries had led her "away from the service of God to the service of man."[76] She hoped to apply the scientific method, in which she firmly believed, to the study of society to understand better, and ultimately to improve, the condition of man.

To that end, Beatrice conceived a plan to allow her to meet a "fair sample of the wage-earning class."[77] In the autumn of 1883, she persuaded Martha Jackson, her mother's poor relation and her lifelong companion, a woman Beatrice dubbed the family "saint," to take her to Bacup, Lancashire to visit some of her Heyworth cousins. As "Miss Jones," a Welsh farmer's daughter, Beatrice learned a good deal about the life of cotton operatives, and gained a new respect for their religiosity and their hardworking ways. She also came to appreciate the importance to them of government regulation through factory legislation, and to see how their cooperative societies and dissenting chapels fostered within them the capacity for self-help and self-government.

Delighted with her successful ruse, Beatrice redoubled her intellectual efforts and began to direct her studies more carefully upon her return. She also continued her active social life as hostess of her father's home. In this connection, Beatrice met Joseph Chamberlain, at that time the popular mayor of Birmingham. A handsome, charismatic man, many years her senior, Chamberlain had

recently become a widower for a second time. Beatrice
found him fascinating; she thought at first she would like
to "study the great man," but soon found her feelings were
far too engaged for mere intellectual research.

A desultory courtship ensued during which time
Beatrice agonized over her "longing for love and support
. . . and, beyond this, the desire for the personal pres-
tige and the importance"[78] she would acquire by becoming
his wife. This longing was counterbalanced by a fear that
that very role would also lead to the destruction of her
intellectual identity, of her ability to decide right or
wrong for herself. Chamberlain had made his position quite
clear; he expected respect and agreement from his women,
his daughters and sister as well as his wife, and Beatrice
herself agreed it was a wife's duty to subordinate her
views to her husband's. The relationship between them
was never clearly defined, and never led to even the
promise of an engagement, but Beatrice could scarcely have
experienced more pain if she had been stood up at the altar.
Whenever she saw him, and she went out of her way to do
so, her own conflict flared up anew.

Beatrice decided it was over between them in May
of 1884. She felt depressed and devoid of all ambition; a
few months later she was making out her will and thinking
"kindly" of death. She continued to suffer because of her
feelings for him, even after he had definitively ended the
relationship by marrying a decidedly docile and attractive

American woman. It was not until 1889, six years after
their first meeting, that Beatrice began to consider
herself cured of her malaise.

In the course of those very same years, despite her
pain and confusion, in part because of it, Beatrice slowly
established herself in her chosen field. Aside from nag-
ging doubts about her own ability, reservations about the
propriety of a professional career for women, and occasional yearnings for the happiness of a home and family,
the material circumstances of her life offered several
roadblocks to success. Her father had a stroke in December
of 1885 which necessitated a move to Gloucestershire. The
relocation and additional domestic responsibilities forced
her to give up her work as a rent collector and tenant
organizer at Whitechapel, a "model" housing project in
the East End. The likelihood of a career seemed more and
more problematic. She continued her studies, however, and
eventually worked out a care-taking arrangement with her
sisters which allowed her four months each year in London.
She found that her work acted as "a narcotic," alleviating
her personal misery and helping her to keep society in
perspective.

Joining her cousin Charles Booth in his massive
study of poverty in London, Beatrice began researching the
living and working conditions on the East End Docks. She
learned a great deal from Booth's meticulous and imaginative methods of collecting and interpreting data. "Dock

Life in East London," her first publication, came out in
1887 and again in 1890 as part of Booth's survey, <u>Life and
Labour in London</u>. For her second project Beatrice tackled
sweated labor in the manufacturing trades. Her methods
for collecting data this time were strictly her own, and
extremely daring, to say nothing of exhausting for a woman
of her background. She trained, very briefly, as a "trouser
hand," then proceeded to work, over a period of weeks, in
one after another of the East End's crowded, ill-ventilated,
tailoring establishments. Beatrice, by her own account,
never learned to sew a decent pants leg, but she had a
good deal of success with the information she garnered
while making the attempt. Five of her articles on sweated
labor were published in 1888, including a literary version,
"Pages of a Workgirl's Diary," which appeared in the
prestigious <u>Nineteenth Century</u>.

Beatrice became something of an expert on "sweat-
ing"; she was asked to submit evidence to a Royal Commission on sweated labor, and did so. Her position was that
some kind of regulation was absolutely necessary to ease
the plight of the workers; factory legislation was impera-
tive to protect workers, especially women workers, from the
harsh conditions and meager pay they were forced to accept.
She was quite sure that the central idea behind all of the
labor legislation was "the direct responsibility . . . of
all employers for the welfare of their workers, of all
property owners for the use of their property," and that

a denial of this concept led to the existence of sweated labor.[79] In short, Beatrice had come a long way from the laissez-faire principles and practices of her parents and the traditions of her class.

Judging by the frequency with which her name appeared in the papers in the course of the year, Beatrice Potter was enjoying quite a vogue in 1888. Occasionally she wondered how much of her notoriety she owed to "the piquante coincidence of a pair of black eyes, a supple figure," and "a turn for laborious statistical research?"[80] And she cautioned herself against unwarranted "inflation from a tiny success, after years of depression."[81] But, try as she might to fight against vanity and ambition, Beatrice was "very happy" with her "tiny success." If only, she mused, she had known before that she "should be proved to possess marketable talent," how much easier "all those weary years of struggle with [herself] and the world" would have been.[82]

Despite her many doubts along the way, working life had proved to be very attractive to Beatrice. "It is full of interest and sympathy and . . . it has the element of growth--one is always growing in a working life," she wrote to an inquiring friend.[83] By this time, there were no doubts as to whether she would continue to work as a social investigator, "dedicated to the search after truth."[84] The only question was what her next project would be. Charles Booth suggested "Women's Work in the East End," but Beatrice decided instead on "Co-operation," a topic in which she had become interested during her trips to Bacup.

Beatrice spent most of 1889 observing or reading about the various kinds of co-operative societies. She committed herself, in advance, to the production of a book, a magazine article, and a series of lectures. Having "broken the ice" with a few lectures to a women's trade union, she now felt free to speak when the spirit moved her, and she was confident that, if she had something to say, she could "say it well."[85] Pouring over co-operative journals and congress reports, Beatrice was impressed with the possibilities of co-operation, that is, of a community of consumers, but she began to realize that workers as well as consumers needed to be protected. She determined to study trade unions too, and extended her travels to include such events as the annual Trade Union Congress. She interviewed and made friends with many trade union leaders, as she had with the co-operators. All of this trudging about, unchaperoned, and mingling with working men, was hardly common practice for upper-class, attractive, young women. But then, Beatrice Potter was not a garden variety, upper-class, young woman dedicated to the pursuits of her class and her sex.

*　*　*

Given Beatrice Potter's extraordinary determination "to learn and to think" in her early years, to do something "with some result" once she reached maturity, and the agonizing doubts she suffered along the way, one is not surprised to find in her musings of this period a commitment to "charity and sympathy towards women of my own class who need it." "Every woman," she wrote in her diary of 1887, "has a mission to other women, and more especially to the women of her own class and circumstances."[86] What is surprising in the light of such statements, and given her own accomplishments, is the position she took with regard to the women's movement.

In the spring of 1889, Beatrice was one of the more prominent signatories of an anti-suffrage appeal circulated by the popular author, Mrs. Humphrey Ward. The "appeal" was published in the June issue of Nineteenth Century and created quite a stir, including harsh replies from Mrs. Fawcett and Mrs. Ashton Dilke, strong supporters of the suffrage bill under attack. The proposal merely advocated extension of the franchise to propertied widows and spinsters—the very women who occupied Beatrice's "own class and circumstance." Unlike Mrs. Blatch or Mrs. Pankhurst, Beatrice's lack of enthusiasm for this bill did not stem from the fact that it enfranchised only single women, or from the fact that it pertained only to women of property. On the contrary, Beatrice did not think any women ought to be given the vote.

Years later, looking back on her negative response to women's suffrage, Beatrice came up with several reasons for responding as she had. She was, she claimed,

"conservative by temperament" and "anti-democratic by
social environment." Too, she "reacted against [her]
father's over-valuation of women relatively to men; and
the narrow outlook and exasperated tone of some of the
pioneers of woman's suffrage had intensified this reaction."[87] But, at the root of her anti-feminism lay the
fact that she "had never suffered the disabilities assumed
to arise from [her] sex."[88] Rather, being a woman spared
her the necessity of getting a high paying job, and there
was a certain "scarcity value" attendant upon being one
of the few women in her trade. As a result, she was
answered more quickly when interrogating, published more
readily when writing, and paid higher rates when published.
Thus, she explained, she had not been able to sympathize
with the difficulties of her sex.

Be that as it may, it is difficult to imagine that
Beatrice Potter could not identify with the problems
faced by women because she herself had never suffered
in that way. That she had never suffered--indeed had
prospered under capitalism--did not keep her from decrying
its effects on those less fortunate than herself. It is
harder still to imagine that she consciously wanted to
perpetuate the scarcity value of her place in the profession. If paid more for each article because she was a
woman, how would that matter to one who was independently
wealthy, and given to frugality as well? Such callousness
in a woman driven by notions of duty to mankind is hard to

fathom. What was it that blocked her imagination when it came to a gender and a set of problems more familiar to her?

One can imagine a certain element of opportunism entering into her calculations. Most of the co-operators and trade unionists she was interviewing in 1888-89 were very conservative on the "woman question." No doubt it helped smooth her way, and added to the uniqueness of her position, to be an attractive, "emancipated" woman doing man's work, yet eschewing women's rights. But it is doubtful that Beatrice would have espoused a cause she did not believe in, or would have turned her back on one she strongly supported, merely for reasons of this sort.

More to the point than "scarcity value" or her father's "over-valuation" of women was Beatrice's own attitudes toward the role and aptitude of women in general. Women, she felt, were very different from men; they were far more "subjective." Whether this was true by virtue of their intrinsic nature or their education, she was not sure.[89] She was sure, however, that women were inferior in intelligence, and that the "mental superiority of men" was greatest in her own class.[90] She assumed that even the most intelligent women were intellectually dependent on men, and she felt that this was as it should be, for women are naturally "dependent and receptive."[91] Women's strength lay in their spirituality; their "spiritual function" was "to be the passive agent bearing a man's life."[92]

For Beatrice, the differences between the sexes were not only learned differences, and functional ones, they were instinctive. She believed that women instinctively longed for wifehood and motherhood, as she herself did on occasion. "Nature is strong," she wrote in her diary in 1884, "and cries out for its natural fulfillment."[93] So deep were these instincts, according to Beatrice, that "it is almost necessary to the health of a woman, physically and mentally, to have definite home duties to fulfill . . . [and] someone dependent on her love and tender care."[94] It followed, given these differences between the sexes, that their educational experiences ought to be different too. Women's education should not be strictly intellectual: "Women should have a real knowledge of the different branches of household work." Their knowledge should be sufficient to enable them to distinguish "between bad and good work," and they should be "taught to apply method to the practical duties of life."[95]

To this point Beatrice's views are consistent with her anti-suffrage stand. An inconsistency arises only when one tries to fit Beatrice herself into the Procrustean bed she had constructed for her sex. She was occasionally aware of this difficulty. How, she wondered, was she going to remedy her own deficiencies in household work when she "dislike[d] all mechanical work and [had] an instinctive feeling that it [was] a waste of time if [she could] possibly work [her] brain."[96] She was aware, too, of her own "masculine intellect" and "independence of thought,"[97] and of her "masculine characteristic of persistent and well defined purpose."[98] Yet she never took these traits into account, when formulating her stereotypical views of women.

In similar vein, she ignored her experiences with other women like herself. From the time Beatrice had "taken to philantrophy as a pursuit and a profession,"[99] in 1885, she had come into contact with the "increasing number of women to whom the matrimonial career is shut and who seek a masculine reward for masculine qualities."[100] She continued "to admire and reverence women most who" were "content to be among the 'unknown saints,'" but she felt it was "no use shutting one's eyes" to the growing number of ambitious women.[101] Her opinion of them, however, was rarely flattering:

> There is in these women something exceedingly
> pathetic, and I would do anything to open careers
> to them in which their somewhat abnormal but use-
> ful qualities would get their own reward. They
> are a product of civilization--and civilization
> should use them for what they fit and be thankful.
> At the best, their lives are sad and without joy
> or light-heartedness.[102]

Feeling as she did about such women, it is not surprising that Beatrice did not want to be identified with them. When she first began her work at Whitechapel, she begged her father not to discuss any of her experiences there lest her "reputation as a pleasant ordinary woman" be damaged. "An interesting hard-working life," she wrote him, "with just a touch of adventure! is so delightful, so long as one does not get stamped with that most damaging stamp 'Eccentricity.'"[103] To a certain extent, Beatrice was merely reflecting, and protecting herself from, the Victorian prejudices against working women. But, she seems to have carried this distinction between herself and other career women to an extreme, and to have maintained it even after her work as a social investigator--including her rather "eccentric" adventure as a trouser hand in the East End--had achieved public acclaim, and she herself had attained a degree of notoriety.

When Beatrice signed the anti-suffrage petition, she not only maintained the distinction between herself and other accomplished women, she cut herself off from a good many professional women and the movement they supported. As she noted at the Ipswich Congress, which she attended shortly after the "appeal" was published, "the little clique of 'exceptional women' with their correct behavior and political aspirations gave me most decidedly the cold shoulder: this in a company of men annoys me more than it should do."[104] For Beatrice, the need to stand apart seems to have been far stronger than the wish for approval from her female peers.

Like E. Nesbit Bland, and many anti-feminists before and since, Beatrice was in the anomalous position of supporting a view of women and their role in society which contrasted sharply with the life she led. However,

the mitigating circumstances surrounding E. Nesbit's views
did not apply to Beatrice. In 1889, she was neither
married to a staunch anti-feminist nor surrounded by
little children continually reminding her of the functional
differences between the sexes. She was not married, not
even involved at the time with any serious suitors. The
most important man in her life, her father, who was by this
time severely disabled by a stroke, had always believed in
women's intrinsic worth and intelligence, and had treated
her as an equal and, in the years between his wife's death
and his own illness, as an advisor in business matters.

Beatrice's anti-suffrage stand, I would suggest,
had less to do with the men in her life and more to do
with the women. Her mother had had no use for women
or girls, especially Beatrice. Richard Potter's views
notwithstanding, to be a female child in the Potter house-
hold--at least to be the eighth female child--was to be
undervalued and "ignored." To be a girl in a house full
of girls, all but one considerably older and therefore
more accomplished, and to be too bright to ignore one's
own deficiencies and too angry to forgive one's neglect,
made it very difficult for Beatrice to get the attention
she desperately wanted. To do so she would have to be
different from the other daughters in the house. Perhaps,
the way out of the difficulty was to be like the adored
father or the much loved brother whose birth and death
overshadowed her formative years. One need not accept

Freud's biologically determinist model of penis envry,
to assume that it was not lost on Beatrice that the child
over whom her mother made such a fuss was a male equipped
with the appropriate appendage.

Beatrice's relationship to her mother was bound to
intensify ner negative feelings about herself and by
extension other women. Whether Beatrice rejected her
mother as a result of the maternal neglect she had suffered,
or accepted her mother and adopted her views of women, she
was likely thereby to reject the feminine role. At the
same time, the societal disadvantages of being a woman were
clearly demonstrated by her mother's unhappiness and
intellectual frustrations. Certainly, Beatrice identified
with and emulated her mother's intellectual habits, although
she did not acknowledge this until after her mother's
death. More important, Beatrice internalized her mother's
hostility to her own sex and adopted her views as to
the inferiority of women--an intellectual debt she never
acknowledged at all. She chose instead to think of her
anti-feminist views as a "reaction" to her father's "over-
valuation" of women.

Beatrice did look to her father, however, in other
equally significant ways. She viewed him, and the masculine role, as a way out of the neglect she suffered and
the unimportance society, but most especially her own
mother, attached to her sex. Beatrice clearly identified
with her father, and this identification accentuated her

feelings of penis envy. "Father," she wrote to him in 1885, "I am a sort of weak edition of you! There is no doubt about it."[105] And at some place in her fantasy world, she probably had always hoped this was literally true. Thus, it was a man's world she chose. Having put up with eight sisters, all but one of whom she had never yet been close to, she wanted little to do with the "screeching sisterhood." (This anti-feminist term, denoting militant feminists, was used by many of Beatrice's contemporaries, but Beatrice used the term more frequently than most. It seems to have been doubly significant for her.) Beatrice delighted in conversing with men, and in being treated like one of them. When one of her Bacup cousins told her "you are far more like a male than a female to talk wi[th]," she was pleased enough to note it in her diary and write of it to her father.[106]

Early on, Beatrice found what appeared to her as a "magic wand" which eased her entrance into a man's world, and compensated her for her biological deprivation. A cigarette for Beatrice was far more than a necessary dose of nicotine. Whenever she described herself in her diaries, from her first experiences in Bacup, sitting with her cotton operative cousins, to her interviews with trade unionists and co-operators, to her political intriguing in her socialist salon on Grosvenor Road, Beatrice always depicted herself with a cigarette. "Over a cigarette," "with cigarettes and coffee," much was accomplished. One

never has the feeling, however, that this was simply an
affectation of a rebellious young woman of the 1880's.
Beatrice was not one to cut her hair or affect the aesthetic
style in dress like E. Nesbit and her Bohemian circle.
The cigarette was of far more psychic significance to
Beatrice than an avant-garde fad.

Defending her position to one of the male
co-operators who questioned her signing of the anti-
suffrage appeal, Beatrice agreed that she was "a woman
who is the personification of emancipation in all ways,"
and suggested that she "clings to her cigarette if she
does not clutch at her vote."[107] The vote, in other words,
was not enough for Beatrice. As she confided to her diary,
"defenders of man's supremacy should fight female use of
tobacco with more vigour than is displayed in the female
use of the vote. It is far more fatal to power. It is the
wand with which possible women of the future will open the
hidden stores of knowledge of men and things and learn to
govern them."[108] Beatrice ultimately recanted on her
anti-suffrage stand, as will be seen, although it took her
twenty years to do so. But she never ceased to wish to be
different and to distinguish herself from her sex. As one
acquaintance commented after a disquieting afternoon with
Beatrice in the mid-1890's, she seemed to demand that
"women, at least, recognize that she was a person apart,
unique in her sex."[109]

Despite such demands, Beatrice's male identification

was far from absolute. In her autobiography she writes of
the divisions within her nature as between "an Ego that
affirms and an Ego that denies,"[110] speaking primarily of
the conflict between her scientific beliefs and her religious faith. This same division and oscillation occurred
with regard to her gender identification. There were two
disparate parts to her personality: a dependent, vain,
feminine one which enjoyed her own good looks and her
"definite home duties," and an ambitious, intelligent,
masculine component with a cigarette if no penis and
a fearless approach to social investigation. She kept
the two in harness, but at the cost of continuing psychosomatic illness and a good deal of inconsistency in her
views.

Two men, in particular, helped Beatrice begin to
resolve her conflicts over her sexual role. Although
never completed, this gradual resolution did much to
increase Beatrice's personal happiness and her productivity, especially in later years. It did less well in
undoing her prejudices against her own sex. After her
mother's death, her role as hostess, confidante, and
business advisor for her beloved father began to ease
her anger over having been born an unwanted female. The
affection and attention of her father was a partial compensation for her previous neglect. Too, the success of her
work as a social investigator in 1888-89 began to do much
toward ameliorating old psychic wounds. But, the key

figure in Beatrice's life, the man who was to help her come to terms with her feminine role and her "masculine intelligence"--or at least effect a truce between the two--was the unlikely figure of Sidney James Webb.

III.   The Partnership: One + One = Eleven

Beatrice and Sidney met in January 1890, introduced by a mutual friend who suggested that Sidney might be a useful resource for Beatrice in her work on co-operatives and trade unions. He was indeed; at their first meeting he drafted a list of relevant manuscripts, periodicals, and records for her. Thus began one of the oddest court-ships, and most productive partnerships, in recent British history.

Beatrice's first impressions of Sidney's exterior and demeanor, noted in her diary, were hardly flattering, but she "liked the man" and saw qualities in him not usually discerned by many of his associates. "There is," she wrote, "a directness of speech, an open-mindedness, an imaginative warm-heartedness which will carry him far."[111] Too, she was impressed with the "encyclopaedic character of his knowledge," and with his genuine and disinterested faith in collectivism.[112] Still more, she was grateful to him: "It was in my first conversation with you last winter that it flashed across my mind that I was, or ought to be, a Socialist--if I was true to the conclusion I had already reached; and by this sudden self-revelation you saved me months, perhaps years, of study."[113]

Sidney, for his part, was flattered by the interest she seemed to take in his work, by her invitations to dine or to visit her at Box House, the Gloucestershire home she shared with her invalid father. One suspects he was smitten rather early in the game--it is not known whether or not he broke out "in spots." At a conference in Glasgow, four months after their first meeting, they came to a "working compact," and Sidney promised "to realize that the chances are a hundred to one that nothing follows but friendship."[114] Subsequent letters indicate how little able or willing Sidney was to keep to the bargain. His occasional outbursts of love, however, never seemed to advance his suit in the least. They only brought forth sad recrimination or stern admonitions to desist. "If you do not take care--you will frighten me back into acquaintanceship. . . . Beware how you tread!"[115] she warned him. "If I find our friendship leads to constant perplexity and anxiety on my side, or if I find that it leads to surmises and expectations in the minds of others, I shall retire absolutely and entirely from it."[116]

Devastated as he was by unrequited love, Sidney assured Beatrice that no matter how she behaved toward him she need not worry that, by continuing their friendship, she would wreck his life: "I am too strong and too ascetic for that. . . . I [am] in love, as Austria goes to war, with 'limited liability.'"[117] Moreover, for all his self-professed deficiencies in the courtly arts, Sidney's

mind was equal to the task, and his ploy was subtle:

> I really must have a Mentor outside the working
> circle, a looker-on who sees most of the game,
> and I hope you will not refuse to repeat the experi-
> ment (as opportunity serves) which has been so
> successful. Another time, if you will allow me
> the chance, I should like to discuss with you the
> general plan of campaign, the arrangement of the
> long rolling fight . . . into which the Fabian
> Society, and I in particular, am being . . .
> drawn.[118]

With this request Beatrice could find no fault. To

smooth the edges of this rough-hewn reformer, to apply her

much wider knowledge of society (her "university" as she

called it) to some of his ideas and methods, and to elimi-

nate the too patently petit-bourgeois elements from his

manner and dress, was indeed an attractive opportunity.

Accordingly, in one letter she suggested that he "not talk

to people in general" about the way he was "edging" into

different organizations and not speak of his "small suc-

cesses" along these lines. "The general impression," she

cautioned, "seems to be that you are manipulating."[119]

"If I were your sister," she wrote him on another occasion,

"I should end up with three small pieces of advice: However

old your coat may be (and that is of no import) brush it.

Take care of your voice and pronunciation: it is the chief

instrument of influence. Don't talk of 'when I am Prime

Minister,' it jars on sensitive ears."[120] Her most fre-

quent injunction, however, was that he "look after the

breadth of the English vowel." Prefiguring Shaw's

Professor Higgins, she also urged that Sidney not "refuse
to recognise the individual existence of 'or,' 'ir,'
'ow,' 'a,' and confound them all in a common 'er.'"[121]

Beatrice was obviously willing to take Sidney in
hand, and to see this project as part of "the women's
role." She suggested that the process was "part of the
mother's instinct," and was the source of "that subtle
usefulness" in friendships between the sexes which existed,
of course, as long as such friendships were "not blurred
by the predominance of lower feeling."[122] But even
Beatrice had trouble at times reconciling the control she
exerted over Sidney with her theories on the relative
superiority of males and the natural dependency of women:

> Would you like to set me a paper on Marshall's
> book (Principles of Economics) and make me work
> out some new diagrams? In that case I shall be
> at your feet, and not you at mine, a wholesome
> reversal of the relationship--more in keeping
> with the relative dignity of Man and Woman--
> bringing into play a formative influence from you
> to me--which will relieve the one-sided strain
> of our relationship.[123]

On a good many occasions, however, Sidney's
unmatched skills at absorbing information and disgorging
it in rapid fire speech or legible longhand provided
sufficient means for a "reversal of the relationship."
And Sidney was not loathe to advance his suit on these
grounds: "I could be as great an adjunct to your intellectual life as you are to my moral being . .. together
we could move the world."[124] In response to the proofs
of her first book on the co-operative movement, he wrote:

"Shall I be quite candid? Do not take it amiss if I
confess to a slight feeling that you have taken too long
over it. The book will not be a very great work; and you
could have written it more quickly."[125] Sidney was even
less encouraging about Beatrice's decision to write a
second book on trade unions: "What I grudge is the spending of your time in the mere (!) writing. Your role is to
think and inspire--you do not write quickly or easily."[126]

His solution to such difficulties was, of course,
to combine forces. The number of pages he himself was
turning out during this period, with lengthy articles for
The Speaker, Nineteenth Century, the Financial Reformer,
and numerous others, in the midst of a good many tracts
written and lectures delivered on behalf of the Fabian
Society, as well as a book, Socialism in England, and the
beginnings of another on the eight-hour day reform movement,
was truly remarkable. "One plus one," he assured her, did
not equal one, but "eleven." She was "not fit to write
this big book alone," but once he got started on it, he
was sure that his would be "the indispensable help which
will turn a good project into a big book."[127]

Eventually, after a year and a half of "shattering"
letters from Beatrice, telling Sidney she could never
love him--and from Sidney, assuring Beatrice that in the
interests of the greater good, he would settle for less--of
progress and setbacks, and of an incredibly single-minded
pursuit on Sidney's part, Beatrice relented. "I cannot

tell how things will settle themselves," she wrote in her diary in May 1891, "I think probably in his way."[128] Not surprisingly, her decision was made in the course of their joint coverage of the Lincoln Co-operative Congress. Beatrice and Sidney were engaged in June, but fearing to cause her father pain, they kept the engagement a secret until after his death. "The world will wonder," Beatrice mused shortly after their engagement. "On the face of it it seems an extraordinary end to the once-brilliant Beatrice Potter . . . to marry an ugly little man with no social position and less means whose only recommendation--so some say--is a certain pushing ability."[129]

They were married six months later, in July of 1892. By this time, Sidney had given up his post at the Colonial Office, and campaigned for and been elected to the London County Council. He had also begun to help Beatrice on her "big book"--the first of their many collaborative efforts. The odd quirk in their relation-ship, which began in their courtship, solidified as did the division of labor between them. Beatrice continued to play the "mentor" and to run Sidney's life, while continuing to think of herself as the weaker and more dependent of the two, referring to Sidney as "the pre-dominant partner of the firm of Webb."[130] She was the partner most concerned with research; he was the active partner, involved in political affairs.

Outward appearances to the contrary, Beatrice had

done extremely well. To marry an energetic, brilliant reformer whose goals matched hers, yet who was not, like Chamberlain, "a leading politician to whose career [she] would have in the end to sacrifice [her] own,"[131] was of the utmost importance to her. Moreover, Sidney had determined from the start not to allow their relationship to get in the way of her work--to be a help not a hindrance-- and this was certainly the case. He habitually rescued her from the fatigue induced by her ambitious research projects, taking over the often onerous task of making sense of the endless numbers of facts and figures.

Beyond this, in marrying Sidney, Beatrice married a man who was completely and abjectly in love with her, a man who had "never wooed another woman,"[132] at least not successfully, and whom she would never have to share. Other women "bored" him, he had little time for friends; his universe was work, and Beatrice was its sun. Such undivided devotion was a powerful inducement to love, and a continuing comfort, to a once neglected little girl.

Beatrice brought to the relationship a great deal, often more than she was willing to acknowledge. Sidney was dependent on her not only for her adroitness in social matters, for her greater familiarity with polite society and the political leaders who belonged to it; he was dependent upon her for warmth, tenderness, and human feeling. When he first met Beatrice, his involvement in his work had been so complete, he did not number the hours devoted to it, for he "did nothing else." The loving comradeship he found with Beatrice expanded the "cramped and joyless life"[133] he was leading and made him content. Without her, he remained in danger of losing his connection to the world of sentiment and emotion, of spiritual and philosophical speculation, amidst his preoccupation with statistical abstracts and political agendas. As he himself suggested, only half in jest, "his relation to the universe, in the spiritual sense," consisted in his "relation" to Beatrice.[134]

Given Sidney's personal asceticism, one can assume that the existence of Beatrice's fortune was, as he claimed, more a deterrent than an inducement to courting her. After their marriage, however, Beatrice's inherited income of £1,000 a year probably did much to ease Sidney's formerly "cramped and joyless life." It certainly freed him from the necessity of working merely for the sake of an income. Both Beatrice and Sidney remained true to their own theories of ethical conduct, arrived at independently, and sought to repay the community in unpaid or poorly paid work for their unearned income; they worked far harder for their money than most. But they had the "luxury" of pursuing "truth," or their version of it, and of engaging in public service, untainted by notions of profit or monetary self-interest.

* * *

In keeping with their public-spirited notions, and with the frugality with which Beatrice's mother had administered her home, Beatrice provided "her boy" with "simple fare," sufficiently nourishing to keep them both working at top capacity. She continued to worry, however, about "the dross" in her nature, that "strong strain of the vain worldling" she had not completely eliminated. "Thank the Gods," she wrote, "there is no trace of such feelings in Sidney."[135] Sidney's salutory effect on her social vanity was well matched by Beatrice's softening effect on Sidney's style. After only three years of marriage, he had "lost his aggressive, self-assertive tone, the slight touch of insolence which was only another form of shyness."[136] They had, she declared, "a perfect union of hearts and heads!"[137]

Beatrice felt the "setting" she established for Sidney suited him, "both in reputation and taste. It satisfies his sense of consistency to adhere to a democratic standard of expenditure; and yet he reaps many of the advantages, in the scope and variety of social intercourse, of belonging to the inner circle of the political and scientific world."[138] This setting was located within "a hard little house"[139] at 41 Grosvenor Road on the Thames Embankment, which they rented for almost forty years. It consisted of ten rooms, sparsely but comfortably furnished, the most important of which was the workroom on the ground floor. The workroom doubled as a dining

room; it was long and narrow, lined with a multitude
of shelves filled with books and blue-books offset by
occasional engravings and photographs of three generations
of Beatrice's family. The Webb establishment was staffed
by two maids, one of whom remained with them for thirty
years, and a personal secretary who aided in their research.

The Webb partnership was neither blessed nor
burdened with children. According to Beatrice, she and
Sidney decided against having children because she was
"too old" (thirty-four) when they were married, and too
worn out with ten years of "brain work." If she had been
younger and had had the choice, she had "no doubt" she
would have chosen motherhood.[140] Unlike Charlotte Shaw,
moreover, Beatrice did occasionally lament the fact that
she had had no children. She talked wistfully in later
years of their having wanted a "Sunday baby," one to be
played with only on their day off.[141]

Despite the fact that Beatrice's attitude toward
sex was consistently Puritanical, such views cannot account
for her childlessness. She was certain that "the world
could do with a good deal more physical self-control . . .
and disinterested love."[142] She rejected "free love"
because it meant sex "for its own sake and not for the
sake of bearing children. And that way madness lies."[143]
And she felt strongly that "man will only evolve upwards
by the subordination of his physical desires and appetites
to the intellectual and spiritual side of his nature."[144]

Nonetheless, it seems doubtful that Beatrice and Sidney maintained a celibate marriage, as did the Shaws. There is, for one, ample evidence of physical affection between them. In the first years of their marriage, Shaw was given to complaining about their incessant "spooning" during the working holidays he shared with them. Beatrice herself referred to the "intervals of 'human nature'" in which she and Sidney indulged,[145] and to the "showers of kisses" which usually resolved any temporary differences that arose over their work.[146] Moreover, in her many references to the fullness of their love and the completeness of their perfect union, there is nothing to suggest any sexual restrictions.

One might speculate that, rather than an aversion to conceiving a child, Beatrice may have had grave reservations about taking care of children. Having received insufficient mothering herself, Beatrice might not have wished to mother; having witnessed the painful consequences of motherhood on her own mother, she might not have wished to inflict them on herself. And one wonders if Beatrice was anxious or willing to share with a child the kind of "mothering" Sidney lavished upon her in his single-minded concern for her well-being, her work, and her happiness. Certainly, the absence of children spared Beatrice a good deal of additional conflict over her role as a woman and as a social scientist, and allowed her time and energy to pursue her work.

The Webbs lived their lives according to a well thought out plan, and they divided their energies judiciously. They researched or wrote for four hours every morning. After lunch Sidney went off to his committee meetings and administrative work; Beatrice rested, visited, read, or worked a little longer at their current project. Their evenings were often spent in the company of friends, fellow workers, students, politicians, or philanthropists-- depending upon what their current interest dictated. The dominant theme of conversation was almost always "social reconstruction"; the evenings the Webbs considered most successful or enjoyable were those in which they learned something, or introduced useful people to those for whom they might be of use, or when they gained support for a pet project.[147] The three month summer holiday of the L.C.C. usually found them gathering data in provincial towns or writing up their results in the country. They often shared their rented summer homes, especially in the early years, with Shaw or Wallas. On these extended vacations they followed the same routine, but included exercise in the afternoon. After 1895, when they purchased bicycles, their favorite recreation was careening through the countryside while discoursing on their current topic of research or the latest political development.

Early on, the Webbs had determined to make their "little home the intellectual headquarters of the Labour Movement," by the writing of tracts, minority reports, and

newspaper articles for labor leaders less able to do so
than they. They hoped thereby "to direct the aims and
methods of the popular party" on questions on which they
considered themselves experts.[148] By the beginning of the
twentieth century, the aims of the Webbs had changed. In
part, their distaste for many of the socialist and trade
union leaders had altered the Webbs' original purposes;
in part, their own shifting interests were responsible for
this change. In the opening years of the century, the
Webbs enjoyed a certain chic, first with Liberal Imperialists, then among Conservative, aristocratic circles. Both
the L.S.E. and Sidney's work on the Conservative Education
Bill were very important in this regard. "It is always
worthwhile . . . to meet those who really have power to
alter things," Beatrice mused after an evening spent with
her favorite Prime Minister, Arthur Balfour.[149]

The Webbs' perfect union, for all its salutory
effects, did involve a certain number of limitations for
each partner. For one, Beatrice steadfastly advised Sidney
not to go into Parliament. Her reasoning centered primarily
on the distastefulness of the parliamentary process as
opposed to the "real" administrative work he was doing on
the L.C.C., and on the special skills of Sidney himself.
No one was more ruthless than Beatrice in enumerating
Sidney's liabilities as a "popular leader." But, as she
confided to her diary, she was, on occasion, suspicious
of her own motives in this regard:

> I sometimes wonder whether I am right in inclining
> Sidney not to go into Parliament. . . . I do not
> feel confident that he would be a big success in
> the House. . . . And then a parliamentary career
> would destroy our united life; would cut at the
> root of a good deal of our joint effort. Perhaps
> that is why I distrust my dislike of his going
> into Parliament; it would take so much away from
> me, personally, would add so many ties and incon-
> veniences. Sooner or later I suppose he will have
> to make the sacrifice--but better later than
> sooner.[150]

Whether Beatrice's needs stood in the way of
her good judgment, or merely coincided with it, is open to
question. At least one journalist of the time proclaimed
Sidney one of the "Men Who Ought to be in Parliament,"
claiming that Sidney's "ability to make himself clearly
understood," his "knowledge of both bookshelves and council
chambers," and his many accomplishments at the L.C.C. were
sufficient to offset defects of style and speech.[151]
Sidney himself seemed willing enough to follow Beatrice's
lead on this. He did not enter Parliament until 1923.[152]

If Sidney's presence and devotion were necessary to
Beatrice's well-being, Sidney himself had the same need of
Beatrice. While she was researching in the provinces and
he was administering in London, he wrote dolefully:

> The apparent advantage of dividing our forces is
> delusive, I have been horribly impressed all this
> week with the loneliness of life except when you
> are there. . . . I get thoroughly nervous and
> depressed, and am miserable; unable to work, or
> read in the evenings. . . . I have been strangely
> incapable. . . . I am afraid . . . we must not
> count on being able to increase our output by
> working apart.[153]

And he too nurtured an image of her which had the effect of

limiting her, which kept her at his side, and behind the
scenes. It was one thing to be manipulated by one's wife,
quite another to be upstaged by her. He was not overly
anxious for her to be involved in the Fabian Society,
for example, unless her services were absolutely necessary.
Thus, Beatrice declined her first invitation to lecture to
the Fabian, writing to Edward Pease: "Not only does my own
courage fail me, but the hidden masculinity of Sidney's
views are discovered in his decided objection to my figur-
ing among the speakers. See how skin-deep are those
professions of advanced opinions, with regard to women,
among your leaders of the Fabian Society."[154]

For her part, since she thought of herself as a
social investigator, and feared tainting her work by
attempts at reform and agitation, she was willing to remain
merely an "observer" in the Fabian Society for many years.
Despite this apparent reticence, the ramifications of
Beatrice's influence were wide: she guided Sidney, he
maneuvered the Fabian Executive, it controlled the Society
itself, and its members then set about permeating a good
many other political social organizations to bring about
desired reforms. As she crowed just before she and Sidney
took off on a nine month tour of America and Australia in
1898:

> We can now feel assured that with the School as
> a teaching body, the Fabian Society as a propa-
> gandist organization, the L.C.C. Progressives as
> an object lesson in electoral success, our books
> as the only elaborate and original work in economic

fact and theory, no young man or woman who is
anxious to study or to work in public affairs can
fail to come under our influence.[155]

No wonder Beatrice was content with what she called "wife's
politics."

In research, however, Beatrice claimed "equality of
recognition."[156] It had been her desire "to discover the
process of social organization" which had sparked Sidney's
interest.[157] In all of their joint research, and for much
that was undertaken singly, the Webbs followed a similar
plan of attack. Beatrice planned the project and was
responsible for formulating the initial questions. Beyond
that she did most of the interviewing, whereas Sidney took
on the larger share of analyzing the endless reams of data,
statistics, records, and minutes of proceedings. Beatrice
usually did a rough draft of a chapter; then Sidney sorted
it out and rewrote it or they worked on it together. Though
Sidney did much of the writing, he did it according to
Beatrice's design.[158]

Their first joint effort, History of Trade Unionism,
published in 1894, was an outgrowth of Beatrice's work on
co-operative societies. The ponderous volume devoted to
the growth and development of trade unions was a mass of
data in search of a theory, a flaw they corrected in their
second tome, Industrial Democracy (1897). In this book,
which was well-received, they analyzed their material and
presented a point of view. Trade unions were necessary,
they claimed, to maintain some equality between the

economic power of the employer and that of the employee,
for "in the higgling of the markets" the freedom of workmen
is only a delusion. They would be one of many institutions
necessary in modern society, if people were "to regain
collectively what has become individually impossible."[159]
Trade unions, the Webbs affirmed, and illustrated with
endless examples, were structured along principles of
democracy: their regulations, although at times seemingly
contradictory, usually functioned to serve the needs of the
members they regulated. They aided in the development of
the personal character of their members as well. And, at
a time when trade unions were but weakly established, the
authors predicted, with some prescience, that unions would
play an important role in the fully democratic state of
the future.

The Webbs' next project, a study of local government, which they began upon their return from America, was
to occupy them intermittently for the next thirty years.
This too was directed by Beatrice, although the preference
for governmental solutions came from Sidney. But Beatrice
also had come to see that "to the Government alone could
be entrusted the provision for future generations."
Universal education, public care for the destitute, the
sick, and the aged, that is, "provision according to
need," involved enterprises outside the "characteristic
activities or desires" of "voluntary organizations" of
consumers or producers.[160] The social institutions which

had gradually taken on most of these duties thus far were local units: parish vestries, county justices, municipal corporations, and, after 1834, boards of guardians. If these bodies were to grow apace with the needs of the governed, it was necessary to discover by what means they were governed, how they had arisen in the past, how they were currently expanding, and how they might be best fitted for the additional tasks they would be undertaking. Such was the task Beatrice envisioned for the Webb partnership.

She outlined a study of the structure, function, and social environment of English local government from the Poor Law Act of 1834 to their own time. But the project proved far more complicated than they had imagined, and they discovered that most local bodies were so firmly rooted in the period between 1688 and 1832 that it would be impossible to restrict their study to the period which followed. Consequently, the Webbs' first volume, published in 1906, covered the development of the parish and the county between 1689 and 1834. It was a dry-as-dust affair, of even more limited interest than their earlier works, although they themselves found local government much more interesting to study than trade unions.

In 1908 the Webbs issued two more volumes for the period before 1834 on the manor and the borough. And in 1920 a fourth volume, Statutory Authorities for Special Purposes, completed their work on local government before 1834. In addition to these, they also published an

occasional study on the workings of particular local
authorities, such as "The History of Liquor Licensing,"
or "English Prisons under Local Authorities." Only in
the case of the poor law did they complete their task as
originally planned. In three volumes, published between
1925 and 1929, they analyzed the structure and function
of boards of guardians from their inception to their
abolition by the Local Government Act of 1929.

In spite of her substantial contribution to the
intellectual content of their work, Beatrice was prone to
comment that Sidney was "stronger brained" than herself,
and able to accomplish four times what she could do,
and that she needed hours to "brood," while he worked
on with machine-like efficiency.[161] (Of course, some of
what she called "brooding" went into the making of a
diary which in the end would be at least as useful to
students of history and sociology as the weighty tomes
composed by the partnership.) "I look at Sidney writing
away," she wrote to Graham Wallas while they were completing their last chapter of Industrial Democracy, "and feel
the essential inferiority of the woman."[162]

It did not seem to matter to Beatrice that Sidney's
fluency with pen and paper and, what Wallas called, his
"almost incredible force and industry"[163] were not in
the least representative of the average intellectual
male.[164] Beatrice inferred from his superior capacity
for work that she herself was inferior in this regard,

and generalized from this to the "essential inferiority"
of all women. Thus, she maintained and justified a set
of long-standing prejudices, many of which were patently
absurd. "I do not much believe," she wrote in 1894, "in
the productive power of women's intellect":

> Strain herself as much as she may, the output is
> small and the ideas thin and wire-drawn from lack
> of matter and wide experiences. Neither do I
> believe that mere training will give her that
> fulness of intellectual life which distinguishes
> the really able man. . . . Think of the many
> hours . . . I idle and mope away simply because
> I can only work my tiny intellect for two or three
> hours at the most.[165]

Similarly, Beatrice reasoned that her ill health--
the insomnia and indigestion which chronically plagued
her--were a sure sign of her own frailty and of that
of women in general. And she persisted in this belief in
spite of the hardiness she showed in a variety of situations. Her speed and stamina on walking or cycling trips,
for example, exhausted many a male companion; her energetic
forays into various provincial towns and cities often left
Sidney utterly depleted. As she admitted in one of her
more candid moments, their stays in rented rooms and
"rough boarding houses" were much harder on Sidney than
on her; he felt the discomfort far more than she did.
"No doubt," she rationalized, "my greater intentness on
the enquiry makes up for a good deal in my case. In his
case the need for investigation is not a part of his
personal life and aims, which are administrative."[166] Just
so she confided:

> Between this diary and myself, I get on better
> at the actual investigation when Sidney is not
> here: he is shy in cross-examining officials . . .
> he hates life in provincial lodgings and seeing
> each day new people. . . . And I am more ruthless
> in exercise of my craft when he is not there to
> observe and perchance disapprove of my little
> tricks of the trade.[167]

Given the disparity between Beatrice's comments about herself and her actual accomplishments, perhaps it is not surprising that she wrote of the "holiness of motherhood" and its "infinite superiority to all occupations for women,"[168] yet remained childless herself. Both the Webbs talked of their pet projects, the L.S.E. and the New Statesman, as their "children"; Sidney, in particular, granted them the kind of attention and selfless care one usually reserves for one's progeny. Unlike Beatrice, however, he showed no signs of having missed the real thing.

*   *   *

The corporate Webb view of the "woman question" reflected Sidney's basic indifference to women, other than Beatrice, and his continued lack of sympathy with the individualist aims of the feminist movement. Too, it reflected the aims of the Webbs as socialists, concerned with working-class problems, a fact which involved them in some very real differences and disputes with the aims, and the leaders, of the feminist movement. Still more, it reflected the distortions in Beatrice's perceptions of herself and her sex, as well as her distaste for being involved with women's politics, that is, with being too closely identified with women--or as a woman.

For all his seeming obtuseness on this issue, Sidney was more alive to the importance of women's politics than Beatrice. During their courtship, he had written to her: "I think you will one day feel the need of more obviously and actively 'repenting' about women's suffrage. Are you acting quite 'honest' about that?"[169] And some months later: "I could wish that you cared to take part in the women's movement in politics . . . but do not cultivate the anti-male prejudice."[170] That it took Beatrice a full fifteen years to "repent," and she never did become active in the women's movement, might be viewed as some indication of Sidney's scant influence on her-- despite her usual claims that he had her "on the lead."

For her part, Beatrice continued to be one kind of woman, while extolling the virtues of another:

> If women are to compete with men, . . . to vie
> with men in acquisition of riches, power or
> learning--then I believe they will harden and
> narrow themselves, degrade the standard of life
> of the men they try to supplant and fail to stimulate
> and inspire their brother-workers to a higher qual-
> ity of effort. And above all, to succeed in the
> struggle they must forego motherhood. . . . And
> what shall we gain? Surely it is enough to have
> half the human race straining every nerve to outrun
> their fellows in the race for subsistence or power?
> Surely we need some human beings who will watch
> and pray, who will observe and aspire, and above
> all, who will guard and love all who are weak,
> unfit or distressed?[171]

One imagines Shaw's retort--straight from his Quintessence of Ibsenism of two years before--to such an outpouring.

Perhaps half the race must "observe and aspire" or "guard and love" the distressed. Need that half all be women? Are all women so constructed? Obviously, Beatrice was no more influenced by Shaw than she was by Sidney on the question of women.

Yet, in the privacy of her diary, Beatrice did wonder whether her views as a collectivist should have some positive bearing on the "woman question." Collectivists believed, after all, that man "should be enlisted and paid directly by the community"; should not women too, she pondered, "be enrolled as servants of the community?" Should not socialists support the "Endowment of Motherhood, . . . raising the 'generation and rearing' of children into an art through the elaboration of a science?" Is not the breeding of future generations "a vastly more important question" than that of the social organization of adult men and women?[172]

After formulating this rather reasonable case in favor of the payment of mothers by the community--an issue taken up by the Fabian Society some fifteen years later-- Beatrice concluded instead:

> But for all that, we cannot take up the Women's question. We cannot hope to attack individualism . . . in its stronghold of the Home and the Family, entrenched behind current religious morality and custom, before we have replaced it by deliberate collective rule in the factory, the mine . . . where anarchy stands condemned, by the great bulk of the people, as meaning oppression and gross injustice between man and man. . . . We can but leave this problem reverently to our children:

preparing their way by cutting at the roots of
prejudice, superstition and rotten custom.[73]

In characteristic fashion, directly after dismissing her
own argument in favor of the "endowment of motherhood,"
Beatrice turned around and impugned her motives for doing
so:

> Often I wonder whether we do our full duty in
> this respect: whether we do not acquiesce timidly
> in the prevailing thought and feeling on these
> remote issues in order to diminish the friction
> for these reforms we have in hand? If so, we
> are short-sightedly practical--we attain our
> means but lose our end.[174]

This candid attempt to see the issue from both sides and
to question her own purposes illustrates one of Beatrice's
most attractive qualities. Still, given the evidence, one
doubts that timid acquiescence had anything to do with the
matter at all.

Beatrice's occasional attempts to understand both
sides of an argument did not apply, at least not for many
years, to the question of votes for women. In retrospect,
she claimed to have realized her mistake regarding women's
suffrage shortly after signing the manifesto against it in
1888.[175] This was hardly the case. As late as 1897, a
female medical student described Mrs. Webb to their mutual
friend, Graham Wallas, as less than enthusiastic for
the cause: "She has suddenly gone very strong against
suffrage, and I long to hear her talk about it."[176]

The one organization with which Beatrice was
associated at about this time, the National Union of Women

Workers, was on record as being opposed to women's suffrage. The N.U.W.W. was not a trade union but a group of women interested in women's issues and women's work. It was dominated by its executive of decorus and dignified bishops' wives whom Beatrice thought "a nice lot, . . . large-minded . . . [with] the pleasant manners of the great world."[177] Louise Creighton, wife of the Bishop of London and guiding spirit of the Union, was a good friend of Beatrice.[178] On at least two occasions, after the N.U.W.W. Conference in Manchester and after the International Women's Congress (1899) in London, Beatrice noted that the "screeching sisterhood" was "trying to invade" the N.U.W.W. She was sure, however, that "Louise's battalions" would "resist the attach."[179] "To the well-bred and conventional ladies who dominate it [the N.U.W.W.] the 'screeching sisterhood' demanding their rights represents all that is detestable."[180]

It is an interesting commentary on Beatrice's antipathy to even the most "well-bred" of women's organizations, that she quixotically terminated her "official connection" with the N.U.W.W. in spite of her affection for it and its leaders. She did so by offering a resolution to dispense with prayers before business meetings, then feeling compelled, as "a religious-minded agnostic," to resign from the Executive when it did not pass. She resigned despite much "regret" at "parting company" with the bishops' wives.[181]

In contrast to her distaste for women's organizations and women's suffrage, Beatrice was involved with several issues of great importance to working-class women. Her work for the Charity Organization Society, her brief stint as a "trouser hand," her investigations into co-operation, and the Webbs' work on trade unionism had made Beatrice something of an expert on sweated labor and factory legislation, particularly with regard to women. Ironically, the more involved with women's issues she became, the more opposed she was to the views espoused by feminist leaders. Based on their own experiences, most middle-class feminists wanted to increase the educational and vocational opportunities open to women, and reduce or remove the legal restraints governing their employment. Most of all, they wished to introduce a greater degree of equality between the sexes. Beatrice was convinced that such proposals were detrimental to working-class women; they required more special treatment and more protective legislation, she thought, not less.

Her first lecture to the Fabian Society in November of 1893--one assumes Sidney had relented--was on "The Sphere of Trade Unionism." She delivered another to the Fabian in 1896 on "Women and the Factory Acts," subsequently turned into a tract, and edited a book, The Case for the Factory Acts. Her position was representative of the Webb general theory of factory legislation: regardless of the sex of the worker, factory legislation increased rather than

decreased their freedom. Beatrice further argued that,
insofar as factory acts tend to push out the small master
in the slums who most frequently hires sweated labor and
to encourage the development of factories, such acts
are beneficial to women workers. The factory system
in general helps women, she stated, since it leads to a
greater market for women's labor. Where she differed most
with feminists, however, was on the subject of special
legislation for women. Though it might be necessary for
the propertied classes to abolish many of the restrictions
surrounding women in order to increase their economic independence, this was not true, she argued, of working-class
women. For them, the absence of regulations led to hard-
ship and degradation.

       In support of the Liberal Bill of 1895 which
extended earlier factory legislation to various sweated
industries, she explained that legal protection does not
replace trade unions; rather it provides the necessary
standards of physical health, surplus of energy, and
sufficient leisure, without which trade unionism is
impossible. To preach trade unionism to sweated workers
was a "cruel mockery" until they had the time and energy
necessary to pursue it. Almost all working-class women,
she insisted, were in favor of the factory acts, for only
a few "strong women" lose out by restrictions on their
hours. It was, therefore, only middle-class women who
feared handicapping their sex in the struggle for employment,

and they did so, she implied, out of ignorance of the real
needs of working-class women.[182] In her diary she was
harsher, suggesting that it was the wives of capitalist
employers in particular, acting out of their class interests, who fought factory legislation.[183]

Beatrice's annoyance with middle-class feminists
on this issue was well founded. Their efforts against the
Factory Bill of 1894, aimed at curtailing some of the worst
abuses of sweated labor had been most effective. And she
felt they had undertaken their campaign to wreck the bill
without any real knowledge of the subject; they concerned
themselves with the principle of equality while remaining
indifferent to the suffering it caused. "In view of
the special heresies of the Woman's Liberal Federation
on factory legislation," wrote Sidney to the faithful
Pease, "Mrs. Webb wants to circularize their 448 Branch
Secretaries" with her tracts on sweated labor and the
factory acts, Fabian lecture lists, and Book Boxes.[184]

Of the joint work the Webbs did in the first
fifteen years of their partnership, one book in particular,
Industrial Democracy, bore on the "woman question." In
Industrial Democracy the Webbs did not spell out their
assumptions about the relationships between the sexes as
Beatrice did in her diaries; they did not declare that
women belong in the home. Yet such notions infused their
work and influenced their conclusions.

As in Beatrice's work on factory legislation they

differentiated between middle-class and working-class
labor, and they argued against sexual equality. In the
middle classes they point out it is common to see men and
women engaged in identical work, but this does not exist
in manual labor or the manufacturing industry. In the
vast majority of trades, the sexes are sharply divided
in different departments or different processes, as a
result of selection by the employers or the workers themselves. Thus, state the authors, in nine-tenths of the
trade unions there are no women, although no exclusionary
measures were taken. Furthermore, "it is unfair and even
cruel, to the vast army of women workers, to uphold the
fiction of the equality of the sexes in the industrial
world, . . . since . . . women constitute a different class
of workers, having different faculties, different needs,
and different expectations from those of men."[185]

The actual number of cases of "sex competition,"
that is, where women are involved in the same trade as
men, without any change in process having taken place,
they claim, is quite small. In these cases, the problem
as they see it is that women will almost always accept
lower pay than men, and will thereby lower the wage rate
for all, or they will be hired to the exclusion of men.
The imposition of the "Standard Rate"--uniform wages for
each trade--which they strongly support in all other
instances will not, however, solve this problem. If
forced to pay equal wages, employers will always prefer

to hire men. Thus, as many trade unionists had discovered,
they need not actively exclude women from their trades to
keep them out, they merely need to uphold the "Standard
Rate."

The solution the Webbs propose to keep both sexes
"healthy and efficient" is the differentiation of tasks,
of effort, and of subsistence, and "the frank recognition
of a classification of work." There should be no underbidding of individuals of one sex by individuals of
another.[186] Both sexes ought to maintain a "Standard
Rate" for their work, with a "clear and sharp distinction
between them," based on different kinds of work, or the
use of different kinds of machines. If this is not possible, "the only way of preventing individual underbidding by
persons of a lower standard of comfort" (i.e., women!) is
to segregate the women in separate establishments or
departments.[187]

In support of this proposal, the Webbs point to
the successful resolution of "sex competition" in the
hoisery trade in 1888-89. By "an ingenious adjustment of
the Standard Rate," the segregation of the sexes was
secured and "the women retained the privilege of working
at a farthing per dozen less than the men," a concession
which gave them a virtual monopoly of their own machine.[188]

The Webbs willingly grant women the "privilege" of
earning less because of certain assumptions they made on
the nature of women's needs, expectations, and abilities.

They assumed:

1. Women can afford to receive less because they are more abstemious, and they can do more for themselves.

2. Women receive a "bounty," that is, a subsidy from the men in their lives, and therefore require less.

3. Most women marry or plan to marry and so require less money in the long run.

4. Most women expect to marry and are unwilling to train themselves so as to deserve more money.

5. Women are weaker and therefore able to do less work, or less important work, or less skillful work.

In making these assumptions, the Webbs ignored other relevant facts about women, such as:

1. Many young women were not earning enough to keep them in their abstemiousness; a good many turned to the streets to supplement their wages.

2. Many women, widows among them, did not have men to provide for them, or subsidize their wages.

3. An increasing number of women did not marry, or married late in life, and therefore needed a decent income.

4. Men's work is often considered more important than women's work, merely because men do is.

5. Increasing mechanization was in the process of reducing the amount of strength needed for many industrial jobs, and thus was minimizing the differences between the sexes.

The remedies which the Webbs suggested can hardly be faulted--more education and training for women to bring their skills up to the level of men, and trade union organizations in order to negotiate for better pay. These organizations, however, ought not to be competitive with those of men: women employees should be organized "either as a woman's branch" or as an "affiliated society" of a men's trade union.[189] Surprisingly, no suggestion was made to educate the public or employers, or to legislate against discriminatory hiring. Government intervention or regulation, their usual panacea, was never broached as a means of insuring impartial hiring and equitable pay between the sexes. Both Webbs continued to be attached to notions of the basic differences between the sexes, and of the essential inferiority of women.

The Webbs, particularly Sidney, were involved with, and most concerned about, the educational process. On this score, their record with reference to women was mixed. By the time Industrial Democracy was published the Webbs had turned their "hopes from propaganda to education, from the working class to the middle class."[190] The single biggest achievement of the partnership, the L.S.E., represented the interests and talents of both partners. "The school was intended to represent all branches of economic and political science, and no differentiation against persons was to be allowed on the grounds of sex, religion, or economic or political views."[191] Many

a Fabian complained that the former was true; proof of the
latter, at least with reference to women, exists in the
statistics of the first class: 291 students were admitted,
of which 87 were women. A number of intelligent young
women in the prewar period took their training at the
L.S.E., and did a practicum in the Fabian Society. A
few went on to a real apprenticeship as secretaries and
researchers for the Webbs' many projects. Most were
exposed to Beatrice herself who lectured at the L.S.E.
two mornings a week, providing a role model for female
scholars, even if she did not "much believe in the productive power of women's intellect."

Unlike the Webbs' non-discriminatory policies at
the L.S.E., Sidney's involvement in the Conservative
Education Bill of 1902-03 once again brought him afoul
of feminists--this time feminists within the Fabian Society.
Sidney had begun working with the Conservative John Gorst
on a bill to expand and consolidate public education in
1896. The plan which he elaborated for London called for
doing away with the London School Board, on which women
were able to serve, and placing all grades and kinds of
educational institutions under the aegis of the L.C.C.,
on which women were not. Barring women from making educational policy, thereby setting women's rights back several
years, had not been a deliberate part of Sidney's program.
After protests by some women Fabians, he submitted a second
plan to the Fabian which called for allowing women to serve

on the L.C.C. Nonetheless, this demand had not appeared in
Sidney's initial draft;[192] it is doubtful that he would
have risked torpedoing his efforts at educational reform
by linking them to women's rights, if he had not been
pressured to do so.

It seems clear that in the fifteen year period
after their marriage, little had changed in the Webbs'
individual, or in their collective view of the "woman
question." Sidney was still rather neutral or indifferent
to the question of women's rights, and far more concerned
with what he considered larger issues than with the petty,
individualist concerns of middle-class women. Beatrice,
too, was put off by the middle-class perspective of the
women's movement, increasingly so with regard to matters
of employment. The more strongly convinced she became that
lower-class women required protection from overwork, the
more committed she became to special legislation for women
instead of legal equality with men, and the more she
found herself in opposition to the women's movement.

IV. Metamorphosis: The Emergence of a Public Figure and a Reluctant Feminist

After years of "wife's politics" and quite research,
Beatrice began, in 1905, to emerge as a public figure,
that is, as a woman engaged in activities she herself had
labeled as "men's work." With a decade and a half of
accomplishments for the "firm" of Webb, with that many

years of Sidney's love and devotion behind her, the conflicts which had beset Beatrice about her role as a woman,
her work, and her place in the universe, began to ease.
They never disappeared completely; physical complaints
and metaphysical angst continued to plague her. Beatrice,
after all, remained Beatrice. But she became better able
to integrate the disparate parts of her nature, her "masculine intelligence" and "woman's dependence," her ambition
and her frailty, to name just a few. Not surprisingly, as
Beatrice began to accept herself as a woman she became more
generous to her sex as a whole, and subtle differences in
her activities and her outlook began to occur.

The first sign of the sea change Beatrice was
undergoing was her ability to stretch "her tiny intellect"
further. Commenting in her diary (November 1904) that she
was spending four hours in the morning analyzing material
on vestries and two or more in the afternoon reading
eighteenth century literature, she noted that "altogether
I find I can manage six or seven hours' study now, as
against the three or four hours of old days."[193] A second
sign was her decision in that same year to give up cigarettes. She stopped smoking, although not permanently,
as she gave up coffee or stopped eating butter and sugar,
in an effort to improve her health. But one wonders if
Beatrice would have been able to give up that symbol of
her male side, if she had not begun to feel successful
and loved in her own right.

In 1905 Beatrice was appointed to the Royal Commission on the Poor Law by her friend, Arthur Balfour--a benchmark in her emergence as a public figure. The original purpose of the twenty member Commission was to inquire into the laws relating to poor persons, and into those methods outside the poor law used for dealing with unemployment. It was then to report on whether any modifications of the poor law or changes in its administration were advisable. Several of the members had previously taken part in the administration of the poor law as guardians or chairmen of boards. A few more were members of the Charity Organization Society, including Octavia Hill, and there were three representatives of the Catholic Church. Beatrice was one of only three members who belonged to the labor or the socialist movement. Most members, like the Chairman Lord George Hamilton, a Conservative ex-cabinet minister, were committed to the principles set up in 1834: "less eligibility" (making the conditions of the workhouse less comfortable than those afforded by the lowest paid kinds of work), "national uniformity," and the "workhouse system," which required the substitution of indoor for outdoor relief so as to put into effect the other two provisions.

From the beginning, Beatrice had difficulties with the Commission; there was no agenda, no procedure for dissent, no committees to divide the multitudinous duties. She felt she had no choice but to protest against the haphazard conduct of affairs, but she did not find dissent a comfortable state to be in:

> It is a new experience for me [she wrote in December
> of 1905] to have to make myself disagreeable in
> order to reach my ends. In private life, one can
> only get one's way by being unusually pleasant. In
> official life--at least as the most insignificant
> member of a Commission overwhelmingly against me
> in opinion--I shall only get my share of control
> by . . . standing on my rights . . . and refusing
> to be overawed by great personages who would like
> to pooh-pooh a woman who attempts to share in the
> control of affairs.[192]

With Sidney's help, Beatrice began drafting "con-
crete proposals" for the Commission concerning the methods,
procedures, and scope of the investigation at hand. She
pressed for the study of "facts" about the relief of
destitution instead of the collection of "casual opinions"
on the defects of the poor law. Seeing clearly that her
most important work would be done "outside the Commission
room," she decided to give it her "best thought but scant
attendance."[195] She went her own way, using her own
resources to collect additional data, and her own methods
of study to analyze them. Naturally she came up with her
own conclusions. The inequities, inadequacies, and
injustices of the poor law being legion, Beatrice found
no end of topics for research, and formulated, in time,
a multitude of proposals for their redress.

Beatrice found it trying "to be official" at
hearings and meetings: "Ah! how hard it is for the quick
witted and somewhat vain woman to be discreet and accurate,"
she lamented.[196] And she was "horribly sensitive" to the
dislike and displeasure of her colleagues. within a matter

of months, however, she thought that she had managed to become "wholly indifferent to the Commission," and merely reminded herself that, being in a minority, it was her business to be hostile to the government. It was necessary only that she be "comfortably and good naturedly hostile."[197] At the same time, Beatrice wondered if the indifference she strove to feel meant she was "becoming masculine-- losing the 'personal note' which is the characteristic of the woman in human intercourse." She was even more dis- concerted when she caught herself "playing the personal note," without feeling it. "Is that," she wondered, "a characteristic of the woman on public bodies?"[198] In fact, what was characteristic of Beatrice herself was her inability to keep the "personal note" out. She failed in her attempts to remain "good naturedly hostile" and, in the end, alienated her colleagues, perhaps needlessly, and misjudged both the Commissioners and the quality of their work.[199] "The poor old Commission," she wrote in November of 1908,

> it is floundering about in its morass of a report.
> . . . Are all men quite so imbecile as that lot
> are? . . . If ever I sit again on a Royal Com-
> mission, I hope my colleagues will be of a superior
> calibre--for really it is shockingly bad for one's
> character to be with such folk--it makes me feel
> intolerably superior.[200]

There is no question that Beatrice had worked herself into a state of complete exhaustion by this time: "brain fog," nervous apprehension, indigestion, and sleep- lessness, all plagued her, in addition to occasional fits

of bad judgment. Despite her worldliness, and the important role she had taken in Sidney's affairs, she had done
all of her wire-pulling behind the scenes. This was her
first performance on stage, and the novelty of the experience took its toll. That it was, in the end, a learning
experience is clearly evident in Beatrice's later work on
committees and commissions--the high-strung behavior was
not repeated. Experience, or the lack of it, rather than
gender seems to have been the determining factor here,
although one doubts that Beatrice would have agreed.

In January 1909, after three years of inquiry, the
Royal Commission issued its "Majority Report of the Poor
Law Commission," proposing the dismantling of the poor law
and the municipalising of its control, while recommending
that the prior organizations for distributing services,
including the boards of guardians, be left in place.
After three years of dissent, Beatrice issued her "Minority
Report of the Poor Law Commission," duly detested but
published by the Commission and, shortly thereafter, by
the Fabian Society. It called for, in addition to the
breakup of the poor law and the abolition of the boards
of guardians, the use of public works to reduce unemployment, and state measures for the rehabilitation and training of the long-term unemployed. To put these ideas into
practice, the Report envisioned a Ministry of Labour
responsible for organizing and linking labor exchanges,
and a Registrar of Public Assistance, manned by a

professional staff, which would assess payments according to need and would enforce obligations upon the recipients of these payments.[201]

Once the Reports were out, the Webbs were unpleasantly surprised and terribly disappointed at the "superior publicity and approval" accorded to the Majority Report. They left on a much needed six week vacation, and when they returned the "war" between the two Reports began. From the spring of 1909 to the summer of 1911, the Webbs threw permeation to the winds and involved themselves in incessant propaganda on behalf of the Minority Report.[202] To this purpose they set up the National Committee for the Promotion of the Break-up of the Poor Law, which in the following year became the National Committee for the Prevention of Destitution. The senior signatory of the Minority Report, Dean Russell Wakefield, presided, Beatrice was honorary secretary, and Sidney was chairman of the executive committee. Starting out with a small staff of paid assistants, the Committee eventually enrolled a large number of voluntary organizers and lecturers, and some 20,000 members. It became, according to G. D. H. Cole, "the most highly organized campaign since the Anti-Corn Law League."[203]

In retrospect, Beatrice suggested that the Webbs' "plunge into propaganda entailed two grave consequences": they had to suspend their research into social institutions, and they "lost touch with Liberal Cabinet Ministers and

. . . Conservative leaders," and became increasingly
involved in the labor movement.[204] Thus, their "social
environment" changed once again, with important consequences for them, and for the postwar labor movement.
While the N.C.P.D. did much to awaken the public to the
fact of poverty and to the need to do something about it,
it did not, in the short run, bring about the kinds of
change it was promoting. The Liberal Government "dished
the Webbs" (in John Burns's celebrated phrase) with their
National Insurance Bill of 1911. It was much less comprehensive than the reforms recommended by the Minority
Report, and it was based on the principle of individual
contribution to a state run plan. The Poor Law remained
in effect until 1929.

*   *   *

If Beatrice's work on the Royal Commission and the
N.C.P.D. did not directly affect government policy, it did
bring about some rather drastic changes in Beatrice herself,
and in the Webb partnership. In the course of her involvement with the Commission, she found herself becoming the
public person she had thus far chosen not to be. It was
one thing to interview labor leaders or public officials
for one's own research and quite another to do so at a
public hearing. And it was quite another, indeed, to take
to the speaker's platform to push for one's reforms.
Beatrice thought it "rather funny to start at my time of
life, on the war path, at the head of a contingent of young

men and women."[205] And she found it very tiring. But she enjoyed her campaigning all the same: "I enjoy it because I have the gift of personal intercourse and it is a gift I have never, until now, made full use of. I genuinely _like_ my fellow mortals whether as individuals or as crowds--I like to interest them, and inspire them and even to order them, in a motherly sort of way. Also I enjoy leadership."[206] Beatrice had discovered in herself "the faculty of the preacher and the teacher," and she wondered at times if she would "be able to withdraw into research."[207]

Naturally, relationships within the "firm" of Webb changed as well. Beatrice noted in 1907: "Just now our usual positions are somewhat reversed: it is he [Sidney] who sits at home and thinks out the common literary work, it is I who am racing around dealing with men and affairs!"[208] After the formation of the N.C.P.D., Beatrice decided that Sidney was "thoroughly happy," partly because their comradeship had "never been so complete."[209] Hitherto they had only researched and written books together, whereas now they were writing, organizing, and speaking together. In fact, Sidney was devoting most of his time to working with Beatrice on the Minority Report. His efforts on behalf of the L.C.C. had been dwindling for some time--he permanently ended his eighteen year tenure in 1910--and he was less active in the Fabian Society and in the management of the L.S.E.

But Sidney was "extraordinarily generous in not

resenting, in the very least," Beatrice's "having nominally to take the front place as the leading Minority Commissioner." "Fortunately," she protested, "in spite of his modesty, everyone knows that he is the back-bone of the Webb firm--even if I do appear, on some occasions, as the figure head."[210] Unfortunately, Sidney did not keep a diary of his private thoughts which might document all of this; Sidney was not one much given to "private" thoughts. His letters of the period show that he was working hard on their projects, and continued to feel, all evidence to the contrary, unproductive while Beatrice was away. The major difference seems to be that she was away far more often than before; the Webbs may have been organizing and lecturing as comrades--but this often took place in different towns at different times. "I can't do anything without you," he wrote her in 1909, "nor settle down to any useful work. It is nice to think you will come back tomorrow."[211] Sidney's letters contain some of the old wistfulness of their early courtship days when the independent and determinedly single Miss Potter had him "on the lead," instead of the reverse, as Beatrice was to insist, in subsequent years. One wonders how Beatrice was able to retain her notions of female dependency in the face of the mutual dependency she shared with Sidney.

Beatrice had been right about her unwillingness "to withdraw into research" after her experiences as a public person--she was not in the least ready to do

so. She determined, instead, to become active at last
in the Fabian Society, and to convert the youth and energy
of the N.C.P.D. into a research organization connected to
the Fabian. The Society which Beatrice planned to convert
was itself threatened by young men of Syndicalist leanings,
and the Webbs, along with the remnant of the "Old Gang"
still remaining, had their hands full in keeping the
Society from being taken over. The Fabian Research Department, which Beatrice duly set up and directed, using her
newfound skills at organizing and her knowledge and experience as a researcher, did in fact fall under the influence
of this new ideology, half French, half medieval in origin.
She remained the titular head and research advisor, but
the leading young men and women, G. D. H. Cole and William
Mellor in particular, were Guild Socialists, and the
findings of the Department often reflected their bent
rather than hers.[212]

Beatrice served on the Fabian Executive from 1912
until her resignation in 1933. The Fabian Executive,
thus, had its first fully active and celebrated female
member since the days of Annie Besant. Having Beatrice
on the Executive, however, mattered little in terms of the
"woman question"; as we have seen, her interests lay elsewhere. She and Sidney gave a course of lectures, for
example, on the "Control of Industry," and she was particularly involved in the combined I.L.P. and Fabian campaign
to establish the "National Minimum"--the Webbs having

awakened at last to the possible importance of that "feather headed" group of socialists. Although annoyed not to be able to get back to their historical research, Beatrice felt "a clear call to leadership in the Labour and Socialist Movement to which we feel that we must respond."[213]

The Webbs also interpreted their "call to leadership" as necessitating a new weekly publication, an "organ of Fabianism." They started "the most risky of their ventures" in 1912, with very little capital and less expertise in newspaper production. But, their first "child," the L.S.E., was well established in the University of London system; Sidney was content to keep a watchful eye on it without resuming the chairmanship, given up in 1911. It was time for another "offspring," especially for Sidney. "Once again he takes the lead," wrote Beatrice. "He is a far more accomplished journalist than I, and he is the reputed father of the new venture."[214]

With Sidney now occupied, Beatrice may have felt fewer pangs about her continued engagement in political activities. "Leadership in the Labour and Socialist Movement" meant, after all, more lecturing, more meetings, more conferences--Beatrice remained very much the public person. She still felt she spent "an unreasonable amount of energy" on the lectures she gave, but she thought she had "gained a certain art in speaking." More important, when she spoke, she did so in her own voice. In writing

she felt she was "parasitic on Sidney," her style was
"a hybrid of his and mine." But, in addressing an audience,
she noted, "I must speak my own words and sentences."[215]

* * *

In the decade before the First World War, the
feminist movement began to take on a new look. Women
became better organized. The newly established and militant
Women's Social and Political Union appeared alongside the
staid National Union of Women's Suffrage Societies.
Tactics changed. Collecting signatures on petitions
and drafting suffrage bills for Members of Parliament
gradually gave way to hunger striking, breaking windows,
and bombing pillar boxes. Indifference on the part of the
Government sometimes gave way to brutality, creating anew
the demand for political equality. Beatrice was not immune
to the increasing pressures and the formidable arguments
in favor of women's rights. Yet, in altering her views on
the "woman question," she was not simply responding to
feminist activism: her own experiences in public life
both sensitized her to the issues and made her more receptive to the reforms proposed.

Official notice of the change in Beatrice's attitude
appeared in the 5 November 1906 issue of the Times, occurring one year after her appointment to the Royal Commission.
It took the form of a letter to Mrs. Millicent Fawcett,
which she authorized Mrs. Fawcett to publish if she wished.
Mrs. Fawcett had asked Beatrice to inform her if she ever

revised her view of women's suffrage; obviously that time
had come.

Beatrice saw granting women the vote as a corollary
to the incursions of the state--the expanded housekeeping
state of which she fully approved--into the area of women's
obligations and responsibilities. In this Beatrice was
following an increasingly common, somewhat conservative
argument, one expressed by G.B.S. and a good many feminists on both sides of the Atlantic. Eschewing any
notions of natural rights for women, or equality between
the sexes, Beatrice wrote:

> The rearing of children, the advancement of learn-
> ing, and the promotion of the spiritual life--which
> I regard as the particular obligations of women--
> are . . . more and more becoming the main preoccu-
> pations of the community as a whole. . . . [Women
> are] feeling a positive obligation to take part
> in directing this new activity. This is . . .
> not a claim to rights or an abandonment of women's
> particular obligations, but a desire more effectively
> to fulfil their functions by sharing the control of
> state action in those directions.[216]

Further, with reference to the demonstrations and dis-
orderliness of the past weeks, she insisted:

> It is cruel to put a fellow-citizen of strong
> convictions in the dilemma of political ineffective-
> ness or unmannerly breaches of the peace. . . . To
> call such behavior vulgar is an undistinguished
> and I may say an illiterate use of language. The
> way out of this unpleasant dilemma . . . is to
> permit this growing consciousness among women . . .
> to find a constitutional channel.[217]

Beatrice recommended "the admission to the franchise of
women as women, whether married or single, propertied or
wage-earning,"[218] thus obviating the socialist or labor

arguments against the suffrage based on fears of strengthening the propertied elements in the electorate. In her diary of that period, she noted:

> For some time I have felt the old prejudice
> evaporating. And as the women suffragists were
> being battered about rather badly, and coarse-
> grained men were saying coarse-grained things,
> I thought I might as well give a friendly pull
> to get the thing out of the mud. . . . I shall
> be thought, by some, to be a pompous prig. The
> movement will stand some of that element now![219]

Within the Fabian Society, Beatrice signaled her acceptance of female suffrage during the battle over the Basis, subsequent to the Wells furor. At the members' meeting in January 1907, Beatrice seconded the resolution which declared, as one of the objects of the Society, the establishment of "equal citizenship of men and women." Mrs. Pember Reeves who had proposed the resolution, did so on the grounds that the franchise would broaden the minds and interests of the women it affected. In characteristic fashion, Beatrice stated the case in terms of what women would do for the government. The suffrage was necessary, she told her Fabian colleagues, "to make the national government as efficient and complete as possible."[220]

It has been suggested that both Beatrice's retraction in the Times and her actions within the Fabian were politically motivated; that is, they represented her part in keeping Fabian feminists from supporting Wells.[221] Pressures within the Fabian Society and Fabian politics no doubt played an important role in convincing Beatrice that it was, at long last, time to recant her anti-suffrage stand. Yet one suspects that other considerations influenced her as well. The unfair and ungentle treatment accorded to the suffragists in the opening years of this last campaign for the vote seems to have "radicalized" a good many "respectable" women. It is interesting in this regard that Louise Creighton, wife of the deceased Bishop Creighton, had submitted a retraction of her anti-suffrage views to the Times in the previous week. Beatrice had always expressed a great respect for the older woman's judgment, and her respectability. In Beatrice's case, one wonders, too, if the difficulties she herself was having at the hands of her fellow Commissioners functioned in the same way. She was finding out, firsthand, that there were some disadvantages to being a woman, disadvantages she had denied ever experiencing in her work as a social investigator.

Having changed her mind on the suffrage question, thereafter Beatrice remained consistent in her support, if not overly active on its behalf. She showed no such constancy in her estimation of women's inherent worth and ability. Basically, she never altered her views that men and women were very different and that men were both preferable and superior to women. As one member of the F.R.D. observed, many of the young researchers resented the Webbs' lack of interest in women compared to men.

Sidney liked "no women," she claimed, and Beatrice thought
them "socially unacceptable or distracting sirens."[222]
Certainly, one finds ample evidence in support of Beatrice's
continuing bias against women in her diaries.[223]

The one aspect of the "woman question" on which
Beatrice expressed the most complete and the most radical
turnabout was the subject of wages. In September 1918,
Beatrice was one of six members appointed to the War
Cabinet Committee on Women in Industry. The object of
the Committee was to determine if a policy of equal wages
between men and women was a feasible policy or would lead
to "an unwarranted increase in national expenditure."[224]
Further, the Committee was to report on whether the
Treasury Agreement of 19 March 1915, pledging the government to pay women workers the same wage as the men they
were replacing, had been carried out by the public departments concerned. In due course, the Committee decided
that the Agreement of 1915 contained no pledge of equal
wages for women doing work previously done by men.

Having conducted her own investigation, in addition
to those of the Committee, Beatrice came to the contrary
conclusion. In so doing she also came to a startling
reversal of almost every point regarding women's wages
the Webbs had enumerated in Industrial Democracy (1897).
Once again Beatrice found herself on a panel with whose
findings she could not agree, and once again, with Sidney's
help, she wrote her own minority report. It was published

by the Fabian Society as: The Wages of Men and Women: Should They Be Equal? In sharp contrast to the findings of Industrial Democracy, Beatrice determined that the wages of men and women should be equal, and that there was no justification for classifying workers by sex and subjecting them thereby to a differential rate. Perhaps more startling to readers of Beatrice's previous works was her decided objection to the extension of the factory acts to women workers only. She suggested instead that the consolidation of the factory acts "should be made the occasion of sweeping away all special provisions differentiating men from women," there being no reason why sex restrictions of any kind should be imposed.[225] Furthermore, the qualitative and quantitative differentials between men's and women's work, made so much of by the Webbs in a number of their earlier books and lectures, seemed to have vanished. In fact, Beatrice found "very striking evidence . . . that in certain occupations in which both men and women are employed . . . the average woman produces . . . a larger output than the common run of men, with greater docility, and a more contented mind, involving less 'worry' to the management."[226]

If statements such as these did not cause readers to rub their eyes and check again the name on the title page, the following might: "I see . . . no ground for differentiating wages according to family obligations, and certainly no justice in making this the basis of any differentiation between men and women as such."[227] The

same is true of her contention that "it cannot be said that

men are in all respects superior to women, or women to

men--and, what is more important, there are in each case

individuals of one sex who are distinctly superior in

productivity to the majority of the other."[228] Indeed

the conclusion she drew, "there is no justice in, and no

economic basis for, the conception of a man's rate and a

woman's rate,"[229] when compared to earlier conclusions

reached by her "firm," begins to make one wonder about

the "objectivity" of descriptive sociology. Finally, in

support of these assertions, Beatrice stated, "It has been

suggested [she is too modest to state by whom] that . . .

a uniform national minimum will lead to the exclusion of

all women from the better paid occupations."[230] But, she

continued, "I find some difficulty in discovering the

ground for this suggestion"; in fact, the evidence shows

that equal wages often lead to "a marked increase" in the

number of women working in a given field.[231]

On one point Beatrice remained consistent with her

previous recommendations; she again called for a "national

minimum" of wages and working conditions--the only differ-

ence being that now the sex of the worker was to have no

influence on that minimum. The new principle Beatrice

suggested here is that wages be adjusted to the cost of

living. The real conflict she foresaw is not between men

and women but between skilled and unskilled labor; her

remedy was a closer correspondence between the occupational
rates of these groups and their efforts and needs.

The dramatic change in Beatrice's position on
women's wages was in keeping with her increasing acceptance
of women in roles other than conventional ones. Too, the
fact that "women of all classes" had, as a result of the
war, "emerged into public life--industrial, social and
militarist,"[232] and that they had performed admirably,
was not lost upon her. Yet, it is well to remember that
Beatrice was responding to other factors too. The pressure
from the feminists among her own investigators was one; her
desire not to preserve "for the woman the right to undercut
the man"[223] was another. While the text of the report
reads, at times, like a paean to equality between the
sexes, one senses from her diaries that Beatrice was more
concerned that women's wages would not be used to bring
down the wages of men after the war, than with actual
equality between the sexes. The times had changed; therefore so had the tactics.

* * *

In charting Beatrice's changing positions on the
"woman question" one can only say that she became a
cautious and rather reluctant feminist after 1905. On
the issue of women's rights, she and Sidney followed
rather than led the way, Sidney for lack of interest,
Beatrice for a panoply of reasons. The effects of her
mother's prejudices against women, and of her mother's

neglect were lasting; not the least of its manifestations was the split between a masculine and a feminine self which Beatrice maintained. Thus, in the first half of her life she battled against the conventions she herself supported: she led the life of an "emancipated woman" while insisting that woman's place was in the home. In time, and with increasing pressure from the outside world, Beatrice was able to expand her notions of what it meant to be a woman, and gradually to relent on some of her strongest anti-feminist positions. With reference to the relative merit and intelligence of the sexes, however, her real prejudices and preferences never disappeared.

In 1933 Beatrice looked back on a "half-century of contemporaries" and came up with the "melancholy reflection": "Where oh! where are the distinguished women-- relatively to men--in art, literature, science, public affairs."[234] Amy Johnson, the pilot, was the only woman she could bring to mind, and she was easily dismissed. Her record, after all, involved only "muscle, nerve and sight," and her speech was "utterly commonplace."[235] Beatrice might well have mentioned herself, by then the first woman member of the British Academy, but then she never had managed to consider her accomplishments as reflecting on, or representative of, her sex as a whole. She only shared with them what she perceived as her weaknesses.

Her pessimism about women, and the shambles that

passed as British foreign and home policy at the time, was not mirrored in her feelings about Stalin's Russia. For the Webbs had decided that the Soviet experiment was, in fact, the "Co-operative Commonwealth" they had envisioned in 1920, and that it was working. Their "last Testament," as Beatrice called it, Soviet Communism, A New Civilization, was published in 1935. She mockingly explained their enthusiasm for Russia--an enthusiasm they had not felt fifteen years before--in another way as well: "Old people often fall in love in extraordinary and ridiculous ways--with their chauffeurs for example. We feel it more dignified to have fallen in love with Soviet Communism."[236]

In one sense, the Webb flirtation with Stalin's Russia represented not only the dark side of their collectivist model, it paralleled their earlier insensitivity to the women's movement. Having little faith in the "average sensual man," and even less, one would assume, in the average sensual woman, and a great deal of faith in the technocrat, the Webbs were always willing to insist on conformity for the sake of the collectivity or the collective good. Individual women seeking individual rights or privileges had no place in their plan, unless those rights might benefit society as a whole.

The Beveridge Report, calling for a great many of the reforms advocated by the Webbs over the previous half-century, came out in 1942. Having by then given up on the

possibility of merely reforming the capitalist system,
Beatrice's response to the Report was tepid. Not surprisingly, she liked least its provision for unemployment
insurance, still believing that the more attractive
unemployment becomes, the more unemployed there would be.
Nonetheless, the Welfare State effected by the Labour
Government after the war owed a great deal to the work
of Beatrice and Sidney, although neither lived to see
it established. Beatrice died in 1943 at the age of
eighty-five, a remarkable age for anyone as frail as
Beatrice had always considered herself to be. Sidney
died four years later.

After a brief campaign by G.B.S., a mere ninety-one
years old himself, the ashes of both the Webbs were removed
from Passfield Corner and buried in Westminster Abbey.
This was the first time in Westminster's nine hundred year
history that a man and his wife had been buried there
together and at the same time.[237] It was a fitting end
for an extraordinary Partnership.

Footnotes

[1]Beatrice Webb, My Apprenticeship (1926; reprint ed., Cambridge: Cambridge University Press, 1979), p. 412.

[2]Sidney Webb to Marjorie Davidson, 12 December 1888, in The Letters of Sidney and Beatrice Webb (1873-1892), vol. 1, ed. Norman Mackenzie (Cambridge: Cambridge University Press, 1978), p. 122.

[3]Sidney Webb, "Reminiscences," St. Martin's Review, December 1928, quoted in Mary Agnes Hamilton, Sidney and Beatrice Webb (London: Sampson, Law, Marston, 1932), p. 18.

[4]Sidney Webb to Beatrice Potter, 9 October 1890, in Letters, vol. 1, p. 204.

[5]S. Webb to B. Potter, 23 September 1891, ibid., p. 308.

[6]Beatrice Webb, Our Partnership (London: Longmans, Green, 1948), p. 3.

[7]Norman MacKenzie, ed., The Letters of Sidney and Beatrice Webb, vol. 1, p. 73.

[8]S. Webb to Sidney Olivier, 7 July 1885, in Letters, vol. 1, p. 89.

[9]According to MacKenzie, in Letters, vol. 1, p. 72, the fact that all three children were sent away simultaneously--"a most unusual action for a family of this relatively low social status"--gives some credence to the claims of the Canadian descendants of Mary Elizabeth Webb. They assert that she was the eldest Webb child, and that she left home at about that time as the result of "a domestic scandal." Webb's extreme reticence with regard to his childhood and his destruction of some family letters, would seem also to support this claim. No documentation has been found, however, to substantiate the story, and it remains no more than speculation.

[10]S. Webb to B. Potter, 6 December 1890, in Letters, vol. 1, p. 237.

[11]The Zetetical Society, quoted in Letters, vol. 1, p. 75.

[12]George Bernard Shaw, "Fruitful Friendships," in his Sixteen Self Sketches (New York: Dodd, Mead, 1949), p. 107.

[13]B. Webb, Our Partnership, pp. 5-6.

[14]S. Webb to M. Davidson, 12 December 1888, in Letters, vol. 1, p. 121.

[15]B. Webb, Our Partnership, p. 3.

[16]S. Webb to B. Potter, 22 September 1890, in Letters, vol. 1, p. 196.

[17]B. Webb, Our Partnership, p. 3.

[18]S. Webb to B. Potter, 13 August 1890, in Letters, vol. 1, p. 170.

[19]S. Webb to Sidney Olivier, 7 July 1885, ibid., p. 89.

[20]Max Beer, A History of British Socialism (London: Allen and Unwin, 1953), pp. 276-80.

[21]S. Webb to M. Davidson, 12 December 1888, in Letters, vol. 1, p. 120.

[22]Sidney Webb, "Policy of the National Minimum," in Modern Socialism, ed. R. C. K. Ensor (London: Harper and Brothers, 1904), p. 109.

[23]S. Webb to G. B. Shaw, 4 November 1884, in Letters, vol. 1, p. 81.

[24]S. Webb to E. Pease, 24 October 1886, ibid, pp. 101-02.

[25]Ibid.

[26]S. Webb to B. Potter, 14 March 1891, in Letters, vol. 1, p. 265.

[27]George Bernard Shaw, The Quintessence of Ibsenism (London: W. Scott, 1891).

[28]S. Webb to B. Potter, 18 September 1891, in Letters, vol. 1, p. 305.

[29]Sidney Webb, "Women's Wages," Fabian News 1, no. 8 (1891).

[30]S. Webb, "Women's Wages," in Sidney and Beatrice Webb, The Problems of Modern Industry (London: Longmans, Green, 1920), p. 63.

[31] Ibid., p. 67.

[32] S. Webb to B. Potter, 24 June 1890, in Letters, vol. 1, p. 155.

[33] Emma Brooke, Transition (Philadelphia: J. B. Lippincott, 1895), p. 118.

[34] S. Webb to Graham Wallas, 17 August 1885, in Letters, vol. 1, p. 93.

[35] Ibid.

[36] S. Webb to M. Davidson, 12 December 1888, ibid., p. 118.

[37] S. Webb to B. Potter, 30 April 1890, ibid., p. 132.

[38] Beatrice Webb's Diary, begun when she was ten years old, and many of her family's letters are in the Passfield Papers at the London School of Economics. She quoted much of this material directly in her two auto-biographical works, My Apprenticeship and Our Partnership. The complete Diaries have recently become available on microfiche: The Diary of Beatrice Webb 1873-1943 (Cambridge: Chadwyck-Healey, 1978).

[39] B. Webb, Apprenticeship, p. 10.

[40] Ibid.

[41] Ibid., p. 11.

[42] Ibid.

[43] B. Potter to Richard Potter, 1885, Letters, vol. 1, p. 42.

[44] B. Webb, Apprenticeship, p. 13.

[45] Ibid., p. 12.

[46] Ibid., p. 3.

[47] Ibid., pp. 12-13.

[48] Ibid., p. 11.

[49] Ibid.

[50] Ibid.

[51] Ibid., p. 12.

[52] Beatrice Webb diary, 24 March 1874, Passfield Papers, British Library of Political and Economic Science (MS hereafter cited as BWD).

[53] Ibid.

[54] Kitty Muggeridge and Ruth Adam, Beatrice Webb, A Life, 1858-1943 (New York: Alfred A. Knopf, 1968), pp. 22-23.

[55] B. Webb, Apprenticeship, p. 17.

[56] BWD, September to December 1873.

[57] Kate preceded and introduced Beatrice to the Charity Organization Society and rent collecting in the East End. She gave her position over to Beatrice when, at the age of thirty-six, she married Leonard, later Lord, Courtney, then Financial Secretary to the Treasury in Gladstone's administration.

[58] BWD, December 1873.

[59] Ibid., 3 October 1879.

[60] Ibid., January 1881.

[61] B. Webb, Apprenticeship, p. 117.

[62] See, for example, BWD, August 1899, for Beatrice's description of her sister Laurentia (Lallie) Holt; November 1914 for her description of sister Georgie Mein.

[63] BWD, 8 April 1884.

[64] Ibid.

[65] B. Webb, Apprenticeship, p. 58.

[66] Ibid., p. 141.

[67] Ibid., p. 60.

[68] Ibid., p. 62.

[69] Ibid., p. 104.

[70] Ibid.

[71] Ibid., p. 106.

[72]Ibid., p. 113.

[73]Ibid., p. 114.

[74]Ibid., p. 118.

[75]BWD, 22 February 1883.

[76]B. Webb, Apprenticeship, p. 150.

[77]Ibid., p. 151.

[78]BWD, April 1884.

[79]B. Webb, Apprenticeship, p. 337.

[80]BWD, December 1888.

[81]Ibid., September 1888.

[82]Ibid., 5 October 1888.

[83]Ibid., December 1888.

[84]Ibid., 26 October 1888.

[85]Ibid., 8 November 1888.

[86]B. Webb, Apprenticeship, p. 319.

[87]Ibid., p. 355.

[88]Ibid.

[89]BWD, 4 November 1882.

[90]Ibid., March 1883.

[91]B. Potter to S. Webb, 2 May 1890, in Letters, vol. 1, p. 133.

[92]Ibid., 11 June 1890, p. 150.

[93]BWD, October 1884.

[94]Ibid., 5 November 1883.

[95]Ibid., 1881.

[96]Ibid.

[97]B. Webb, Apprenticeship, p. 291.

[98] Ibid., p. 352.

[99] B. Potter to Richard Potter, Summer 1885, in Letters, vol. 1, p. 36.

[100] Ibid., November 1885, p. 48.

[101] Ibid.

[102] Ibid.

[103] Ibid., August 1885, p. 40.

[104] BWD, 1889.

[105] B. Potter to R. Potter, November 1885, in Letters, vol. 1, p. 47.

[106] B. Webb, Apprenticeship, p. 156.

[107] BWD, September 1889.

[108] BWD (n.d.), quoted in Muggeridge, Beatrice Webb, p. 76.

[109] Harriot Stanton Blatch and Alma Lutz, Challenging Years (New York: G. P. Putnam's Sons, 1940; Westport, Conn.: Hyperion Press, 1976), p. 79.

[110] B. Webb, Apprenticeship, p. xliii.

[111] BWD, 14 February 1890.

[112] Ibid.

[113] B. Potter to S. Webb, 5 February 1890, in Letters, vol. 1, p. 133.

[114] B. Webb, Apprenticeship, p. 410.

[115] B. Potter to S. Webb, 22 June 1890, in Letters, vol. 1, p. 154.

[116] Ibid., 29 May 1890, pp. 139-40.

[117] S. Webb to B. Potter, 30 May 1890, ibid., p. 141.

[118] Ibid., 30 April 1890, p. 132.

[119] B. Potter to S. Webb, 11 June 1890, ibid., p. 149.

[120]Ibid., 11 August 1890, p. 166.

[121]Ibid., September 1890, p. 186.

[122]Ibid., 2 May 1890, p. 133.

[123]Ibid., 11 August 1890, p. 166.

[124]S. Webb to B. Potter, 30 May 1890, ibid., p. 143.

[125]Ibid., 14 March 1891, p. 264.

[126]Ibid., 6 April 1891, p. 267.

[127]Ibid., 14 September 1891, p. 299.

[128]BWD, May 1891.

[129]Ibid., 20 June 1891.

[130]B. Webb, Apprenticeship, p. 402.

[131]B. Potter to S. Webb, 7 December 1890, in Letters, vol. 1, p. 238.

[132]S. Webb to B. Potter, 5 December 1890, ibid., p. 236.

[133]Ibid., 6 April 1891, p. 269.

[134]B. Webb, Partnership, p. 292.

[135]Ibid., p. 20.

[136]BWD, December 1895.

[137]B. Webb to S. Webb, February 1896, in The Letters of Sidney and Beatrice Webb (1892-1912), vol. 2, ed. Norman MacKenzie (Cambridge: Cambridge University Press, 1978), p. 41.

[138]B. Webb, Partnership, p. 214.

[139]H. G. Wells's fictional description of the Baileys, alias the Webbs, and their home was less than flattering. See H. G. Wells, The New Machiavelli (New York: Duffield, 1914), p. 16.

[140]BWD, 25 July 1894.

141Blanch Patch, _Thirty Years With G.B.S._ (London: Victor Gollancz, 1951), p. 17.

142B. Webb, _Partnership_, p. 170.

143Ibid., p. 360.

144BWD, 30 November 1906.

145B. Webb, _Apprenticeship_, p. 414.

146B. Webb, _Partnership_, p. 52.

147Ibid., p. 292.

148Ibid., p. 116.

149Ibid., p. 313.

150Ibid., p. 117.

151["Philo"] "Men Who Ought to Be in Parliament, III," _New Age_, March 12, 1896.

152According to Beatrice, Sidney had "a repulsion for public speaking . . . partly because he hates putting himself forward," and partly because he did not enjoy "popular approval . . . it bores him." B. Webb, _Partnership_, p. 472. Despite this antipathy, he campaigned with "boyish pleasure," and he set off for Parliament, at the age of sixty-three, "like a boy going for his first term to a public school." _Beatrice Webb's Diaries, 1912-1924_, p. 234.

153S. Webb to B. Webb, 1899, in B. Webb, _Partnership_, p. 184.

154B. Webb to Edward Pease, 18 April 1893, Fabian Papers, Box A5, Nuffield College, Oxford.

155B. Webb, _Partnership_, p. 145.

156Ibid., p. 292.

157Ibid., p. 107.

158Frank W. Galton, "Investigating with the Webbs," in _The Webbs and Their Work_, ed. Margaret Cole (London: Frederick Muller, 1949), p. 29.

159Sidney and Beatrice Webb, _Industrial Democracy_ (London: Longmans, Green, 1902), p. 850.

[160]B. Webb, _Partnership_, p. 149.

[161]Ibid., p. 53.

[162]B. Webb to Graham Wallas, July 1897, in _Letters_, vol. 2, p. 55.

[163]Graham Wallas, "Socialism and the Fabian Society," in _Men and Ideas_, ed. May Wallas (London: George Allen and Unwin, 1940), p. 105.

[164]Looking back on the early Fabian Society, Wallas reported that Sidney "taught us to work, and to forget that at Oxford and Cambridge one reserved the afternoon for rest." When a member of the Executive complained in 1887 that he had no time for "exercise and amusement," Webb responded that "he should find exercise in walking to lectures and amusement in delivering them." Wallas, "Socialism and the Fabian Society," p. 105.

[165]BWD, 25 July 1894.

[166]B. Webb, _Partnership_, p. 165.

[167]Ibid., pp. 157-58.

[168]BWD, 25 July 1894.

[169]S. Webb to B. Potter, 21 August 1890, in _Letters_, vol. 1, p. 183.

[170]Ibid., 30 November 1890, p. 232.

[171]BWD, 28 July 1894.

[172]Ibid.

[173]Ibid.

[174]Ibid.

[175]B. Webb, _Apprenticeship_, p. 354.

[176]Female Medical Student (name undecipherable) to Graham Wallas, 16 January 1897, Graham Wallas Collection, Box I, British Library of Political and Economic Science.

[177]B. Webb, _Partnership_, p. 135.

[178]She and her husband had been particularly helpful and supportive to Beatrice in the late 1880's, when Creighton was a Cambridge don and Beatrice a young

sociologist just finding her way. It was said, after Creighton was appointed to the immensely prestigious position of Bishop in 1897, that "the Creightons are in full possession of London, and that the Webbs are in full possession of the Creightons." Medical Student to G. Wallas, 16 January 1897, Wallas Collection.

[179]B. Webb, Partnership, p. 136.

[180]Ibid., p. 188.

[181]Ibid., p. 135.

[182]Beatrice Webb, "Women and the Factory Acts," Fabian Tract No. 67 (London: Fabian Society, 1896).

[183]B. Webb, Partnership, p. 205.

[184]S. Webb to E. Pease, 3 February 1896, Fabian Papers, Box A3, Nuffield College, Oxford.

[185]Beatrice and Sidney Webb, Industrial Democracy, pp. 405-06.

[186]Ibid., p. 506.

[187]Ibid., p. 504.

[188]Ibid., pp. 502-03.

[189]Ibid., p. 504.

[190]B. Webb, Partnership, p. 92.

[191]W. A. S. Hewins, The Apologia of an Imperialist, quoted in B. Webb, Partnership, p. 89.

[192]See "Resolution adopted by the Fabian Society," 2 May 1902, 8 May 1903, Passfield Papers, Box IX.

[193]B. Webb, Partnership, p. 478.

[194]Ibid., p. 324.

[195]Ibid., p. 328.

[196]Ibid., p. 341.

[197]Ibid., p. 377.

[198]Ibid.

[199]One of these colleagues, Sir Samuel Provis, served on another committee with Beatrice, some ten years later, and they became "warm friends."

[200]B. Webb, Partnership, pp. 419-20.

[201]Joan Simeon Clarke, "The Break-up of the Poor Law," in The Webbs and Their Work, p. 101.

[202]What set the Report apart from legislation which was to follow, was Beatrice's partiality for the "non-contributory principle" with regard to state aid, and her characteristic insistence "that any grant from the community to the individual, beyond what it does for all, . . . be conditional on better conduct." She felt that there was a "fatal defect" in any insurance scheme, because "the state got nothing for its money," beneficiaries "felt they had a right to the allowance whatever their conduct." B. Webb, Partnership, p. 417. The concept in the Report which was of most lasting value, though of little short-range impact, and around which the whole document revolved, was that of the "national minimum of civilized life." It called for a minimum level of wages, sanitation, and working conditions for all, enforced by legislation and government boards; it was, in 1909, years ahead of its time.

[203]G. D. N. Cole, "Beatrice Webb as an Economist," in The Webbs and Their Work, p. 273.

[204]B. Webb, Partnership, pp. 422-23.

[205]Ibid., p. 428.

[206]BWD, 31 December 1909.

[207]Ibid., 24 May 1910.

[208]Ibid., 3 May 1907.

[209]Ibid., 31 December 1909.

[210]Ibid.

[211]S. Webb to B. Webb, 3 July 1909, in Letters, vol. 2, p. 330.

[212]Relations between the Fabian and the F.R.D. were often stormy until 1917, when the latter broke off completely, renaming itself the Labour Research Department.

[213]Beatrice Webb's Diaries (1912-1924), ed. Margaret I. Cole (London: Longmans, Green, 1952), p. 6.

[214]Ibid., p. 12.

[215]Ibid., p. 16.

[216]B. Webb to Mrs. Fawcett, 2 November 1906, quoted in full in B. Webb, Partnership, pp. 362-63.

[217]Ibid.

[218]Ibid.

[219]Ibid., p. 361.

[220]Fabian News 11, no. 11 (1907): 18.

[221]Margaret Cole, Beatrice Webb (New York: Harcourt Brace, 1946), p. 221.

[222]Margaret Cole, "Labour Research," in The Webbs and Their Work, ed. Margaret Cole, p. 159.

[223]See, for example, BWD, 28 September 1913.

[224]Mrs. Sidney Webb, The Wages of Men and Women: Should They Be Equal? (London: George Allen and Unwin, 1919; London: University Microfilm International, 1981), p. 4.

[225]Ibid., p. 40.

[226]Ibid., p. 37.

[227]Ibid., p. 44.

[228]Ibid., p. 55.

[229]Ibid.

[230]Ibid., p. 58.

[231]Ibid.

[232]Beatrice Webb's Diaries, p. 34.

[233]Ibid., p. 146.

[234]BWD, June 1933.

[235]Ibid.

[236]Quoted in Muggeridge, _Beatrice Webb_, p. 245.

[237]Ibid., p. 258.

Chapter 5

CONCLUSION

Considering the record of the Fabian Society
between 1884 and 1914, one cannot deny that the times were
not always propitious for the support of women's rights.
Nor does one wish to dispute that many of the decisions to
adopt or to champion certain measures rather than feminist
proposals were based on rational, well-founded priorities.
It is entirely comprehensible that the Fabian Society as a
whole, and its principal Executors in particular, believed
that the passage of an eight-hours bill, or the creation of
a municipal gas and water system, was more important for
the well-being of the collectivity than were matters of
female suffrage or equal wages. Similarly, that the Fabians
often did not wish to imperil reforms involving the
redistribution of wealth, by encumbering them with proposals
for the re-ordering of family life or sexual roles, was
eminently sensible. Then as now, myriad reformers have
hesitated to slow the progress of one set of reforms by
burdening it with the exactions of another. And nowhere
is this more true than in the seemingly related but often
conflicting claims of women and the working classes.

Yet, I would argue, in the case of these Fabian
couples the fine line between practical politics and

personal bias was often crossed. Their willingness to support unpopular or less than urgent measures (as, for example, the Conservative Education Bill of 1903), was as constant as their unwillingness to champion feminist claims (such as the right of married women to work) even when no other reforms would seem to be endangered thereby. The prejudices against women's rights which kept them from supporting feminist measures were, often as not, their own prejudices rather than, or in addition to, those of the people they were trying to convert.

*   *   *

Charlotte Shaw, E. Nesbit Bland, and Beatrice Webb present three variations of paradoxical behavior: each professed one set of views about the nature of women and behaved according to another. Charlotte Shaw was the most clearly feminist of the three. After her introduction to advanced ideas on the subject, Charlotte became concerned with expanding women's opportunities through access to the vote, to administrative and political positions, and to professional training. In later years, she marched in suffrage demonstrations, sat on the Executive of the Fabian Women's Group, and refused to let her husband declare her income as part of his own on his tax return.

Yet, in spite of her feminist activities, the role she adopted in her marriage was a fairly conventional one; the emancipation she demanded for her sex, she failed to pursue in her own life. As a research sociologist, she

got no further than "arranging her material." Thus, the
freedom Charlotte gained was largely of a negative sort;
she was free not to be a sexual object because she remained
celibate, even after marriage. She was never exploited by
an inequitable employer, paying her less than a male
counterpart, because she did not work at all. Her domain
was the house and the hotel; her chief concern was her
husband and his work.

Edith Nesbit Bland thought feminists boring, she
never supported women's suffrage, and she delivered a
lecture to the Fabian Women's Group on the physical
disabilities of women, that is, why they were less suited
to working than men. In her children's novels, girls cried
and were afraid of everything, boys were brave, and smart,
and interested in everything. Women were mothers who worried
about cook quitting, and men were fathers who went to work
and worried about serious matters. And yet Edith Nesbit
dreamt of being a great poet when she was quite young, and
retained elements of that dream through most of her life.
When she was first married she rescued her family from
financial disaster by a multitude of talents and efforts.
For many years thereafter she was the chief bread winner.
She who professed to believe in the differences between the
sexes, was a tree-climbing, boat-rowing, unconventional
female whose artistic talents and earning capacity often
exceeded her husband's.

Beatrice Webb's views on the "woman question" were

the most paradoxical of all. Convinced of woman's intellectual inferiority and lack of staying power, certain that woman's role was to nourish and to love, she was appalled by the efforts of the "screeching sisterhood" to secure their rights. According to Beatrice, women needed to be protected from overworking by special factory legislation, protected from losing their jobs by being granted lower wages, and from political contamination by being denied the vote.

Yet, for all her faith in male superiority, for all her arguments about the enormous differences between the sexes, Beatrice herself spent several years trudging about the countryside researching the work conditions and voluntary organizations of the laboring classes. And she stretched her "tiny intellect" to formulate innovative sociological theories about them. That her own actions required stamina, her theories intellectual ability, and her work intense ambition, never stood in the way of Beatrice's perception of the inferior stamina, intellect, and ambition of the female of the species. Just so, her belief that motherhood provided the raison d'etre of womankind did not induce her to marry early, or inspire her to have children of her own.

One must conclude that being a woman socialist, even a middle-class, evolutionary socialist, did not necessarily lead one to become a feminist. Similarly, being a feminist no more guaranteed emancipated behavior than being an anti-feminist prevented it.

* * *

If Charlotte Shaw was adept at saying one thing and doing another, she was no more so than her husband. Capable of the most profound statements in support of women's emancipation, George Bernard Shaw often turned his back on the women's movement. No playwright ever did more, he claimed, to shake "the whole rotten convention as to women's place and worth in human society." [1] Yet, when the nitty-gritty issues of women's emancipation were the topics at hand, Shaw was not always there to be counted. Theoretically expanding women's domain was one thing, working for their rights was another. He was perfectly willing to destroy any notions of women's weakness, inherent inferiority, and reputed asexuality--he was always ready to try to bring people's notions of the sexes in closer alignment with reality--but he was not willing to work overtime at securing women the vote, or equal wages, or readier access to the job market. While he wrote three tracts for the Fabian Society in which equal political rights for women was recommended, he delivered a greater number of words on why political equality was not really his concern or that of the Society's.

Clearly Shaw was the only of the three men under study who could be characterized as a feminist. He was also the only one of the three to marry a woman without a career or major interest of her own, that is, a woman who did not fit the image of women he himself drew. Similarly, Shaw was the only one to advocate freer sexual relations, from extramarital sex, to child bearing outside of marriage, to easier divorce procedures. And, for all his liberated thinking, he lived for forty years in a sexless marriage, decreed by his wife but accepted by himself.

Of the six characters under study, Hubert Bland was the most unflattering in his opinion of women, the most assertive in his anti-feminism. Women could do little, he maintained, and they deserved less. In his conservative masterplan for moral regeneration, marriage was important, divorce out of the question, and women belonged in the home. Moreover, socialism, being the most virtuous form of government, did not in the least portend the emancipation of women. Within the Fabian Society, therefore, he opposed most measures concerned with securing additional rights or representation for women, and he broadcast his anti-feminist views ad nauseum both within and without the Society's hallowed lecture halls and committee rooms.

As we have seen, Hubert's private behavior was blatantly inconsonant with, indeed made a mockery of, his public stance. While espousing the importance of marriage, he committed most of his time and energy to extra-marital affairs. Perpetually insisting that women belonged in the home and had insufficient talent or ability to warrant work elsewhere, he was, nonetheless, married to a woman who worked throughout their married years and whose work was quite well-received, and often better compensated than his.

According to Sidney Webb there was no "woman question,"

women were merely undereducated, underorganized, somewhat less productive, and more prone to absenteeism. If women remained in the home, raising children, the race would be stronger and they themselves happier. But Sidney bore women no particular malice, he certainly credited them with more intelligence than Beatrice did, and a higher standard of morality than did Hubert Bland. Webb found women "boring," and they "moved outside his plane," but he was apt to ignore them rather than to malign them. In so far as women represented relationships and emotions and individualistic needs, he could not understand them; he himself believed in expertise and education and the general welfare. The world of feeling and introspection was not one he visited frequently, and the less he was in touch with the "feminine side" of his nature, the less likely he was to give credence to women's arguments of any sort.

Given that Webb's lack of sympathy with women's problems was basically a failure of imagination and feeling (his course of action in the Fabian Society vacillated between benign neglect of women's problems and complete misunderstanding of their needs) the possibilities for wifely influence and intervention were enormous. If Beatrice had so chosen she could easily have been Sidney's Egeria, counseling him on the difficulties exceptional women faced, or on how far from the mark the stereotype of women often fell. This did not happen, for reasons which had more to do with Beatrice than with Sidney. Sidney did not generalize from Beatrice's experience to that of other women because

Beatrice herself did not. What this meant for Sidney was that the woman who reputedly kept him in contact with the universe, who opened up the few avenues to emotion or introspection that existed for him, did so in the context of her own male-centered cosmos. Instead of enlightening Sidney on questions relating to women, she obscured the issues, underrated the female participants, and weighted the battle against them.

Since the Fabian Society's overall response to the "woman question" was in the final analysis most congruent with the views of Sidney Webb, Beatrice's failure was a significant one. Yet what was true of the Webbs was also true of the Blands and Shaws. All three wives might have played more meaningful roles in winning their husbands over to support for women's rights, or in making sure their support was overt and consistent. Had Charlotte been more forceful in her beliefs and wielded more influence over G.B.S. in political and intellectual matters, his feminist efforts might not have been so checkered, particularly in the first decade of their marriage. Had Edith been more secure in herself and in her marriage, she might have had the temerity to translate her artistic insights on women's potential into real demands for women's rights. At the least, she might have seen through Hubert's baldly self-serving views, challenged his misogyny, and charged him with maintaining a more rational perspective.

*   *   *

After a close look at these three couples, Fabian vacillation on the "woman question" becomes easier to understand. For them (as for most of us) the public battle between the sexes echoed the private battle within the family. The complexity of their attitudes toward issues of gender, amply apparent in their marriages, clearly informed their decisions as Fabians. Questions of political expediency, temporal propitiousness, or ideological coherence were relevant and contributory to the feminist or anti-feminist decisions of these Fabian couples, but they were secondary at best, used more to reinforce existing opinions than to form new ones. No wonder, then, that the ideal of sexual equality, which appeared to be an idea whose time had come, bedeviled its detractors and eluded its advocates.

Footnotes

[1]G.B.S., "An Aside," in <u>Myself and My Friends</u>,
by Lillah McCarthy (London: Thorton Butterworth, 1933),
p. 8.

SELECTED BIBLIOGRAPHY

I. Unpublished Sources

Bland, E. Nesbit. Correspondence. Society of Authors Collection. British Library, London.

Fabian Society. Records, Correspondence, 1884-1914. Nuffield College Library, Oxford.

Passfield Papers. Beatrice and Sidney Webb Correspondence, Documents. Beatrice Webb Diaries. British Library of Political and Economic Science, London.

Pease, Edward R. "Recollections for My Sons" (1930). Unpublished manuscript. In the possession of the Pease family.

Pease, Nicolas A. "Retrospect." Unpublished manuscript. In the possession of the Pease family.

Shaw, Charlotte. Papers. 37 vols. British Library, London.

Shaw, George Bernard. Papers. 236 vols. British Library, London.

Wallas, Graham. Papers. British Library of Political and Economic Science, London.

II. Primary Sources

Besant, Annie. The Law of Population: Its Consequences, and Its Bearing upon Human Conduct and Morals. London: Freethought, 1889.

----------. An Autobiography. London: T. Fisher Unwin, 1893.

----------. "Autobiographical Sketches." Our Corner 3-5 (January 1884-June 1885).

----------. "Review of Women in the Past, Present and Future, by August Bebel." Our Corner 6 (August 1885): 94-98.

----------. "Modern Socialism." Our Corner 7 (1886): 263-70.

Bland, E. Nesbit. Songs of Love and Empire. Westminster: Archibald Constable, 1898.

Bland, E. Nesbit. The Story of the Treasure Seekers (1899),
The WouldbeGoods (1901), and New Treasure Seekers
(1904). In her The Bastable Children. New York:
Coward McCann, 1929.

----------. The Red House. New York: Harper and Row,
1902.

----------. The Literary Sense. New York: Macmillan,
1903.

----------. Five Children and It (1902), The Phoenix and
the Carpet (1904), and The Story of the Amulet (1906).
In her The Five Children. New York: Coward-McCann,
1930.

----------. The Railway Children. 1906. Reprint.
Middlesex: Puffin Books, 1960.

----------. Ballads and Lyrics of Socialism, 1883-1908.
London: A. C. Fifield, 1908.

----------. Daphne in Fitzroy Street. New York: Doubleday,
Page, 1909.

----------. The Magic City. 1910. Reprint. London:
Ernest Benn, 1958.

----------. Harding's Luck. 1909. Reprint. London:
Ernest Benn, 1961.

----------. The Wonderful Garden. London: Ernest Benn,
1911.

----------. "My School-Days." The Girl's Own Paper
(October 1896-September 1897).

"Bland, Fabian" [pseudonym for Hubert and Edith Nesbit
Bland]. The Prophet's Mantle. London: Henry J.
Drane, 1889.

Bland, Hubert. With the Eyes of a Man. London: T. Werner
Laurie, 1905.

----------. Letters to a Daughter. London: T. Werner
Laurie, 1906.

----------. The Happy Moralist. London: T. Werner
Laurie, 1907.

----------. Olivia's Latchkey. London: T. Werner Laurie,
1913.

Bland, Hubert. Essays by Hubert Bland. London: Max Goschen, 1914.

----------. "Books." To-Day (April 1886-May 1888).

Blatch, Harriot Stanton. "Specialization of Function in Women." Guntons Magazine 10 (May 1896).

----------, and Lutz, Alma. Challenging Years, the Memoirs of Harriot Stanton Blatch. 1940. Reprint. Westport, Conn.: Hyperion Press, 1976.

Brieux, Eugene. Woman on Her Own. In Three Plays by Brieux. Trans. Charlotte Shaw. London: Fifield, 1911.

Brooke, Emma. A Superfluous Woman. London: William Heinemann, 1894.

----------. Transition. Philadelphia: J. B. Lippencott, 1895.

----------. A Tabulation of Factory Laws of European Countries. London: Grant Richards, 1898.

Chesterton, Mrs. Cecil. The Chestertons. London: Chapman and Hall, 1941.

Edwards, Joseph, ed. The Labour Annual. 1885. Reprint. Brighton, Sussex: Harvester Press, 1971.

Fabian Women's Group. "The Working Life of Women." By Miss B. L. Hutchins. Fabian Tract No. 157, Fabian Women's Group Series No. 1. London: Fabian Society, 1911.

----------. "Three Years' Work of the Women's Group." London: Fabian Society, 1911.

----------. "Family Life on a   a Week." By Mrs. Pember Reeves. Fabian Tract No. 162, F.W.G. Series No. 2. London: Fabian Society, 1912.

----------. "Women and Prisons." By Helen Blagg and Charlotte Wilson. Fabian Tract No. 163, F.W.G. Series No. 3. London: Fabian Society, 1912.

----------. "The Economic Foundations of the Women's Movement." By Mabel Atkinson. Fabian Tract No. 175, F.W.G. Series No. 4. London: Fabian Society, 1914.

Fabian Women's Group. Women Workers in Seven Professions.
    Ed. Edith Morley. London: George Routledge and
    Sons, 1914.

Fabian Society. Annual Report. London: Fabian Society,
    1890-1914.

----------. "Executive Minutes." London: Fabian Society,
    1890-1914.

----------. Fabian News 1-24 (1890-1914).

----------. "A Manifesto." By George Bernard Shaw.
    Fabian Tract No. 2. London: Fabian Society, 1884.

----------. "The True Radical Program." Fabian Tract
    No. 6. London: Fabian Society, 1888.

----------. "Facts for Londoners." Fabian Tract No. 8.
    London: Fabian Society, 1889.

----------. "The Workers' Political Program." Fabian
    Tract No. 11. London: Fabian Society, 1890.

----------. "The New Reform Bill." Fabian Tract No. 14.
    London: Fabian Society, 1891.

----------. "Questions for Parliamentary Candidates."
    Fabian Tract No. 24. London: Fabian Society, 1891.

----------. "Questions for School Board Candidates."
    Fabian Tract No. 25. London: Fabian Society, 1891.

----------. "Questions for Town Councillors." Fabian
    Tract No. 27. London: Fabian Society, 1891.

----------. "Questions for County Councillors." Fabian
    Tract No. 28. London: Fabian Society, 1891.

----------. "Early History of the Fabian Society." Fabian
    Tract No. 41. London: Fabian Society, 1892.

----------. "The Unemployed." Fabian Tract No. 47.
    London: Fabian Society, 1893.

----------. "Women as Councillors." Fabian Tract No. 93.
    London: Fabian Society, 1900.

----------. "The London Education Act, How To Make the
    Best of It." Fabian Tract No. 117. London: Fabian
    Society, 1904.

Fabian Society. "The Abolition of Poor Law Guardians." Fabian Tract No. 126. London: Fabian Society, 1906.

----------. "The Decline in the Birth Rate." By Sidney Webb. Fabian Tract No. 131. London: Fabian Society, 1907.

Fawcett, Millicent Garrett. What I Remember. 1925. Reprint. Westport, Conn.: Hyperion Press, 1976.

Galton, Frank W. "Investigating with the Webbs." In The Webbs and Their Work. Ed. Margaret Cole. London: Frederick Muller, 1949.

Hobson, S. G. Pilgrim to the Left. London: Edward Arnold, 1938.

Lees, Edith. Attainment. London: Alton Rivers, 1909.

Olivier, Sidney. Letters and Selected Writings. Ed. Margaret Olivier. London: George Allen and Unwin, 1948.

Pankhurst, E. Sylvia. The Suffragette Movement. London: Longmans, Green, 1931.

Patch, Blanche. Thirty Years with G.B.S. London: Victor Gollancz, 1951.

Pease, Edward R. The History of the Fabian Society. 1916. Reprint. New York: Barnes and Noble, 1963.

----------. "Webb and the Fabian Society." In The Webbs and Their Work. Ed. Margaret Cole. London: Frederick Muller, 1949.

Pethick-Lawrence, Emmeline. My Part in a Changing World. London: Victor Gollancz, 1938.

Shaw, Charlotte. "Forward." In Damaged Goods. By E. Brieux. London: Fifield, 1914.

Shaw, George Bernard. The Quintessence of Ibsenism. London: Walter Scott, 1891.

----------. The Philanderer. In The Collected Works of Bernard Shaw. Vol. 7. 1898. Reprint. New York: William H. Wise, 1930.

----------, ed. Fabian Essays in Socialism. London: Walter Scott, 1908.

Shaw, George Bernard. Press Cuttings. In his Translations and Tomfooleries. New York: Brentano's, 1926.

----------. Essays in Fabian Socialism. London: Constable, 1932.

----------. "An Aside." In Myself and My Friends. By Lillah McCarthy. London: Thorton Butterworth, 1933.

----------. Prefaces. London: Constable, 1934.

----------. Selected Plays of George Bernard Shaw. 4 vols. New York: Dodd, Mead, 1948-1957.

----------. Sixteen Self Sketches. New York: Dodd, Mead, 1949.

----------. "Woman-Man in Petticoats" (1927). In Platform and Pulpit. Ed. Dan H. Laurence. New York: Hill and Wang, 1961.

----------. Bernard Shaw's Letters to Granville Barker. Ed. C. B. Purdom. New York: Theatre Arts Books, 1957.

----------. Selected Non-dramatic Writings of Bernard Shaw. Ed. Dan H. Laurence. Boston: Houghton Mifflin, 1965.

----------. Bernard Shaw: Collected Letters 1874-1897. Ed. Dan H. Laurence. London: Max Reinhardt, 1965.

Townshend, Emily. Some Memories for Her Friends. London: Privately printed at the Curwen Press, 1936.

Wallas, Ada. Daguerreotypes. London: George Allen and Unwin, 1929.

----------. Before the Blue Stockings. London: George Allen and Unwin, 1929.

Wallas, Graham. The Great Society, a Psychological Analysis. Lincoln: University of Nebraska Press, 1967.

----------. Men and Ideas. Ed. May Wallas. London: George Allen and Unwin, 1940.

Webb, Beatrice, ed. The Case for the Factory Acts. London: Grant Richards, 1901.

Webb, Beatrice. The Wages of Men and Women: Should They Be Equal? London: George Allen and Unwin, 1919.

----------. Beatrice Webb's American Diary, 1898. Ed. David A. Shannon. Madison: University of Wisconsin Press, 1963.

----------. My Apprenticeship. 1926. Reprint. Cambridge: Cambridge University Press, 1979.

----------. Our Partnership. London: Longmans, Green, 1948.

----------. Beatrice Webb's Diaries 1912-1924. Ed. Margaret I. Cole. London: Longmans, Green, 1952.

Webb, Sidney. "Policy of the National Minimum." In Modern Socialism. Ed. R. C. K. Ensor. London: Harper and Brothers, 1904.

----------, and Webb, Beatrice. Industrial Democracy. London: Longmans, Green, 1902.

----------, and ----------. The Problems of Modern Industry. London: Longmans, Green, 1920.

----------, and ----------. The Letters of Sidney and Beatrice Webb (1873-1892), vol. 1. Ed. Norman MacKenzie. Cambridge: Cambridge University Press, 1978.

----------, and ----------. The Letters of Sidney and Beatrice Webb (1892-1912), vol. 2. Ed. Norman MacKenzie, 1978.

Wells, H. G. Socialism and the Family. Boston: Ball, 1908.

----------. The New Machiavelli. New York: Duffield, 1914.

----------. Experiment in Autobiography. New York: Macmillan, 1934.

III. Secondary Sources

Banks, J. A., and Banks, Olive. Feminism and Family Planning in Victorian England. Liverpool: Liverpool University Press, 1964.

Bebel, August. Women in the Past, Present and Future.
    London: Modern Press, 1885.

Beckson, Karl, ed. Aesthetes and Decadents of the 1890's,
    an Anthology of British Poetry and Prose. Rev. ed.
    Chicago: Academy Chicago, 1981.

Beer, Max. A History of British Socialism. London:
    Allen and Unwin, 1953.

Bell, Anthea. E. Nesbit. London: Bodley Head, 1960.

Blackburn, Helen. Women's Suffrage. 1902. Reprint.
    New York: Source Book Press, 1970.

Boxer, Marilyn. "Socialism Meets Feminism in France,
    1879-1813." Ph.D. dissertation, University of
    California, Riverside, 1975.

Bridenthal, Renate, and Koonz, Claudia, eds. Becoming
    Visible, Women in European History. Boston: Houghton
    Mifflin, 1977.

Britain, Ian. Fiabianism and Culture: A Study in British
    Socialism and the Arts, 1884-1918. New York: Cambridge
    University Press, 1982.

Chodorow, Nancy. The Reproduction of Mothering: Psycho-
    analysis and the Sociology of Gender. Berkeley:
    University of California Press, 1978.

Cole, Margaret. The Story of Fabian Socialism. Stanford:
    Stanford University Press, 1961.

De Beauvoir, Simone. The Second Sex. Trans. H. M. Parshley.
    New York: Alfred A. Knopf, 1953.

Degler, Carl N. At Odds: Women and the Family in America
    from the Revolution to the Present. New York: Oxford
    University Press, 1980.

Dervin, Daniel. Bernard Shaw: A Psychological Study.
    London: Associated University Presses, 1975.

Dowse, Robert E. Left in the Centre, the Independent
    Labour Party 1893-1940. Evanston, Ill.: Northwestern
    University Press, 1966.

Dunbar, Janet. Mrs. G.B.S.: A Portrait. New York:
    Harper and Row, 1963.

Engels, Frederick. The Origin of the Family, Private

  Property, and the State. Reprint. New York: International Publishers, 1972.

Ervine, St. John. Bernard Shaw: His Life, Work, and Friends. New York: William Morrow, 1956.

Evans, Sara. Personal Politics: The Roots of Women's Liberation in the Civil Rights Movement and the New Left. New York: Alfred A. Knopf, 1979.

Fletcher, Ronald. The Family and Marriage in Britain. Baltimore: Penguin Books, 1962.

Fremantle, Anne. This Little Band of Prophets. New York: New American Library, 1959.

Freud, Sigmund. The Standard Edition of the Complete Works of Sigmund Freud, vols. 19, 21, and 22. Trans and ed. James Strachey. London: Hogarth Press, 1953-74.

Hamilton, Mary Agnes. Sidney and Beatrice Webb. London: Sampson, Law, Marston, 1932.

Henderson, Archibald. George Bernard Shaw: Man of the Century. New York: Appleton-Century-Crofts, 1956.

Hobsbawm, Eric J. Labouring Men: Studies in the History of Labour. London: Weidenfeld and Nicolson, 1964.

----------, ed. Labour's Turning Point, 1880-1900. Cranbury, N.J.: Associated University Presses, 1974.

Hollis, Patricia. Women in Public: The Women's Movement 1850-1900. London: George Allen and Unwin, 1979.

Horney, Karen. Feminine Psychology. New York: W. W. Norton, 1967.

----------. "The Problem of Feminine Masochism." In Psychoanalysis and Women. Ed. Jean Baker Miller. Harmondsworth, Middlesex: Penguin Books, 1973.

Hynes, Samuel. The Edwardian Turn of Mind. Princeton, N.J.: Princeton University Prses, 1968.

Klein, Melanie. Love, Guilt and Reparation, and Other Works 1921-1945. London: Hogarth Press, 1975.

Kraditor, Aileen S. The Ideas of the Woman Suffrage Movement, 1890-1920. New York: Columbia University Press, 1965.

Lee, Patrick C., and Stewart, Robert S., eds. Sex Differ-
    ences: Cultural and Developmental Dimensions. New
    York: Urizen Books, 1976.

Lutz, Alma. Created Equal, a Biography of Elizabeth Cady
    Stanton. New York: John Day, 1940.

Lynd, Helen M. England in the Eighteen-Eighties: Toward
    a Social Basis for Freedom. London: Oxford University
    Press, 1945.

MacKenzie, Norman, and MacKenzie, Jeanne. The Fabians.
    New York: Simon and Schuster, 1977.

Maccoby, Eleanor, and Jacklin, Carol Nagy. The Psychology
    of Sex Differences. Stanford: Stanford University
    Press, 1974.

Marx, Karl, and Engels, Frederick. The Communist Manifesto.
    Reprint. New York: International Publishers, 1948.

McBriar, A. M. Fabian Socialism and English Politics
    1884-1918. Cambridge: Cambridge University Press,
    1962.

Mill, John Stuart, and Mill, Harriet Taylor. Essays on
    Sex Equality. Ed. Alice S. Rossi. Chicago: University
    of Chicago Press, 1970.

Mitchell, David. The Fighting Pankhursts. New York:
    Macmillan, 1967.

----------. Queen Christabel. London: MacDonald and
    James, 1977.

Mitchell, Juliet. Women's Estate. New York: Random
    House, 1971.

Moore, Doris Langley. E. Nesbit, a Biography. New York:
    Chilton Books, 1966.

Morgan, David. Suffragists and Liberals. Oxford:
    Blackwell, 1975.

Muggeridge, Kitty, and Adam, Ruth. Beatrice Webb, a
    Life, 1858-1943. New York: Alfred A. Knopf, 1968.

Murray, Janet Horowitz. Strong-Minded Women and Other
    Lost Voices from Nineteenth-Century England. New York:
    Pantheon Books, 1982.

Nethercot, Arthur H. The First Five Lives of Annie Besant. Chicago: University of Chicago Press, 1960.

Pearson, Hesketh. Bernard Shaw: His Life and His Personality. London: Methuen, 1961.

Peters, Margot. Bernard Shaw and the Actresses. New York: Doubleday, 1980.

Quataert, Jean H. Reluctant Feminists in German Social Democracy, 1885-1917. Princeton, N.J.: Princeton University Press, 1979.

Ramelson, Marian. The Petticoat Rebellion. London: Lawrence and Wishart, 1967.

Rosaldo, Michell, and Lamphere, Louise, eds. Women, Culture, and Society. Stanford: Stanford University Press, 1974.

Rosen, Andrew. Rise Up Women! The Militant Campaign of the Women's Social and Political Union, 1903-14. London: Routledge and Kegan Paul, 1974.

Rover, Constance. Women's Suffrage and Party Politics in Britain, 1866-1914. London: Routledge and Kegan Paul, 1967.

Rosbotham, Sheila. Women, Resistance, and Revolution. New York: Pantheon Books, 1973.

----------. Hidden from History. New York: Random House, 1974.

----------. A New World for Women: Stella Browne-- Socialist Feminist. London: Pluto Press, 1977.

Silver, Arnold. Bernard Shaw: The Darker Side. Stanford: Stanford University Press, 1982.

Sinclair, Keith. William Pember Reeves. Oxford: Clarendon Press, 1965.

Soffer, Reba N. Ethics and Society in England. Berkeley: University of California Press, 1978.

Strachey, Ray. The Cause. Port Washington, N.Y.: Kennikat Press, 1969.

Streatfield, Noel. Magic and the Magician (E. Nesbit and her Children's Books). London: Abelard Schuman, 1958.

Strouse, Jean, ed. Women and Analysis. New York: Grossman, 1974.

Thompson, E. P. William Morris. New York: Pantheon Books, 1976.

Thompson, Laurence. The Enthusiasts: A Biography of John and Katharine Bruce Glasier. London: Gollancz, 1971.

Tsuzuki, Chushichi. H. M. Hyndman and British Socialism. London: Oxford University Press, 1961.

Vicinus, Martha, ed. Suffer and Be Still, Women in the Victorian Age. Bloomington: Indiana University Press, 1972.

Waters, Mary-Alice. "Feminism and the Marxist Movement." International Socialist Review 33, no. 9 (1972): 8-23.

Watson, Barbara Bellow. A Shavian Guide to the Intelligent Woman. New York: W. W. Norton, 1964.

Weintraub, Rodelle. Fabian Feminist. University Park: Pennsylvania State University Press, 1977.

Wiener, Martin J. Between Two Worlds: The Political Thought of Graham Wallas. Oxford: Clarendon Press, 1971.

Williams, Juanita H. The Psychology of Women. New York: W. W. Norton, 1977.

Wilson, Elizabeth. Women and the Welfare State. London: Tavistock, 1977.

INDEX

Actresses' Franchise League, 141
American Woman Suffrage
    Association, 26
Anti-Puritan League, 186
Associative housing, 29
Atkinson, Mabel, 44, 45, 46

Back to Methusela, 96
Balfour, Arthur, 330, 353
Ballads and Lyrics of
    Socialism, 201
Bergson, Henri, 67-68
Besant, Annie, 8, 13-19, 27, 144,
    168, 174
Besant, Frank, 14
Beveridge Report, 372
Birth Control, 15, 139
Blagg, Helen, 44
Bland, Edith Nesbit, 48
  anti-feminism, 163,200,
    236-237, 258-259, 389
  children's literature, 205-237
  and Fabian Society, 199-200
  and Hubert Bland, 237-241,
    257-258
  poetry, 201-205
  and sexual stereotyping, 216,
    219-221, 224, 226, 232,
    235-236
  and sibling society, 210, 235
Bland, Fabian, 239
Bland, Hubert, 7, 10, 19, 47, 48,
    49, 272
  anti-feminism, 181-194,
    250-255, 392
  and Edith Nesbit Bland,
    237-241, 257-258
  and Fabian Society, 170-172,
    174-177
  and George Bernard Shaw,
    173-174
Bland, Iris, 199
Bland, John, 247
Bland, Paul, 199
Bland, Rosamund, 239, 247-248,
    272
Blatch, Harriot Stanton, 24-30,
    56, 184
Blatch, Henry, 26

Blatch, Nora, 26
Blavatsky, Madame, 27
Booth, Charles, 303-304, 305-306
Bradlaugh, Charles 15
Bridgemen, Miss, 24
Brieux, Eugene, 140-142
Bright, Mrs. Jacob, 27, 139
Brooke, Emma, 22, 24
Brownlow, Mrs., 24
Burns, John, 45
Burrows, Herbert, 168
Butler, Samuel, 67, 68, 75

Campbell, Mrs. Patrick, 143-144
    146-147
Candida, 70
Carpenter, Edward, 4
Chamberlain, Joseph, 301-303
Charity Organization Society, 353
Chesterton, Cecil, 179
Chesterton, Mrs. Cecil, 169
Clery, General, 112, 115
Cole, G. D. H., 357, 361
Comte, Auguste, 282, 289
Conservative Education Bill, 179,
    330, 350, 388
Co-operative societies, 306
Councils, borough, 64-65
Creighton, Louise, 342, 366

Damaged Goods, 142
Davidson, Thomas, 4, 167
Diggle, J.R., 168
Dilke, Mrs. Ashton, 307
Divorce, 75-76
Divorce Law Reform Union, 138-139
Dunraven Exclusion Act, 31, 64

Ellis, Havelock, 4
Equal Franchise Committee, 27
Equality League of Self -
    Supporting Women, 56
Essays by Hubert, 252
Fabian Essays in Socialism,
    9-10, 47, 62, 64, 175
Fabian News, 16, 20, 32
Fabian Society
  Basis, 5, 10, 35, 36
  Biology Group, 185-186

Book Boxes, 9
Central Group, 20-21
Executive Committee, 7, 8
formed, 5
lectures, 8-9
middle-class organization, 2, 6
Pamphlet Committee, 200
Parliamentary Committee,
    174-175
provincial societies, 10
Research Department, 361
Wells's Special Committee,
    35-36, 131
women members, 6, 11, 37
Women's Committee, 20
Women's Group, 39-46, 135, 185
and women's movement, 3, 12,
    20, 22, 23, 29-33, 41
Fabian Summer School, 147
Fabius Cunctator, 5
Factory legislation, 29-30, 304,
    343-345, 368
Fagan, Mrs., 21, 23
Fathers, supplementary, 77-78,
    89-90
Fawcett, Millicent, 307, 363
Fellowship of the New Life, 4
Five Children and It, 223
Freedom, 13
Fry, Roger, 145

Garrett, Mrs., 24
Gautier, Theophile, 107
George, Henry, 92
Getting Married, 74, 76
Girls Own Paper, 207
Gorst, John, 350
Grover, Miss, 20, 21
Gurley, Elizabeth (Mrs. George
    Carr Shaw), 87-90, 93-94

Haddon, Miss, 5
Hamilton, Lord George, 353
Hampstead Historic Society, 13,
    283
Harben, Henry, 45
Harding's Luck, 231-233
Headlam, Stewart, 18, 168
Heartbreak House, 94
Hewins, William, 286

Hill, Octavia, 353
History of Trade Unionism, 333
History of Woman Suffrage, 26
Hoatson, Alice, 243-244, 247
Hobson, S.G., 171
House of Arden, 231
Hutchins, B.L., 43
Hutchinson, Henry H., 10, 286
Hyndman, Henry Mayers, 92, 166

Ibsen, Henrik, 65, 69, 287
Independent Labour Party, 2, 53,
    175
Industrial Democracy, 333, 345,
    367
Irrational Knot, 74, 93

Jackson, Martha, 301
Johnson, Amy, 371

Kirby, Mary Susanna (Mrs. Horace
    Payne-Townshend), 105-107,
    111-112
Klein, Melanie, 252
Knowledge Is the Door, 145
Knowlton, Dr., 15
Kropotkin, Prince, 13

Labor Exchanges, 74
Lacey, Mary, 21
Laura Gay, 294
Law of Population, 18
Lawrence, T.E., 149-150, 151
Lays and Legends, 239
Lee, George John Vandalear, 89
Le Gallienne, Richard, 241
Letters to a Daughter, 191, 248
Liberal Imperialists, 67
Life and Labour in London, 304
Local Government Act, 285
London County Council, 31, 41,
    285, 350-351
London Daily Chronicle, 168
London School of Economics,
    117-119, 130, 286, 330, 338,
    349-350, 362
London School of Medicine for
    Women, 118

MacDonald, Ramsey, 4, 30

Magic City, 237
Major Barbara, 72
Mallet, Mrs. C., 19-20, 21, 24
Man and Superman, 63, 68, 71
   73
Manchester Sunday Chronicle,
   168
Manhood Suffrage Bill, 137-138
Marx, Karl, 1, 13, 283-284
Matchmakers' Union, 18
Maternité, 140, 141
Mellor, William, 361
Mill, John Stuart, 81, 277, 279,
   282-283, 287
Mills, James Porter, 144-145, 146
Minimum wage, 33, 369, 384
Modern Utopia, 230
Moore, Doris Langley, 243
Morris, William, 230
Munthe, Axel, 113-115

National Insurance Bill, 135, 358
National Reformer, 15
National Secular Society, 15
National Union of Women Workers,
   341-342
National Union of Women's
   Suffrage Societies, 363
National Woman Suffrage
   Association, 24, 26
Nesbit, Edith. See Bland, Edith
   Nesbit
Nesbit, John Collis, 194-195
New Independent Party, 136
New Statesman, 338
New Treasure Seekers, 216-217,
   218
Newcombe, Bertha, 95-96
Nineteenth Century, 304, 307

Oakeshott, J.F., 23, 24, 29
Olivia's Latchkey, 182, 187,
   252
Olivier, Sidney, 8, 18, 19, 24,
   47-48, 175, 278, 282
Our Corner, 16
Overruled, 96, 143

Pankhurst, Christabel, 144
Pankhurst, Emmeline, 27, 30

Patterson, Jenny, 95
Payne-Townshend, Charlotte. See
    Shaw, Charlotte
Payne-Townshend, Horace, 104-105
Pease, Edward, 4, 7, 19, 24, 47,
    128, 146, 170, 200
Peddie, R.A., 24
Pethick-Lawrence, Mrs., 37
Philanderer, 69
Phillips, W.L., 6
Phoenix and the Carpet, 223,
    225
Poor Law, 353-358
Potter, Beatrice. See Webb,
    Beatrice
Potter, Laurencina Heyworth,
    292-295
Potter, Richard, 291-292
Press Cuttings, 82
Prophet's Mantle, 238
Protective tariffs, 179-180
Pygmalion, 99, 144, 146

Railway Children, 217-222
Reeves, Amber, 272
Reeves, Mrs. Pember, 39-40,
    43-44, 135, 365
Reform Bill, 110
Rosebery, Lord, 67

Sanders, Stephen, 45
Seven Pillars of Wisdom, 149
Shakespeare, William, 256-257
Shaw, Charlotte, 39, 48
  and Fabian Society, 116-117,
    127-135
  and feminism, 107-110, 388-389
  and George Bernard Shaw, 119,
    120-127, 146-147
  relationship with mother,
    105-106, 111-112
  suitors, 112-115
  and women's suffrage, 137-138
Shaw, George Bernard, 5, 7, 9-10,
    18, 19, 24, 29, 30, 36, 47,
    48, 49, 153, 175, 176, 180,
    190, 239-240, 246, 279,
    339-340, 373
  and Charlotte Shaw, 119,
    120-127, 146-147

and eugenics, 68-69, 71-73, 77
and feminism, 60-86, 391-392
and Hubert Bland, 173-174
relationships with women, 95-99
and socialism, 62-63, 66-69
and women's suffrage, 63, 81-85
Shaw, George Carr, 86-87, 91
Shaw, Lucy, 90, 92-93
Social Democratic Federation, 2,
    5, 92, 166, 199
Socialism, 5, 66-69
and feminism, 1-2
Socialism in England, 322
Socialist League, 2
Songs of Love and Empire, 203
South African War, 30, 177-178
Soviet Communism, 372
Spencer, Herbert, 298
Stacey, Elizabeth Mary, 276
Stanton, Elizabeth Cady, 24, 26,
    56
Story of Amulet, 223-224,
    227-228, 229-230
Suffrage, women's, 20, 22, 41,
    63, 81-85, 137-138, 363-366
Sunday husbands, 77-78, 89-90
Sylvia's Home Journal, 243

Taylor, Helen, 279
Terry, Ellen, 97, 120
Theosophical Society, 18, 27, 54
Three Plays by Brieux, 141
To-day, 168, 172
Trade unions, 18, 333-334, 344,
    347, 349
Treasure Seekers, 208-209, 218
Tucker, Thomas Terry, 261

Unemployment insurance, 373
Unions. See Trade unions
Unsocial Socialist, 172

Vassar, 25
Venereal disease, 142
Vitalism, 67-68

Wages, 17, 23, 33, 42, 45,
    346-348, 367-370
Wages of Men and Women, 368
Wakefield, Dean Russell, 357

Wallas, Graham, 8, 18, 19, 47,
    119, 170, 175, 180, 336, 341
Walter, B., 20
Ward, Mrs. Humphrey, 307
Webb, Beatrice, 24, 29-30, 48,
    89, 96, 99, 102, 116, 117,
    119, 121, 129, 144, 146, 170
  anti-feminism, 274, 307-316,
    339-340, 351, 389-390,
    393-394
  and Fabian Society, 361
  relationship with mother,
    292-295, 314
  and Sidney Webb, 318-338
  and women's suffrage, 363-366
Webb, Mary Elizabeth, 374
Webb, Sidney, 7, 10, 19, 37-39,
    45, 47, 48, 49, 67, 116, 117,
    119, 130, 146, 170, 175, 176
  and Beatrice Webb, 318-338
  committeeman, 280-281, 284, 285
  and woman question, 274,
    287-289, 338-339, 392-394
Wells, H.G., 33-36, 37, 131,
    134, 169, 171, 184, 230, 247,
    249-250, 272
Wells, Jane, 272
Wilson, Charlotte, 7, 12-13, 39,
    44, 135, 174
Woman on Her Own, 141
Woman's Local Government Bill, 32
Women's Political Union, 56
Women's Social and Political
    Union, 33, 142, 363
Women's suffrage, 20, 22, 41, 63,
    81-85, 137-138, 363-366
Wonderful Garden, 270
Wouldbegoods, 216, 218

Zetetical Society, 279

For Product Safety Concerns and Information please contact our EU
representative GPSR@taylorandfrancis.com
Taylor & Francis Verlag GmbH, Kaufingerstraße 24, 80331 München, Germany

www.ingramcontent.com/pod-product-compliance
Lightning Source LLC
Chambersburg PA
CBHW050558270326
41926CB00012B/2101